The Event Planning Toolkit

The Event Planning Toolkit

Your Guide to Organizing Extraordinary Meetings and Events

LINDA JOYCE JONES

Foreword by David Adler

ROWMAN & LITTLEFIELD
Lanham • Boulder • New York • London

Published by Rowman & Littlefield
An imprint of The Rowman & Littlefield Publishing Group, Inc.
4501 Forbes Boulevard, Suite 200, Lanham, Maryland 20706
www.rowman.com

86-90 Paul Street, London EC2A 4NE

British Library Cataloguing in Publication Information Available

Library of Congress Cataloging-in-Publication Data
Names: Jones, Linda Joyce, 1959– author.
Title: The event planning toolkit : your guide to organizing extraordinary
    meetings and events / Linda Joyce Jones ; foreword by David Adler.
Description: Lanham : Rowman & Littlefield, [2020] | Includes bibliographical
    references and index. | Summary: "'The Event Planning Toolkit' is a how-to
    guide offering the information you need to execute any event with precision
    and enjoy the big day with less stress and fewer unpleasant surprises. You will
    learn how to manage your scope, time and resources, as well as identify goals,
    create budgets, find the right venue, assemble a strong team, and more"—
    Provided by publisher.
Identifiers: LCCN 2020024028 (print) | LCCN 2020024029 (ebook) | ISBN
    9781538141052 (cloth ; alk. paper) | ISBN 9781538173923 (paper ; alk. paper) |
    ISBN 9781538141069 (epub)
Subjects: LCSH: Special events—Planning. | Special events—Management.
Classification: LCC GT3405 .J656 2020 (print) | LCC GT3405 (ebook) | DDC
    394.2—dc23
LC record available at https://lccn.loc.gov/2020024028
LC ebook record available at https://lccn.loc.gov/2020024029

Contents

Foreword   ix

Introduction   1

SECTION I: The Essentials   **13**

1 Becoming a Project Manager   15

2 Scope   21

3 Time   25

4 Resources   29

SECTION II: Creating an Action Plan   **35**

5 Identifying Your Goals   37

6 Understanding Your Budget   43

7 Finding the Right Venue   57

8 Assembling Your Team   71

9 Designing Your Action Plan   81

SECTION III: Designing an Event to Remember   **93**

10 Working with Your Venue   95

11 Food and Beverage   103

12 Room Configurations   111

13 Selecting a Theme   119

14 Creating a Program   125

15 Trade Shows and Expos   143

16 Choosing Speakers and Presenters   149

SECTION IV: Logistics   **157**

17 Nuts and Bolts   159

18 Selecting Service Providers   169

19 Contract Negotiations   177

20 Technology   187

21 Safety and Security   195

22 Marketing and Publicity   203

23 The Main Event   213

SECTION V: The Real Secret to Event Planning Success   **221**

24 Communicate Effectively   223

25 Stay Organized   231

26 Stay Focused   239

27 Measure Your Success   243

28 Learn from the Experts   249

29 Rise to the Occasion   257

Appendix: Worksheets and Checklists   263
    Goal Statement   264
    Budget   266
    Team and Volunteer Details   269
    RFP Template   270
    Venue Evaluation   274
    Sleeping Room Evaluation   279

Action Plan   282
Service Provider Details   290
Exhibitor Details   291
Speaker Details   293
Planning Meeting Preparation   295
Planning Meeting   297
Event Script   299
Event Debrief Meeting   305
Event Participant Survey   307

Acknowledgments   309

Notes   311

Index   313

About the Author   325

Foreword

If planning is about preparation, organization, arrangement, forethought, design, drafting, working out, setting up, and groundwork, then the book you are about to read is the road map for planning successful events.

Linda Jones, with more than twenty-five years of event planning experience, has been able to condense her knowledge into the playbook for both experienced and first-time planners. Even one bit of her wisdom could be the difference between extreme embarrassment and being hailed as a conquering hero.

That old admonition to "Never let them see you sweat" will not be an issue if you always keep by your side a copy of *The Event Planning Toolkit: Your Guide to Planning Extraordinary Meetings and Events*. You may not even want to let anyone know you have this formula that enables you to plan like a pro, even on the first go.

Know the vocabulary and the pitfalls. Negotiate like an old hand. Make decisions with confidence. Understand concepts like force majeure, plus contracts, hotel room block rules, food and beverage protocols, proper load in and load out, union and safety rules, new invitation and registration options, and more.

With the global outbreak of COVID-19, the world has changed, and how we come together will never be the same. And yet the fundamentals of human gatherings remain: we are social animals and connect more meaningfully face-to-face.

Event planning is more important now, postpandemic, than ever before. We must remember to look for occasions for joy, especially when our trials seem hardest. So advised Antarctic explorer Ernest Shackleton, who in the early twentieth century successfully guided his entire crew to safety and eventual rescue through months of hunger and peril after the devastating wreck of their ship, *Endurance*. Even on the darkest days, we must "celebrate everything."

Event planners are critical to the mission of any organization or community meetings and festivities, allowing the work to be more effective. Post-COVID-19, event organizers will become "chief connection officers" on both an informal and a formal level.

This is a book for all levels of planning experience, from the hidden planners to the experienced pros. If you get handed the assignment of preparing a meeting, a conference, a holiday party, a convention, or afterwork cocktails, know that there is a process to everything. This book reveals the processes transparently.

As a veteran in the event world, I have seen many books written to help the planning process. This one is an exceptional work written in a straightforward way that makes any task easy to understand and any challenge surmountable. This is the kind of book that will get all dogeared and is destined to become the new go-to manual for the industry and the new standard of excellence.

David Adler
Founder and Chairman, BizBash

Introduction

When was the last time you experienced a mountaintop moment, when your heart was full and your sense of happiness and well-being seemed like a tangible thing? Was the feeling born from achieving a long-awaited goal, receiving a moment of inspiration, or just experiencing a feeling of togetherness or being a part of something sublime? Perhaps it was at a concert where the music transported you to another place and time. Perhaps it was an awards ceremony where you were recognized for your hard-won accomplishments. It could have been an occasion where you got the feeling that the speaker was delivering a message meant specifically for you. Or maybe you were honoring someone you love at a milestone celebration.

Mountaintop moments can be organic, but most of the time they are born out of intentional thought and careful planning. Someone envisioned an occasion that would transform the ordinary into the extraordinary. Someone decided that there was something worth celebrating. Someone thought that the ultimate goal was worth the time and effort.

Someone decided to create and organize an event.

Is that someone you? If you are reading this book, you probably have an important event in your future and will play a big part in making it a success. It could be a corporate conference or association meeting, a community event or fundraiser, or a personal celebration, and *you* are being asked to rise to the occasion and get the job done.

Many people find the thought of planning an event to be an intimidating prospect. They think they're not organized enough or that they don't have the experience required to pull it off. But whatever the occasion, the path to success is pretty straightforward; it's a matter of thinking through the details and using a proven strategy to create an action plan and executing it on time and on budget.

Don't worry—*The Event Planning Toolkit: Your Guide to Planning Extraordinary Meetings and Events* will be your guide from start to finish. Whether your event is held in a boardroom, a conference room, or a party room, this book will help you master the details for almost any occasion. Refer to this text again and again as you move through the seasons of your life to create amazing events for your business, your community, your family, and your world.

WHY DO WE GATHER?

Gathering is a way for us to make a difference, to make someone feel special, or to achieve a goal. Gathering isn't essential to life, but I maintain that it is essential to living a meaningful life. A special gathering is an opportunity to connect with others who are part of the same family, association, or community. We gather to recognize a special moment, further a joint cause, or encourage one another to grow in knowledge or faith. Sometimes we gather with people we are intimately familiar with, and sometimes we gather with people we've never met but who share a common bond or interest. Sometimes a passion for something can be so strong that it draws you in and compels you to seek out others with the same passion.

Quilters would still make quilts even if they never attended a quilters' convention, but where else could they go to talk to other quilters, see hundreds of examples of heirloom-quality pieces all in one place, and learn about new tools and techniques? Accountants could learn how to use a software program without ever attending a live training event, but they would never get the benefit of networking face-to-face with others using the same program, sharing best practices, rubbing elbows with the team that created the tools they use every day, and perhaps lobbying for future enhancements. The seasons could come and go without a single fall festival, spring concert, holiday work party, or family reunion, but what would the fun be in that?

Alice Waters—chef, restaurateur, and author of several books on food and cooking—believes that there's no better way to way to spice things up than to celebrate life's important occasions. "This is the power of gathering," she says. "It inspires us—delightfully—to be more hopeful, more joyful, more thoughtful: in a word, more alive."[1]

Our modern history is filled with iconic gatherings—from the raucous, chaotic beauty of Woodstock, where a music festival on a farm in rural New York defined a counterculture; to the royal wedding of Charles and Di, celebrated around the globe in street parties and in small family gatherings by the glow of TV sets; to the keynote address at the Macworld Conference and Expo in 2007, where Steve Jobs announced the first-generation iPhone and changed the way we connect forever. Events can help tell the story of an individual or an era, and creating them can be rewarding and even life changing.

These mountaintop moments can have profound personal and professional impact. They can motivate, inspire, and sustain us through times of stress and struggle. But someone must first decide to invest time and effort before an event becomes a reality. The rewards can be extraordinary when you decide that someone will be you.

WHO IS THIS KIT FOR?

The Event Planning Toolkit is designed for anyone tasked with planning an event but isn't quite sure where to start. It is a predicament that can arise at any time, and sometimes without much warning. And while it's easy to find examples in the news and on social media of the fabulous work of professional event planners, for the majority of us in the real world—the business professional, the employee, the association member, the community volunteer, the parent, spouse, sibling, or friend—hiring a professional to run the show is typically not an option. It will be our responsibility to step up and do the work to produce our own special occasions.

Business Management, Administration, and Staff

You've seen it: every job description written by every company, large or small, details all the specific responsibilities for the position and ends with the universal line, "and other duties as may be assigned." This is often where the accidental event planner is born. You may have started a new job or a taken on a new role that—surprise!—includes planning company events. Many times those who work in administration, human resources, or sales and marketing end up organizing the customer conference, management retreat, training event, community outreach effort, holiday party, trade show, or business expo with little or no formal training in event management.

Don't be intimidated or reluctant to raise your hand to help plan an important event at work. It not only shows initiative to go above and beyond typical professional duties but also provides an opportunity to demonstrate leadership and organizational skills. You could get the chance to bring a new perspective and a fresh voice to existing events that may have gotten stale over time. There is also the potential that you will be collaborating with colleagues in a position of management or leadership who will see your work in action. Planning and executing these projects could raise your profile and increase your value to the organization.

Association Members and Community Organizers

If you are a member of a club or association, it's highly likely that you will eventually be asked to serve on the planning committee for an event. It could be a formal gala or award ceremony, a charity golf outing or silent auction, an arts festival, sporting event, concert, or annual conference. This might place you in the category of an accidental or even reluctant event planner. You will be expected to attend planning meetings and get your assignments completed on a specific schedule, and you must learn how to incorporate these obligations into your already-busy life.

Parent, Spouses, Siblings, and Friends

Milestone celebrations underscore our personal lives, from baby showers and bridal showers to graduation and anniversary parties. You never know when you'll need to step up and organize a fundraiser for a sick friend, a block party for the neighborhood, or a dinner party for your book club.

If you have kids, you may be asked to help organize a cheerleading competition, a swim team banquet, or the elementary school's winter carnival. Later on there are the weddings, receptions, and birthday parties, and there are always the holidays—oh my, the holidays!

The Future Event Professional?

You may have found your way to this book because you've already dipped your toe into the world of professional event planning and you're thinking it may be something you want to pursue. If so, welcome, and congratulations! You are on your way to a rewarding and satisfying career. Use this book as a map to set you on the right path to event planning success.

At one point or another, each of us will have to incorporate a special event into our packed schedule. You may already be having trouble managing a full calendar, or perhaps you tend to procrastinate or become overwhelmed when your to-do list gets too long. Or maybe you simply don't think you have the organizational skills to pull off an important event. Perhaps you're a "big-picture" person, a visionary who might have trouble identifying the important details.

Think about an event that you considered memorable. What was it that sticks with you? Did something unexpected happen? Did the organizers create something extraordinary by adding special touches to surprise and delight? Were the venue and decor stunning? Or was it simply that the content and programming were so compelling that they stuck with you all these years?

These are the kinds of events that are worth every minute of effort and determination. These are the kinds of events that you can create for your guests.

Whatever special occasion is in your future, the important thing you need to know is that *you can do this.* You have the ability to produce an event that will make a difference, achieve a goal, and make someone feel special. All you need are a few tools and tips to get you on the right path, as contained in this toolkit. Consider this book your own personal event planner, working alongside you every step of the way to solve problems, inspire creativity, create value, reduce time-wasting mistakes, and ensure that your event is a smash hit.

WHAT'S INCLUDED IN THE KIT?

The Event Planning Toolkit is a reference guide that provides you with the information you need to prepare and execute each aspect of your event with precision and to enjoy the big day with less stress and fewer unpleasant surprises. Professional event planners will tell you that every minute you spend ahead of time creating your plan will prevent missteps later and add to your success.

This toolkit provides the assistance you need to make your event a real triumph. You'll learn how to create an action plan that includes all of the details you need to help you be more confident in shaping your special occasion.

The kit includes:

- Project management essentials that will keep you on track
- An action planning guide
- Design elements that can take your event to the next level
- Tips for managing crucial event logistics
- Details that can take your event from good to great

- The real secret to event planning success
- A comprehensive appendix full of reproducible worksheets and checklists

The Essentials

Section I contains a high-level explanation of how to apply basic project management concepts to the event planning process, using specific examples to contrast and compare event project planning to other projects you may have organized in the past. It shows you how to evaluate the scope of the event and calculate how much time it will take to achieve your goals and explains the importance of being realistic in your time assessment. It also explains how to determine each type of resource that will be necessary: the equipment, time, help, space, and money you will have at your disposal and where those resources will come from.

Action-Plan Creation

Section II jumps into the foundational components upon which a successful event is built. Readers will begin to understand the importance of taking time at the outset to define goals you wish to achieve with your event and how these goals will dictate every other decision you make in creating your special occasion. It includes a deep dive into the subject of the all-important budget and how to determine both the available revenue and expenses that will be incurred. You will learn how to attract sponsors and how to properly price an event. This section includes an exhaustive list of the variety of venues available and discusses how to ask the right questions so you can select the perfect location. It also contains a chapter about how to assemble a team to carry out the vision and track the tasks that are assigned to them.

How to Design an Event to Remember

Section III considers the elements that will define the look and feel of the event. These are the things the participants will hear, see, feel, and taste, the things that they'll be talking about long after the event is over.

This section addresses how to establish a theme that can be incorporated in the food, decor, and program to set the desired tone, including many examples and case studies. Next you will learn how to develop a program and agenda, select speakers and presenters, develop a realistic food and beverage budget, and control costs. This section also includes some great examples of entertainment components that can help set the tone and elevate the fun and excitement at your event.

Logistics

Section IV addresses many of the details that are often missed by a novice event planner. Here you will learn how to find and negotiate with vendors for a variety of products and services and how to select the best vendors for your project and the specific terms that should be included in any binding contract. Next you'll find a chapter on the variety of logistics you may need to consider, including electricity, lighting, sound and technology, parking, restroom facilities, and trash management. A discussion on the importance of performing a thorough risk assessment will prepare you for virtually any scenario. This section concludes by teaching you how to best reach your target audience through social media and other, more traditional methods.

The Real Secret to Event Planning Success

Section V is devoted to sharing the personal best practices I've developed over the years that have helped me achieve success in the world of project management and event planning. I describe how being organized, focused, and calm can help you overcome obstacles, have fun, and create wonderful memories for your community, family, and colleagues. I've also asked other meeting and event professionals to weigh in with their best advice.

Worksheets and Checklists

The appendix is designed to take all of the guesswork out of your event plan by providing everything you need to get started. This all-important section is filled with the tools that I've used over and over again to organize events of every size and theme. They are easy to follow, and the online versions are customizable to match the needs of your particular event. Here you will find tools for broad use, such as a goal setting worksheet or budget development, and other, more event-specific documents, including worksheets for speaker details, volunteers, and exhibitors.

HOW SHOULD YOU USE THE KIT?

If you've ever played an organized sport, you've likely had a coach who used a playbook—a guide for the team, outlining the approach used to win the game. It often includes a schedule for practices and drills, an assessment of each team member's strengths and weaknesses, and plays to be used to overcome the challenges the opposing team will bring.

The Event Planning Toolkit is your playbook. The strategies found in these pages can be applied to any event that comes your way. You may not use every single play you learn for every event you plan, but this book will help you develop the tools to address arising needs. As you journey with me through the next few chapters, you will learn how to create a customized plan for each of your events by using relevant worksheets and checklists. For example, when you read chapter 5 on establishing goals, head to the appendix to complete the goal setting worksheet when planning for your next event. From there you'll move on to complete a budget worksheet, venue selection checklist, and so on.

Once you've worked through each relevant section and completed each worksheet and checklist, before you know it, you will have cleared a path toward true event planning success. Store your customized worksheets in a dedicated location on your computer, in a shareable folder in the cloud using Dropbox or Google Drive, or print them out and organize them in an actual three-ring binder, and—poof!—you've created a portable, living action plan that will accompany you to each site visit, planning session, and vendor appointment.

MY JOURNEY

From the beginning of my adult life until today, regardless of my official job title, I have found myself responsible for planning projects and events of every scope and occasion. It started when as a student in high school I directed the school play. By my early twenties I was planning customer events at a private tennis club where my title was actually office manager. When my children came along and we settled into a new community, I got involved by organizing playgroups, block parties, book clubs, and ladies' retreats.

As my career path shifted toward local government, I found myself chairing the local bicentennial committee, coordinating a year's worth of events, including a formal gala, a parade, a series of concerts at the local amphitheater, and dozens of other commemorative events. When the State of Ohio celebrated its bicentennial, I helped organize our local celebration. For many years I chaired or co-chaired one of the largest juried arts and crafts shows in the United States, and, as an HR professional in the software industry, I have organized dozens of corporate conferences, planning retreats, fundraisers, and employee events.

Throughout my life I have been a student of and over time have become an expert in project management and event planning out of sheer necessity. It doesn't hurt that planning these special occasions turned out to be a true passion of mine (it feeds a dominant organizing gene inside of me). I've had lots of successes, a few missteps, and a ton of fun working with people from all walks of life to plan events both large and small. This has enriched my life, and I hope that for you as well. For, as author Anne Lamott writes, "It is one of the greatest feelings known to humans, the feeling of being the host, of hosting people, of being the person to whom they come for food and drink and company."[2]

My purpose in writing this book is to share my event planning experiences and a few lessons learned so that you can avoid the stress that sometimes arises when planning an event, be inspired, and dive into your next occasion with nothing short of gusto.

I have been privileged to continue my education in both the art and the science of event management by working with and learning from many event management experts. I will be forever grateful for and humbled by their willingness to provide readers the benefit of their experiences and wisdom in this book.

WHERE TO BEGIN?

No two events are exactly alike. Even those occurring on the same day and at the same time every year can have strikingly different outcomes. It can actually be an exciting challenge to examine an event you've organized in the past and find ways to make it better the next time around. You could develop a new theme that makes the event more casual and inviting. You could discover a great new event app that increases attendee engagement. Or you could come up with a different room configuration to provide better flow. You could change up the menu to provide a food experience that is cool and inventive. You could land a great sponsor that provides the resources to afford a sought-after keynote speaker. Or you could create an awesome networking event that will be remembered long after the last business card is exchanged.

Soon you will learn how exciting it can be to get messy in the details. This is the gooey-rich good stuff, people! I'm talking about taking on the things that will change your event from so-so to an occasion that satisfies and delights everyone involved.

The book I have written is not intended to organize the creative process right out of your planning. After decades taking on event planning of every scale, I can confidently say that there is no single right way to do any of this; there are many paths to your goal. But I promise that if you take the time to think through the details and create a thorough action plan, you will have a calmer, more organized, more satisfying journey. It's all laid out in the toolkit.

Every expert was once a beginner. The only way to transition from amateur to authority is to learn all you can from those who have walked this way before you; then experiment, troubleshoot, and gain perspective; and eventually apply your own unique point of view, relying on your own experience and intuition. As with learning anything, mastery only comes with time and practice.

My sincere hope is that in *The Event Planning Toolkit* you discover some novel approach or fresh perspective that you can apply to your next event and find the courage and confidence to take on any new project or assignment that comes your way.

Before we dive in, I'll leave you with this. My friend Stephanie is an artist, marathon runner, and world traveler. She inspires me with her willingness to take any new challenge head-on and work hard for what she wants to achieve. She offers advice to anyone thinking about creating something new or attempting something they think beyond their capabilities: "My friends, go out and get all the things you've ever wanted. That sweet, mountaintop victory is so delicious when you arrive. It's worth every step forward and setback you take on your journey!"

I believe that everyone has what it takes to organize an amazing event. Success doesn't require a degree or years of professional event planning experience. All you really need is a willingness to jump in and do the work. Your future will be influenced by the voice inside your head telling you that you can or you can't. It is time for you to believe in yourself and your abilities.

Let's do this!

THE ESSENTIALS

You have probably played the role of project manager many times in your life. If you've ever redecorated a house, created something with your hands, conducted an experiment, chaired a committee, raised a garden, planned a family vacation, or completed a complicated work assignment, you understand that the key to your success is managing the scope, time, and resources you have available to you to create a quality result that is on time and on budget. You are already an experienced project manager!

Planning an event is really no different. Whatever the occasion, applying basic project management skills to your plan will ensure that you meet your objectives. It's a matter of identifying the goals you want to achieve, determining the resources available, creating a task list and a schedule to accomplish each task, and making decisions along the way that will keep things on track.

It's been said that in life you shouldn't sweat the small stuff, but event planners know that a successful event is composed of a perfectly organized, ginormous pile of small stuff! The time and attention you give to those details will help ensure the results you want to achieve and reduce the stress that sometimes comes with executing such an elaborate project.

At times the stress of professional event planning could be comparable to the stress borne by an airline pilot or shouldered by a first responder. And while it's extremely rare that an event professional would ever have to deal with a life-or-death crisis, the physical demands, deadline demands, and public interaction involved with planning an event can create an extremely pressure-filled environment. So, in planning your event, your best line of defense is to do everything in your power to plan ahead for every possible scenario.

Who remembers getting a paint-by-number set as a kid? The painting was divided into hundreds of tiny, irregular patches, each containing a number corresponding to a paint color provided in a little plastic pot. Using a small paintbrush, you painstakingly filled in each patch with tiny swipes of paint. After you completed every section of the canvas, your meticulous attention to detail was rewarded as you beheld your beautiful Van Gogh or Monet reproduction. It was only by having enough discipline and persistence to complete each tiny section that you were able to enjoy the completed final product.

This notion of "sweating the small stuff" is all about realizing your goals one small step at a time—setting objectives, identifying deliverables, creating an action plan, and then breaking that action plan down into manageable tasks and activities that make up that glorious big picture you visualized.

1

Becoming a Project Manager

You can apply project management principles to an event of any size. It could be something relatively small like a holiday party or company picnic. Or it could be something larger like a business conference, concert, or fundraiser. The only real difference in the planning of different events is their budget, the number of days you have until the event, the number of tasks that will need to be completed, and how much help you will have to complete them. The principles remain the same.

Successful event planners need to have a thorough understanding of everything that is available to them to create the best-quality event possible. The very best way to minimize risk and avoid disaster is by being realistic and using your resources wisely. A sales manager at an event venue once told me, "You can't expect a filet mignon event if you only have a fried chicken budget!" While her delivery may have been a little harsh, she offered a valuable lesson: You need to face the fact that there are limits to what can be accomplished if you are short on time, help, or money.

In the 1959 book *Betty Crocker's Guide to Easy Entertaining: How to Have Guests and Enjoy Them*, Betty says that "The first step, and a very important one, is deciding what kind of a party you can give most gracefully with the equipment, time, space, help, and money at your disposal."[1] This probably sounds familiar because it is the foundation for every successful project you've ever undertaken. Ladies and gentlemen, let me introduce you to one of the unsung pioneers of modern-day project management and event planning: Ms. Betty Crocker! She nailed it; every project begins with identifying the desired outcome and then applying all necessary resources in an efficient and productive manner to achieve that outcome within an acceptable time frame.

A project manager must learn to demonstrate certain qualities or skills in order to be effective. Below I've listed the top ten traits that I believe are important to becoming a truly skilled project manager. As you read this list, remember that these are things we can all aspire to be. They are *not* prerequisites for getting started; we all have skills and abilities to bring to the table, but no one person can possess them all right out of the gate. Even seasoned event professionals get frustrated or tired or loses their ability to stay positive. They will sometimes miss a deadline or struggle to stay neutral when trying to resolve conflicts. So, as you take a deep breath and dive into the event planning arena, just keep these traits in mind. Make a mental pledge to incorporate them as often as possible into your thoughts, words, and actions, and before you know it, they will start to become second nature.

Once you understand the importance of these qualities and competencies and identify where you may need help from others, you can create a team that collectively possesses these skills and many more. Over time you will acquire this expertise as you learn from your predecessors, from your team, and eventually from your own experiences.

1. *An effective project manager is a leader.* Leaders provide the structure and processes necessary for their teams and their projects to succeed. They can look at a project from twenty thousand feet and see the whole picture, keeping it top of mind even when the details seem overwhelming. They understand the environment they are working in and know what is necessary to achieving the established goals.

Leaders show appreciation for hard work, recognize those efforts publicly, and at all times treats their team with respect. They are willing to share their knowledge and perspective by mentoring those who are new to the team.

2. *An effective project manager is organized.* The ability to successfully organize people, schedules, and tasks is the very definition of project management. To be organized, a project manager must thoroughly document the approved action plan, organize and assign work, and track dates and deadlines. They understand what is urgent and what is important at any given moment. They know how to prioritize resources and escalate tasks that require attention.

3. *An effective project manager is a problem-solver.* This means they have the ability to assess a problem, brainstorm potential solutions with the right people, make a decision, and stand behind that decision. When a problem arises, a project manager will need to spend some time thinking about how to avoid the same problem in the future, but they mustn't get stuck in anger or blame. An effective problem-solver is agile; they don't allow an issue to fester and grow. They have the ability to address a problem head-on and react quickly. Once they fully understand the problem and how it happened, they must focus on potential solutions. This means generating as many solutions as possible, researching and evaluating those solutions, and then selecting and implementing the decision that seems best for the situation.

4. *An effective project manager possesses conflict resolution skills.* At times a project manager may have to navigate disagreements within the team and make decisions that won't necessarily be popular. When trying to resolve conflict on a team, it's important that the people on each side of the conflict feel like their position is being heard and respected. That means that the project manager must be extremely attentive and composed, remaining as calm and neutral as possible while gathering the information from all parties. They must

control the conversation and not permit personal attacks or defensiveness to get in the way of an acceptable compromise or solution.

5. *An effective project manager has business acumen.* Any experience a project manager has in business fundamentals—financial management, budgeting, marketing, human-relation skills, technical skills, logistics, risk management, or contract negotiation—will be extremely valuable to managing an event. If the project manager doesn't personally have this kind of experience, they must surround themselves with people who do. The value of having team members who possess these skills cannot be overstated.

6. *An effective project manager has a positive attitude.* A project manager must model appropriate behavior and be ready to forge ahead with courage and determination no matter the circumstances. They should try to create an atmosphere of positivity from the very first organizational meeting. After all, this team is going to all be working together to create something extraordinary! The manager's level of enthusiasm and passion for this project, whether high or low, will be felt and mirrored by the team and ultimately the guests.

   A positive attitude can be hard to come by for anyone who is physically, emotionally, or mentally exhausted. Self-care is vital to creating stamina and sustaining momentum on an event with a long lifespan. A solid exercise, sleep, and nutrition plan is essential for a project manager to be consistently effective and available to their team when necessary. It's also important to build a personal and professional network of people who support the team's endeavors—people to lean on when things start to feel overwhelming or when extra help is needed.

7. *An effective project manager possesses good communication skills.* This means working to adopt a communication style that is clear and straightforward. They should be able to effectively and efficiently convey to others what needs to be accomplished in order to achieve their goals. Project managers must lead by example, but they definitely don't have to have all of the answers. They know that effective

communication is most definitely a two-way street, and they know how to encourage and inspire others to bring their own ideas to the table. They recognize that it is more important to listen than to be heard and will ask lots of questions in order to receive input before making final decisions.

8. *An effective project manager knows when to delegate.* The day will come when a project manager may have to step away from planning a particular event, either by choice or by necessity. By delegating important tasks from the outset, the manager provides opportunities to show others what they are capable of. Being a martyr by doing everything themselves ("If I want it done right, I'll have to do it myself!") is bad for the individual and bad for the project. If a project manager hangs on to that mindset, never challenging team members to push comfort zones to learn and grow into individual roles, they are sentencing themselves to a lot of hard work, undue stress, and ultimately total burnout. They will also destroy any chance for their team members to use their own initiative and creativity to introduce new ideas and perspectives. A project manager should carefully select team members who have proven themselves able (and, more important, willing) to take on certain elements of the action plan, and then give them the autonomy to run with it.

Embracing delegation means that the project manager is creating a leadership succession plan that will allow them to step aside with confidence when the time comes, knowing that the event preparation will continue without missing a beat. Of course, former managers will often make themselves available for input and advice if necessary. But what a wonderful legacy they are creating: long after their individual contribution has been made, they are able to leave an event better than they found it and watch the remaining team construct something beautiful.

9. *An effective project manager is ethical.* A good reputation, once lost, is almost impossible to regain. An ethical leader does the right thing even when no one is looking. They establish a code of conduct at

the outset and make sure the entire team agrees to uphold that code with their words and their actions. The project manager is consistent and always has good follow-through so that the team as well as all other project stakeholders know that they can be trusted to get the job done.

Trust is always at the core of great teamwork. Project managers recognize people for their effort; they give credit where credit is due. They also take ownership when they or one of their team members makes a mistake. When it comes to working with third-party vendors, ethical project managers negotiate in good faith and hold vendors accountable for their deliverables. They also make sure that they and their team uphold all agreed-upon terms. A leader must walk the walk if they want to be known as a person of integrity.

10. *An effective project manager is kind.* Kindness may not be a trait that immediately comes to mind when you think about project management, but I believe it is essential to the process. People who are treated with kindness will be more motivated to perform, and those leaders who encourage their teams to operate in an atmosphere of kindness, peace, and calm will have more favorable outcomes. Every successful event professional I've ever met genuinely cares about their team, their audience, and their stakeholders and possesses a basic desire to serve others and to create real connections between people.

2

Scope

The scope of an event encompasses all of the deliverables, the elements that must be present to achieve your objectives. Scope is made up of many components, including the length of the event, the depth of the program, the tasks that must be completed, and the added extras that make your event special. The scope is always dependent on the available time and resources.

A seasoned project manager spends a lot of their project planning time evaluating the *time/quality/cost triangle*. The concept is this: You may be able to achieve one or two of these elements and still achieve a satisfactory result, but you can't skimp on all three, nor can you always expect to achieve all three. It's a matter of deciding which elements are most important. This is a basic project management principle that can easily be applied to event planning.

If you're trying to execute a project quickly and cheaply, you will probably have to make a few sacrifices on quality or the depth of scope. Say, for instance, that your local high school football team goes to the state championship as the underdog and wins in spectacular fashion. A celebration is definitely in order, but it needs to happen very quickly, using a budget that will be scraped together in a short window of time through donations solicited from local businesses. In this case, the scope of the event must be narrowly defined: the players and their accomplishments can and must be honored and celebrated, but without spending a lot of money. It's time to book the biggest gymnasium you can find, bring on the high school marching band, and put the rest of your volunteers in charge of making signs and rallying citizens to line the streets as the champions arrive home.

If you want a quality result and need it to happen fast, you must be prepared to apply more resources to the project. If you've been tasked with arranging a meet-and-greet reception for a political candidate who has suddenly decided to make a stop in your city, there's no time to waste. When you have little or no notice, you may have to enlist more paid staff in order to get the job done. You'll need to consider additional costs, such as last-minute travel arrangements, premium rates from quality vendors willing to squeeze your event into their schedules, additional security, and expedited printing and shipping fees.

If you're looking for an inexpensive solution and still want to achieve a quality result, you may have to wait longer than you'd like for the desired outcome. If you've decided to plan a wedding on a budget, for example, you may have to wait for an off-season date so you're not paying premium prices for venues or services, or you may have to devote more personal time to completing DIY projects, like creating your own website, invitations, and table favors.

If you're organizing a conference and don't have enough time to book three days' worth of speakers and presenters, or if you don't have the budget to pay for the speaking fees, travel, and lodging for high-profile speakers, you'll need to consider shortening your event or finding quality local speakers who can provide relevant content for your attendees at little or no charge. If offering three plated meals each day is too rich for your budget, you may have to consider not including breakfast in the registration fee or perhaps providing an early evening reception with some finger foods rather than a complete dinner. If you are serving alcohol, you may opt for a simple selection of house beers and wines instead of a top-shelf, full-service bar.

It's easy to see how calibrating time, quality, and cost can help you quickly adjust the scope of your event to match your resources while providing a high-quality experience.

AN IDEA FLOURISHES

Once upon a time, the two hundredth anniversary of the founding of the village where I lived and worked was fast approaching. In a desire to commemorate this very special time in the history of our community, a core group of interested citizens began to meet the year prior to organize a special weekend celebration, and I was happy to volunteer to coordinate the activities.

As planning and discussion continued that year, excitement began to spread throughout the community; it seemed that everyone, young and old, wanted to be a part of the festivities. Additional ideas were brought forward, and the celebration began to expand. The local historical society decided that a full-length, hardbound commemorative book was in order, a combination of historic photos and documents, alongside dozens of interviews and commentary from long-time residents. Other people started to come up with additional incredible ideas. Before long, we were planning a walking tour of historic homes, a multilocation quilt show, a founder's ball, a historic lecture series, a concert series that included the US Air Force Band of Flight, a golf outing, a fashion show, and an Independence Day extravaganza that spanned three days and was to include fireworks and a parade! The scope of our original weekend celebration had quickly grown to an entire year's worth of events, more than twenty-five separate occasions in all.

When you allow the scope of your event to grow, everything else must grow in proportion. There was no way we could have pulled off all of these additional activities with the original planning committee; we simply didn't have the capacity to organize such a complex schedule on our own. Each individual event required a set of resources that was specifically committed to executing that particular occasion. In addition to fundraising needs (including donor solicitations, sponsorships, and government grants), each event had its own time line and action plan, as well as a volunteer committee, venues, equipment, and publicity. People stepped up with their time, talents, and resources, which ensured that the community would have a year-long celebration that we would always remember.

Managing *scope creep* is important if your event is on a strict budget or if you are short on time. It can be tempting to include more elements to your event to add value, increase excitement, and engage attendees. But trying to do too much and doing it poorly will not generate the impression you are trying to achieve. Instead, focus on trimming down your agenda and skillfully executing fewer but more significant things for greater impact.

3

Time

It's easy to misjudge the time it takes to carefully plan and execute an event. In fact, the most memorable occasions were most likely planned well in advance, with plenty of attention paid to each detail along the way so that they only appeared effortless in their execution.

When planning, often you will be working on a recurring event with a date set in stone—a conference that always takes place the second full week in October, a fashion show falling every year in conjunction with New York Fashion Week, or a music festival people flock to every Memorial Day weekend. In such a case, you can start implementing your plan much earlier and take your cues from the previous years' events and the longtime team members who already know the event inside and out. They will be able to help you create a reasonable time line; they know that the contract for the trash removal company always gets negotiated immediately following the prior year's event and that all sponsor contracts have to be signed, sealed, and delivered six months prior to the start of the occasion so that all of the deliverables in those contracts can be achieved. They know that the most popular musicians and entertainers must be signed early if you want to have any chance of getting them on your program since they book their engagements a year or two in advance and will not typically squeeze in another gig once their performance schedule is full.

But there may be times where you have no control over the date of your event or how much time you have to prepare. Sometimes events are initiated by people who have no understanding of how much time is actually necessary to execute the event successfully. Any boss who decides in November that it would be fun to host a holiday party for the entire staff and their significant others at the most luxurious hotel in the city or the most popular nightspot in town clearly doesn't realize that the most sought-after venues are reserved months or even years in advance, as are most respected service providers. Time is not on your side in this scenario; even if you are able to find a venue on such short notice, there are dozens of other tasks you'll have to arrange very quickly, starting with invitations and followed by selecting a food and beverage menu, entertainment, decor, and so on.

Begin confirming the event elements essential to a successful result as early as possible. Once the foundational components are established, you'll be able to do a budget assessment and begin to incorporate other elements that will add value and interest, as time and resources allow.

And always remember the time/quality/cost triangle: If you find yourself planning an event with very little time to prepare, be prepared to compromise on certain elements, such as venue selection, and expect to pay a premium for some of the resources you will require or pay expedited shipping and handling fees for equipment or supplies.

UNDERSTANDING YOUR TIME LINE

The very best way to manage the time line for your entire event is to always, always strive to be proactive rather than reactive. What does this look like? It means controlling the situation by making things happen instead of merely reacting to something after it has occurred. It means looking ahead to upcoming meetings, appointments, deadlines, and to-do items and thinking about what you can do right now to bring them closer to completion.

A proactive time line means that you've gathered the details about lead times for products and services so you can place a final order on a timely basis. Let's say you want to provide a T-shirt for approximately two hundred volunteers for each day of your technology convention, and the supplier needs a six-week lead time in order to get the shirts, add your logo, and deliver them to you a week before your event begins. If your event begins on September 15, then you need to be prepared to deliver your camera-ready artwork and a list of quantities, sizes, and colors of the shirt you've selected no later than August 1. This means you need to (1) determine your budget per shirt, (2) select a shirt style, (3) create a logo, (4) verify exactly how many volunteers you will have, and (5) determine what size shirt each person will need . . . all before July 1. If you aren't deep into this whole process by early May, you are going to be doing a lot of unnecessary scrambling in July.

Another example of how a proactive approach can benefit the planning process is in the area of communication. The best practice is simple: communicate early and often. An invitation that adequately explains the who, what, when, where, and so on will eliminate a lot of questions and phone calls later. An FAQ page on your registration website with every conceivable question answered will save you time wading through dozens of e-mails down the road: "Which hotels are within easy walking distance to the convention center?" "What's the dress code?" "What should I bring to the retreat?"

If your event requires that groups of people meet regularly to report on planning progress and to assign new action items, a proactive approach includes sending out meeting reminders. What a waste of time it would be to have key team members miss an essential meeting because they just forgot the date and time! A simple reminder could have prevented the situation altogether. Before your meeting, check in with committee chairs to discuss progress on outstanding items, or perhaps meet with your core team ahead of the larger team meeting to troubleshoot known issues before they become a larger problem and suck up valuable meeting time.

UNDERSTANDING DEPENDENCIES

As with any project, a big part of managing your event time line is having a firm grasp on which tasks are dependent on others—which must be completed before work can begin on the next priority.

A great example of a dependent task is a printed conference program. It's one of the last things that will be completed on your to-do list, because it's contingent on so many other elements of your conference. The program will include a list of sponsors, including logos and artwork, descriptions, and sponsorship levels. It will include a comprehensive schedule, complete with a list of tracks and sessions. It will include bios of speakers, session descriptions and times, and meeting room locations. It will also include maps of the venue and the surrounding area, frequently asked questions, after-hours event info, and information about next year's event, including dates and location. There are dozens or even perhaps hundreds of tasks that must be completed before the program can go to print; contracts must be signed, speakers must be secured, along with bios and session descriptions, decisions about future meeting dates must be made, and artwork from vendors and sponsors must be secured. Understanding these dependencies is crucial to creating a sensible time line you can establish to accomplish your goals.

If you are in a time crunch, it will soon become evident that you probably can't do everything by yourself; you will need to expand your team to divide and conquer the to-do list, or something will surely be missed. Less time means one of two things: either more resources will be needed or the scope of the event will have to be reduced. It's all part of the time/quality/cost triangle.

4

Resources

Organizing any event requires the careful management of many resources. The word *resource* is often used synonymously with the word *money*. But when we're talking about resources in event planning, the word has a much broader meaning; we're talking about space, people, and equipment in addition to money. A resource is anything you will need to fully execute your project.

"Your circumstances are not the reason you can't succeed," says leadership consultant Cy Wakeman, author of *No Ego*. "They are the reality in which you must succeed."[1] This is especially true for those who are planning an event. Rarely will the circumstances be ideal; most of us won't have unlimited funds, unlimited time, and an overabundance of volunteers. Rather, we'll have to stick to a budget, make timely decisions, and use our resources wisely and efficiently in order to pull off the event.

SPACE

The space or venue you choose will dictate the number of guests you can accommodate. Perhaps many spaces are required for your event. If you're planning a conference, for example, you'll be assessing meeting rooms and banquet facilities, as well as storage facilities, registration space, and exhibit halls. If you're hosting a convention in a city center, you'll need to know the number of parking facilities and nearby hotels with availability. If you are hosting a virtual event, you will need to know the number of participants that can log in to your event at any given time. And if you're hosting an outdoor music festival, you'll need to find a space that can accommodate multiple stage areas, parking for thousands of vehicles, and infrastructure to support not only the lighting and sound for the musicians but also food trucks, safety services, and restroom facilities.

PEOPLE

One of your most important resources in planning your event is the team that will assist you in executing your plan. Planning an event of most any size is going to require a lot of help; it won't be a solitary exercise. You'll quickly burn out (and potentially fail) if you try to manage an event of any scale without soliciting help from others. The conductor of an orchestra would be pretty lonely without a stage full of talented musicians, each delivering their unique contribution with skill and beauty. Surrounding yourself with the right people will help you create an experience that will be remembered for years to come.

When thinking about the people to include on your team, you are going to have to not only formulate the group that will work alongside you but also select professionals who will deliver other elements central to your event. It could be as simple as ordering a birthday cake and a bouncy house for your child's next birthday or contracting with a well-respected audiovisual firm to create an atmosphere full of color and whimsy for the annual gala. Choosing your partners wisely will eliminate a lot of hassle and distress on the day of your event.

If you are planning an annual event, it is vital that you form strong relationships with the people who have planned it in the past. Many times, associations will have a core team of individuals with several years of experience planning all or part of an event who have phased out because their term of office expired or they just got burned out and decided to take a break. These individuals are a goldmine of information and an important resource to those newly elected committee members and volunteers.

If you are new to an event planning committee, you may walk in with a laundry list of great ideas and innovations; if so, fantastic! But before you present your ideas for change, spend some time gaining a little perspective on why things have been done a certain way in the past. Seek out those who came before you, buy them a cup of coffee, and learn from them. Better yet, if you're newly appointed and will assume a planning position next year, shadow the person who has your job this time around. Attend the meetings, be a fly on the wall, listen, and take tons of notes. Once you fully understand the intent behind decisions previously made, you'll be in a better position to introduce new alternatives or ideas that could make the planning process more efficient or an after-hours event more successful.

CONNECTION

Everything is made easier for an event planner who knows how to leverage their connections. Every connection in your personal and professional life—every social media connection, coworker, family member, friend, and acquaintance—has the potential to be a valuable resource when you are organizing an event.

If you are attending a networking event, save every business card you receive, and on the back of each one, make a note for future reference about where you met them and how you connected. If you attend a conference, make friends in the buffet line. Collect information from the presenters, the sales manager, the A/V team, the caterer, and the entertainers. Follow all of your new contacts on LinkedIn, Twitter, Instagram, or Pinterest. Everyone you meet could be a resource for a future event.

This strategy has served me well time and time again. The speaker at a lunch and learn I attended for human resource professionals ended up being the perfect keynote for a client conference. An exhibitor at a trade show told me about a great venue he found for a civic organization he volunteered for, and it became one my favorite venues to use for an annual corporate conference. I attended a breakout session presented by a legal expert and reached out to her when I was project planning and needed legal services in her area of expertise.

Remember that if you plan to leverage the power of connection in this way, you must be willing to pay it forward. When a fellow presenter at my TEDx talk asked me to meet with a group of novice event planners for a regional technology association to help them plan their annual event, I was happy to help. I listened to their plans and challenges, helped them avoid a few potential pitfalls, and provided some tips and tricks that put them on the right path to creating a solid action plan.

Always be generous with your time and talents when you are approached by a connection you have made. I promise it will reap rewards down the road.

EQUIPMENT

Equipment needs will vary widely based on the type of event you are planning. If you're in charge of a large fair, festival, or outdoor show spanning many acres of ground, you'll need to procure golf carts and utility vehicles to move people and supplies. You will need a radio system to communicate with your team and with security officials. You'll also be responsible for acquiring the right number of portable restrooms, trash dumpsters, generators, tents, and staging. If you are planning a trade show, you'll require not only tables, chairs, signage, and pipe and drape but also fork trucks, lifts, and other equipment for safely moving and installing large displays. And if you're planning a party, gala, or award ceremony, you will need to work to secure the equipment necessary to produce compelling audio and video presentations as well as lighting, decor, awards, programs, and other equipment and supplies that will create a visually stunning and unforgettable event.

When attempting to secure equipment and supplies for your event, ask your vendors whether they would be willing to provide their products or services at a reduced rate in exchange for sponsorship. This is a great way to keep costs under control and provide your vendor and partners with some valuable advertising and market exposure.

MONEY

Your budget will determine how extravagant you can be with the food, flowers, and the quality of the speakers and entertainment you provide. When assessing your budget, explore every possible source, including registration fees, sponsorships, and in-kind services.

When you assess all of your available resources and realize that you have some gaps, you are going to have to either adjust the scope of your event or get creative. Try bartering for services, buying flowers wholesale and creating your own centerpieces, borrowing equipment, repurposing decor from previous events, or taking advantage of free or nearly free public venues.

Meetings and events professional Margie Nolting once worked with a group that wanted to host a conference but didn't have any real budget, so she helped them book an all-inclusive cruise. She was able to find an available cruise ship, and the conference registration fee for the attendees didn't extend beyond the per-person cost of the cruise. The meeting spaces on the ship were well appointed, and all of them were included at no extra charge (including the built-in audiovisual equipment). Evening events included a cabaret show already included as part of the cruise amenities. Margie says, "The only major cost to the organization was the bar bill for the after-hours party, which was held around the pool. It ended up being an inexpensive but highly successful event for the company, and the attendees had an unconventional but fantastic experience."

Resource planning is a process that must begin very early in determining the scope of your event. The first step is to brainstorm all of the resources you can think of that will be needed to pull off what you hope to achieve and then to create a comprehensive list. Next, thoroughly inventory everything available to you that is known—staff and volunteers who have made firm commitments, equipment and supplies immediately available or already in stock, cash on hand, and so on. Discuss the gaps that exist between the wants list and the haves list, and start planning how you will close the gap. This could involve assigning team members to obtain quotes, solicit volunteers, or reach out to patrons or sponsors who might be willing to help. As the project manager, it will be your job to find ways to reduce the scope of your event if your resources don't match what you hope to achieve.

II

CREATING AN ACTION PLAN

Screenwriters use a script to tell their story. Chefs work from a recipe to get consistent results. Travelers use GPS to get turn-by-turn directions in order to arrive at their destination. Use any analogy you like, but the same principles hold true in event planning: you must create a plan in order to achieve the desired outcome.

Imagine that you've been asked by your boss to plan the annual company golf scramble to benefit a local charity. The date is four months away. Not only will you have to cover the costs of hosting the event, but your boss also needs to be able to present a hefty check to that worthy cause! What do you do first?

While you may be tempted to start immediately publicizing and registering people for the event, there are a lot of things you need to know before you can create a registration form or determine what the registration fee should be.

What is your fundraising goal? What is the maximum number of people you can accommodate? What is the per-person charge for greens fees and cart rental? How will people register? Who will be in charge of acquiring your sponsorships? What other expenses do you need to budget for (website, registration software, insurance, security, administrative costs, and so on)? How many people will you need to staff your event (parking logistics, registration table, hole monitors, and the like)?

What food and beverage options will you provide to your attendees throughout the day? Will you have a door-prize raffle or silent auction, split the pot, or host other fundraising activities before or after the round of golf has concluded? What is your backup plan in case it rains?

I could go on, but you get the picture. It quickly becomes apparent that you have a lot of questions that will require answers before you can even begin establishing the registration fee and promoting your event! An event has many moving parts and requires a lot of thought and planning in order to succeed.

It's time to begin creating your action plan. To begin, you must create your foundation: visualize the goals you want to achieve, understand your budget, find the right venue, and assemble an effective team.

5

Identifying Your Goals

A goal statement paints the picture of what you want to accomplish with your event. It is a twenty-five- to fifty-word "elevator pitch" that anyone on your team should be able to recite from memory and describes the purpose of the event at a high level. A clearly stated goal statement will provide the foundation you need to make effective decisions throughout the entire planning process.

It's important to involve your entire team when working through the goal statement process. Ask them about their expectations, and determine where everyone agrees and where compromise will need to occur. This is not a solitary endeavor; it's important to get your team's perspective in this exercise.

When documenting your goals, you should be able to describe why the goal is important, what resources and action steps are required to achieve this goal, and the people or teams that will be responsible for performing those actions. Use the Goal Statement worksheet in the appendix to work through each phase, and you will have a lot more confidence that your team's efforts will be focused and effective.

OBJECTIVES

What is the purpose of your event? What objectives do you hope to achieve when all is said and done? Whether it's a customer event, a

trade show, a retreat, a fundraiser, a family event, or an annual convention for a civic organization, identifying and documenting all of your
objectives, and then making sure everyone involved understands those
objectives, is the best way to ensure that your time and resources are
spent wisely and efficiently.

This is the point in the planning process where you will identify additional stakeholders. Before you can completely articulate your goals,
you need to identify all of the parties invested in the success of your
event. Surprisingly, this list for your event could be quite long. When
thinking about goals, consider the expectations of each stakeholder and
what you want to achieve on their behalf.

A corporate event can have many stakeholders, each with a number
of objectives. The executive and management teams want to strengthen
their relationships with their clients; exhibitors want to share information on their products and collect qualified leads; sponsors are looking
for opportunities to highlight their brand. Speakers and keynotes will
want to educate and inspire, and participants want to be educated and
inspired. Accomplishing multiple objectives requires a lot of planning
and effort, but it can be done. If done well, your event will be remembered for years.

Once everyone understands the purpose behind your event, it also
becomes much easier to enlist the right team members to create an action plan and task list that will achieve your objectives.

DELIVERABLES

It's time to get specific, to identify the deliverables you will produce at
your event in order to achieve your goals. This will involve some serious brainstorming with your team. What kinds of activities can you
include in your program that will deliver the goods? A vague statement
like "Help attendees grow their businesses" is an objective, not a deliverable. A better deliverable statement would be "To include workshops on
topics like social media marketing, financial management, and effective
recruiting for small-business owners."

If you're planning a conference for aspiring writers, examples of deliverables would include a speaker lineup that includes published authors willing to share their successful writing journeys as well as a wide variety of publishing-industry experts. It would also include an opportunity for writers of a wide variety of genres to pitch their writing to agents and publishers looking for new projects.

SUCCESS CRITERIA

In this phase, you will discuss how you will know when you have achieved success. You will identify all of the desired outcomes and how you will measure your success at achieving the outcomes. Examples of measurable outcomes include numbers of tickets sold, dollars raised, or sales closed. Success can also be measured through survey results, exit polling, and social media activity.

OBSTACLES

As you work through this goal setting exercise, remember what you've learned about the fundamentals of effective project management: Is there anything related to scope, time, or resources that will limit your ability to achieve your objectives? If you've only been allotted a single day for a planning retreat, there will be a limit to what you can effectively accomplish; your goal statement and objectives must be finely tuned to ensure that only the most important topics make it onto the agenda. If you have a budget set in stone, you will have to carefully plan your event to stay within those guidelines. Every project has constraints; identifying these challenges is the first step to overcoming them.

SAMPLE GOAL STATEMENTS

Following are a few examples of goal statements for several different kinds of events. As you think about these goals, consider what the objectives, deliverables, success criteria, obstacles, and action plans might look like for each type of event.

- "Our intentions for the Fifteenth Annual Customer Conference are to build and strengthen relationships with our clients, educate attendees on how to fully utilize our products to help them be successful, and market new products and services that will help them work smarter while improving our profitability."
- "The goals of the Summer Writer's Workshop are to attract a widely diverse group of aspiring authors of all genres, help them find their community and accountability partners, provide education from industry experts who can provide guidance on a wide-ranging array of topics, and offer attendees the opportunity to pitch their work to agents, editors, and publishers."
- "The purpose of the John Smith Memorial Run is to honor the memory of John and his many contributions to our community, raise awareness of the devastating disease that took his life far too soon, and raise at least $10,000 to help find a cure."
- "The goals of the Annual Arts Festival are to (1) provide a venue for a carefully selected group of talented artisans to demonstrate their processes and sell their creations, (2) offer an opportunity for local nonprofit organizations to raise money by operating all food and beverage booths, and (3) promote our community as a great place to live, work, play, and create."

OTHER EVENT GOALS

Following are some additional goals you may consider when planning your event:

- Raising money
- Raising awareness
- Community building
- Recruitment
- Impressing stakeholders
- Creating a buzz
- Building loyalty

- Strengthening reputation
- Creating a spiritual or emotional experience
- Providing an opportunity to achieve a personal or professional goal
- Arranging access to buyers or sellers
- Providing a showcase
- Building rapport
- Improving customer relationships
- Improving employee or partner relationships
- Entertaining
- Having fun
- Hosting a competition
- Celebrating a milestone
- Recognizing someone special
- Creating a networking opportunity
- Team building

UNEXPECTED RESULTS

Our company holds a basket raffle every December. We randomly assign six or seven people to a team. They come up with a basket theme, purchase the contents, assemble the basket, and put it on display in the office. Raffle tickets are sold over a couple of weeks, and the winning tickets are drawn at our annual holiday luncheon. The proceeds of the raffle are donated to a local charity or nonprofit that is nominated by one of our team members.

Organizing this simple little event has turned out to be beneficial in several ways. Initially our goal was simply to create a team-building opportunity, to have team members who didn't work side-by-side on a daily basis work together to come up with a plan to get the basket assembled and on display before the deadline. The teams seemed to have a great time working together on this project, but it also became quite popular because the people who buy tickets have the chance to win some really cool and creative baskets. Best of all, we've been able to write some hefty checks over the years to organizations doing fantastic things in our local community. Our primary goal to create a team-building event ended up having some great secondary outcomes.

IT'S ALL ABOUT CREATING CHANGE

Phil Mershon, director of events at Social Media Marketing World, the world's largest social media marketing conference, reminds us that when it comes to creating great events, "our goal should always be to create experiences that will change people." Think about what your attendees will be talking about on their ride home or when they get back to their office. What did they experience at your event? How were they changed? Were they inspired, educated, delighted, or bored? What do you want them to remember six months or a year from now? Would all of your stakeholders consider your event a success?

Clarifying your goals will make all the difference between a mediocre occasion and a marvelous signature event that people will be talking about long after it's over.

6

Understanding Your Budget

Creating a detailed budget is crucial to planning an event. Until you have a firm grasp on all sources of revenue available and all expenses you will incur, you are operating on nothing but guesswork, and that's a dangerous way to operate.

LET'S TALK ABOUT REVENUE

A variety of potential revenue sources are available to you, depending on the kind of event you're planning. If it's a corporate event, such as a conference or trade show, you may be utilizing a combination of company funds, sponsorship fees, exhibitor fees, and registration income. If you're organizing a ticketed event, such as a concert or fundraiser, you'll be counting on robust ticket sales and possibly donations to achieve your goal. If you're planning a private event, such as a birthday party or wedding, you may be using your own resources to cover most of the cost, or perhaps you'll be using private contributions or bartering with family, friends, and acquaintances for in-kind services to keep costs under control.

Ticket Sales or Registration Fees

If you're relying on ticket sales or admission fees to cover your costs, proceed directly to the expenses section of this chapter ("Let's Talk about Expenses") and get to work! Until you have a comprehensive picture of the expenses you will incur, you can't possibly know how much to charge in order to cover those costs, let alone make a profit. You also need to know how many people you can reasonably expect to attend your event. If you're hoping for five hundred guests, play it safe by dividing your total overhead expenses by four hundred tickets to calculate the ticket price. That way, if ticket sales fall a little short, you'll still have your basic expenses covered.

When it comes to a ticketed event, it's imperative that you have a team ready to promote your event to maximize attendance. Be sure to use a tracking system that allows you to see how registrations are going during the weeks leading up to the event so you can regularly assess expected revenue and make adjustments to expenses if it looks like you won't reach your goal.

Sponsorships

Sponsorships can be local, regional, national, or international corporations or organizations that have agreed to provide money, products, or services that you would otherwise have to pay for. They agree to do this typically in exchange for marketing or promotion (it benefits them because your audience is also their audience). Or perhaps they simply have a desire to be involved in the community and want recognition on your social media sites, program, and signage.

When seeking corporate sponsors to provide either money or in-kind products and services, you must begin courting them early. Corporations typically create an annual budget for sponsorships or community involvement. If their budget is established in January, chances are that their funds for charitable giving will be allocated early on in the year, so you'll probably be out of luck if you wait until September to submit your request. Identify the companies you want to approach, and inquire about their budget cycle so that you know when you'll need to approach them with a sponsorship request.

Most larger companies will post their policies and procedures regarding benevolent giving or sponsorships on their company website. Perhaps they only sponsor nonprofit events, or maybe they focus on supporting events that benefit children or encourage health and wellness. You're going to have a leg up on the other organizations competing for those dollars if you know what the company expects to see when receiving a request for donations. You may be required to complete an online application form explaining your event and your mission.

If a potential sponsor declines a primary sponsorship level, get creative by providing promotional sponsorship opportunities. This involves logo placement on notebooks, lanyards, water-refill stations, conference bags, and walkways. Ask if they can sponsor a particular keynote speaker or session relevant to their mission. Other events that could be sponsored include networking events, breaks, or receptions.

If a company declines to donate cash, don't give up. Ask whether they have any product or service that could benefit your event. Perhaps they can donate shirts or refreshments for your volunteers or donate a pen or other item for a goody bag or silent auction.

Event operations and project management expert Allison McKnight explains that in order to attract and retain sponsors for your event, you must understand their motivation—why they would want to be seen at your event and how can you actively integrate their brand and have attendees fully engaged with their product. Allison told me about a time when she was looking for sewing machines to give away as prizes for a costume-making contest at a large expo. "I had a staff member go to a sewing convention and strike up a conversation with a sewing machine manufacturer," she says. "In the end, they ended up giving us machines in exchange for a large exhibit booth at our event where they could present live demonstrations and workshops for things like embroidery and ruffle making." This is the kind of big-time creative thinking that can grow your sponsorship dollars, generate fabulous opportunities to wow your audience, and offer your sponsors a huge return on their investment.

Brian Monahan is vice president of sales and business development for Prestige AV and Creative Services, a company that not only provides third-party services for events of all sizes but also acts as in-house technology provider for many hotels and convention centers. Prestige is often asked to provide some of their services for free in exchange for promotion as an event sponsor. His best advice? "If you are seeking sponsors, you must think of them as a customer: What is your plan to serve them as a customer and deliver the ROI? For instance, being offered a table at your gala doesn't provide the same return on investment as receiving access to your network, a thank-you on your letterhead, or a reference to another organization who might need our services."

Many sponsors have confided to me that they often feel like an afterthought or even a nuisance when they show up at an event they've sponsored. Remember that sponsors are the reason you can pay for quality speakers or entertainment and keep ticket prices low. They provide a lot of value to your event and will require value in return. The good news is that you can provide much of that value and create a long-lasting relationship with your sponsors at little or no cost! It costs nothing to introduce sponsors during key portions of your event, include them in your printed collateral and on your website, give them access to your attendee contact information, or write a recommendation letter for their services to your sister association in the next state.

Donations

Is there someone you can approach to match giving? Individual donations could increase if people knew that their dollars would be matched by a corporation or other benefactor. If you decide to use a fundraising website so that giving can continue after your event is over, be sure to link the donation site to your event website and social media pages.

Acquiring sponsorships and donations can be a time-consuming job. If you're relying on these sources as a large portion of your revenue, you must have team members dedicated to this task in order for your event to be successful.

Fundraisers

There are all sorts of events with fundraising as the primary goal. Perhaps you're raising money for a family in troubled financial straits after a medical crisis or other emergency. Or maybe you're organizing on behalf of a church or school organization raising funds to pay for new equipment or to offset certain expenses. A club or association will often have an ongoing mission to raise funds that provide scholarships or support agencies counting on donations in order to operate. Or you could be hosting an annual event for a nonprofit that relies on the success of the event to fund their year-round activities and help them achieve multiple goals.

Creating a fundraising event that is entertaining, meaningful, and profitable can be a bit of a trick. Every dollar you spend on event expenses is a dollar that you can't use for the greater good. One key to profitable fundraising is the ability to solicit donation items that can be raffled or auctioned; you must also seek out contributions to offset your overhead expenses. If you're hosting a spaghetti dinner to raise money for uniforms for the high school marching band, see whether you can get the ingredients for the meal donated from a local grocery store. If you're hosting a gala that includes a live auction to raise big money for medical research, you'll need to use every contact you and your team have to find patrons who will donate big-ticket items—luxury vacations, jewelry, artwork, autographed memorabilia, or box seats to a concert or sporting event.

Put a face to the cause you're attempting to support: play a video for your guests or, better yet, invite a guest speaker who can tell a compelling story of how they benefited from the proceeds of the fundraiser. Making an emotional connection with your potential audience will help drive donations.

Fundraisers can take many forms:

- *Basket raffle.* Donated items are assembled into themed baskets. Two-part tickets are sold, and people decide which basket they would like to win most, placing one side of their ticket in that basket. A winning ticket is drawn for each basket.

- *Splitting the pot.* Two-part tickets are sold, with one side going into a drawing and the other kept by the buyer. Once sales are closed, a winning ticket is drawn, and the winner receives 50 percent of the total proceeds from the ticket sales, with the other 50 percent going toward the fundraiser. Many times I've seen the winner of a split-the-pot contest end up donating their portion of the winnings in order to benefit the cause.

- *Silent auction.* Items are displayed in a public area. All attendees are assigned a bid number, and the number is recorded. A bid sheet is set next to each auction item. Attendees bid on items using their bid number, so no one knows whom they're bidding against. Bidders are responsible for continually visiting the items they are bidding on and adding a higher bid to the bid sheet if someone has bid against them. A specific time is set for bidding to close, and the person with the highest bid is the winner of the auction item. A silent auction is an easy fundraiser to transition to a virtual event using an online meeting tool such as Zoom.

- *Mystery auction.* Items are displayed in a public area, and a sealed container is placed in front of each item up for bid. Bidders write their name and the maximum price they are willing to pay for the item, having no idea whether their bid is higher or lower than other bids. When bidding closes, the container is opened, and the highest bidder wins the contents.

- *Live auction.* Items are on display in a public area, and potential bidders are registered and issued a bid number. An auctioneer describes each item, including its estimated value. Bids are solicited, and when the bidding stops, the highest bidder is the winner. The key to a live auction is your auctioneer: they don't necessarily have to be a professional, but they must be lively, fun, and able to engage the audience and encourage them to continue to raise the bid.

- *Quarter auction.* Donations are received for the auction from direct-sales representatives (makeup, jewelry, kitchen products, cleaning products, and so on). The reps are each provided with a space to display items for direct purchase as well. Attendees purchase a numbered auction paddle or paddles, and when an item comes up on the auction block, they can choose to bid by raising their paddles and placing the required number of quarters in the bid bucket for each paddle. When all bids are made, the emcee draws numbers corresponding to the paddles until a successful bidder is drawn. Money is made through the sale of auction paddles, the quarter bids, other raffles, and perhaps food and beverage sales.
- *Reverse raffle.* Two oversized decks of playing cards are required for the reverse raffle. In one deck, punch a hole in the top of each card, and thread a loop of yarn big enough for people to wear the card around their neck. Sell the cards for $20 or $50 per person, and pull cards one at a time from the other deck throughout the evening, eliminating players, until you get to the last card and person standing. That person wins the grand prize, which could be a portion of the sales or a donated item.
- *Goal sponsorship.* These are the "-athon" events. Sponsors are solicited for people participating in a twelve- or twenty-four-hour walkathon, readathon, swimathon, rockathon, and on and on. The possibilities are endless. Usually each participant is required to secure a minimum amount of sponsor dollars before they can participate. Sponsors agree to pay a certain amount for each hour of activity completed by the participant.
- *Tournament or race sponsorship.* This type of fundraiser works well for golf tournaments, video game tournaments, poker tournaments, bike races, and footraces (5ks, 10ks, and so on).
- *Cornhole, darts, shuffleboard tournaments, and the like.* Participants pay a fee to enter the tournament and follow the rules set by the organizers. High scorers win cash or other prizes.

- *Hosting a meal.* Pancake breakfasts, spaghetti dinners, fish fries—all these events typically start with a club or civic organization that needs to raise some money on a local level. This kind of fundraiser requires a team of people to secure donations of ingredients, a facility to host the event, and teams to prepare the food, serve it, and clean up after it's all over. This is a great type of fundraiser, and it has the potential to build up a community or neighborhood by strengthening interpersonal relationships.
- *Hosting a concert, play, or other performance.* Secure entertainers—like a soloist, band, acting troupe, comedian, or choir—who volunteer to perform for free or at a reduced fee, and then sell tickets to support your cause.
- *Carnival.* Schools are great at organizing these kinds of events. Tickets are sold to play games at various booths, with inexpensive prizes for winners.
- *Festival.* This is a themed event that provides entertainment in the form of food, vendors and artists, games, rides, and music. Many festivals are created around specific food items. Where I live, there are annual festivals that celebrate everything from sauerkraut to pumpkins to strawberries! Other festivals celebrate music, art, and culture. Festivals typically generate revenue from some combination of ticket sales, booth rentals, food and beverage sales, and sponsorships.
- *Bake sale.* Volunteers make and donate every imaginable kind of treat—cookies, brownies, candy, cakes, pies—and sell them, typically at a companion event that has a larger draw, such as a festival or sporting event.
- *Art show.* This fundraiser involves selling admission tickets to an art display at a local studio or museum. Consider partnering with a local college or high school arts program.
- *Fashion show.* Here the beneficiary organization partners with a clothing designer or department store to create a themed show, such as "Back to School" or "What's New for Spring," where the beneficiary receives a percentage of all sales. For an added twist, find a museum or

theater company and have models show off their collection of vintage clothing. As an added touch, provide an afternoon tea or a light meal.

- *Car wash.* Partnering with a company that has adequate facilities to handle traffic flow created by dozens of vehicles entering and exiting to get a car wash performed by a large group of volunteers. This is typically done for a suggested donation, and is a favorite way to raise funds for cheerleading squads, marching bands, and so on.

- *Cake walk.* This is usually part of a larger carnival or festival, where donated cakes or other sweets are won by ticket purchasers. To set it up, place large numbers on the floor in a circle. Participants walk around the circle as music plays (think musical chairs). When the music stops, everyone stands on one of the numbers. Then a number is drawn from a bucket, and the person standing on that number gets their pick of the sweet treats. As an alternative, you can organize a *toy walk.* Or, if your players are adults, change it up and get donations for a *purse walk* or *book walk.*

- *Games of chance.* Bingo, poker, pull tabs—in each of these games where money is bet, the winner splits the pot with the beneficiary organization. Check the legality of conducting games of chance in your location before including these kinds activities at your event.

LET'S TALK ABOUT EXPENSES

The variety of expenses you will incur for your event will fluctuate by the type of occasion you are planning. In addition, the cost for each item will vary depending on your goals and available resources.

Take some time to obtain quotes from at least two reputable vendors on the big-ticket items so that you know you are getting a fair price and can be confident in your budget estimate. Prepare a comprehensive *request for proposal* (RFP) for the big contracts; when the contractors use your bid format, it will be easier to make side-by-side comparisons.

The following are a few basic categories that you should consider as you begin to construct your budget; add other categories as needed, depending on the type of event you're planning.

Venue

Unless you're planning an event in a place that you control (such as your home or business), you will most likely have costs involved in your site selection. The items included in your venue charge could include everything from meeting room fees and A/V charges to equipment rentals, labor charges, and sleeping rooms for your team and guests.

Decor

This category includes flowers, lighting, table decor, paper products, staging, banners, and all kinds of signage. It also includes registration kiosks, backdrops, soft seating, and theme-related items.

Food and Beverage

Food and beverage expenses can easily account for a third of the total budget for certain kinds of events. If you're planning a wedding, you're probably planning for a cocktail hour, a plated meal or buffet, an open bar, and a wedding cake. But if you're planning a corporate conference, you may need to plan for three meals a day, plus an all-day beverage station, afternoon break food, hors d'oeuvres at a welcome reception, and snacks or finger foods for after-hour events. Also don't forget linens, serving pieces, bar- and waitstaff, and taxes and gratuities (see more on this below). If you're organizing a fair or festival, you will need to have lots of options for a variety of food preferences and lots of beverage options, including easy access to drinking water.

Program

Program costs might include fees for speakers, including lodging and transportation. They can also include fees for entertainers and support staff, production costs, virtual meeting platforms, and costs supplies for individual activities. If your event has an audiovisual component, costs can include everything from online registration to procuring the best vendors for sound, lighting, wireless networks, social media walls, and so on.

Prizes and Giveaways

This can include swag bags or party favors, auction items, ribbons or trophies or plaques for contest winners or award recipients, door prizes, and thank-you gifts for speakers, dignitaries, team members, and volunteers.

Publicity and Promotion

There can be many components in this category, including advertising, publicity packets, graphic design, website and online registration tools, paper and stationery, postage, photography and videography, and printing costs for brochures, programs, and signage.

Logistics

Spend some time making sure to capture every other possible expense when creating your budget. Logistical expenses could include telephones or two-way radios, transportation, fuel and mileage, liability insurance, safety equipment, security, volunteer expenses, portable restrooms, trash removal, and other services.

Hidden Expenses

These are the budget-busters that can all too easily be overlooked in the initial budgeting process. There are several items that you must consider before you can finalize your budget:

- *Taxes and service fees.* When reviewing a banquet menu from a venue, such as a conference center or hotel, it's important to know that the per-person price on the banquet menu is not the final price. Look at the line of small print all the way at the bottom of the banquet menu, and you'll see that there's almost always a service fee added to cover taxes and gratuity, which typically ranges from 22 to 30 percent. If you're calculating the cost to feed one hundred people a plated meal with a stated price of $50, the price just went from $5,000 to $6,500. If your budget only allows for $50 per person for food, you'll have to select a lesser-priced item to stay within your limits.

- *Other gratuities.* There are many aspects of your event where tips may need to be factored into your budget. These range from the driver who picks up your keynote speaker at the airport and delivers them to the hotel or venue and the bus drivers who transport your participants from one venue to another to bartenders, musicians, and other entertainers.
- *Freight and storage.* If you must have items shipped directly to your venue, be sure to incorporate the freight charges and any storage fees that may be charged by the venue.
- *Labor and overtime.* Check the fine print on all your contracts to be sure you understand the additional fees you will incur if you exceed the contracted time limits for your service providers. These fees can rack up quickly.
- *Merchant fees.* If you allow attendees to pay for their registrations through sites such as PayPal, there will be a service fee deducted from their total payment. Likewise, many online registration platforms have a fee associated with credit card payments accepted through their site, depending on the type of plan you choose. In some instances, it's possible to pass that fee on to the attendee so that you will still receive your stated full ticket price (think Ticketmaster).
- *Contingencies.* As a rule, it's a good idea to add a 10 percent contingency to your budget to cover unexpected expenses, such as legal fees, insurance premiums, additional security, tips, surcharges, or emergency runs to the office supply store or copy shop.

MONEY-SAVING TIPS

- Partner with another event team to share resources (equipment, etc.) that you may only need once or twice a year.
- Ask the venue about other events going on in the facility at the same time as your event, and check out that event's website. Are there any speakers or presenters whom your attendees would be interested in

hearing? Most speakers would *love* the chance to land two speaking gigs on the same day and would most likely discount their typical speaking fee in such a case if asked.

- If you can't afford to provide all meals for your event, consider organizing a dine-around. This is where a small group of between six and ten people sign up to share a meal at a local restaurant. The group could consist strictly of attendees who want to get to know other attendees, or network, or just share some good conversation. Another option is a hosted dine-around, where sponsors, vendors, or speakers make the arrangements for the table and facilitate a topic-based event of special interest to attendees. The planning of a dine-around can be simple or complex, depending on the format. To keep it simple, just reserve the tables at local restaurants (make sure the restaurant knows everyone will be paying with a separate check), provide a signup method—either online or at the registration desk—designate a meetup spot, and you're done! In order to avoid a lot of no-shows, you might consider charging a reservation fee to hold their spot at a specific table.

The earlier you begin the budgeting process and identify the monetary constraints you are working with, the easier it will be to adjust the scope of your event or work on solutions to improve your resources—like working on additional sponsors, adjusting your ticket price or registration fee, or modifying your food and beverage offerings.

7

Finding the Right Venue

Now that you have established your goals, have created an action plan, and understand your budget, it's time to find the perfect venue for your event. When researching your options, you'll need to consider all aspects of the space, including the overall size, parking availability, equipment, and configuration options (see the Venue Evaluation worksheet in the appendix).

All venues have a website where they post information about their facilities and services. At a minimum, you should be able to study their photo gallery and banquet menu, the layout of each space available, and the capacity of each space based on room configuration. The website should also include a list of amenities, maps and directions including proximity to local airports, sleeping room information (if any), and an online form to complete in order to get the proposal process going.

TYPES OF VENUES
To help you get started, examine the pros and cons of the various venue types to determine which one is perfect for your event.

Banquet Facilities
These facilities are designed specifically to hold special one-day events like parties, receptions, and fundraisers. These venues will typically offer

a variety of packages that include food, beverages, sound, decor, and service personnel. Some simply charge for use of the building and leave it to you to bring in everything else you may need. This type of venue can be quite affordable and is ideal for an event only lasting a few hours and where sleeping rooms aren't required.

Banquet facilities may or may not have a liquor license or bartending services. Be sure that you and your guests understand and abide by the particular license restrictions at your venue. The venue could be at risk of losing their license if your party violates the rules associated with their particular license.

Hotels

If your event involves getting people together from a variety of locations, such as a training session or shareholders' meeting, consider a hotel that can provide both meeting space and sleeping rooms. Many hotels will offer discounted or free meeting space and banquet rooms if you can guarantee that a certain number of sleeping rooms will be reserved by your group or that you will spend a certain dollar amount on food and beverages. Certain hotels can also provide beautiful spaces to hold weddings, receptions, and rehearsal dinners.

Conference and Convention Centers

If you are involved in planning a large event, you are going to need a partner that fully understands the accompanying special challenges. Convention centers will have the coordinating team, equipment, and service staff best prepared to serve your needs for a large or multiday conference or trade show. If you need lots of meeting space and the ability to feed hundreds or even thousands of people a hot meal in a short window of time, this is the kind of facility you should be exploring.

Participants must come prepared to pay for parking unless you are able to work out a voucher system with the parking facility and pay for their parking fees out of your budget. You may need to provide transportation to and from nearby hotels throughout your event. Because the meeting rooms can be spread out over several wings, you will also have to incorporate more time between sessions for your attendees to move from one room to another.

Lodges, Camps, and Retreat Centers

If you're interested in something a little more rustic, consider the facilities offered at state parks, scout camps, or retreat centers. You may not have free Wi-Fi or flat-screen televisions in your room (you may not have a television at all), but that's the point of selecting these kinds of locations: they're perfect when you want to have a captive audience with few distractions—think team-building events, spiritual retreats, or reunions. You'll definitely want to check out these facilities in person; many of them were built decades ago, so you'll want to see the condition of the meeting rooms, sleeping rooms, and shower and bathroom facilities firsthand.

I once attended a retreat at a nature lodge that was simply beautiful. It was nestled in the woods far from any city or town. There was no cell phone service, no Internet, no television, and—wait for it—no flush toilets! There was one shower room for ten guests that included two tiny shower stalls and two compost toilets. A couple of attendees were unpleasantly surprised by the accommodations, but they soldiered through, and it turned out to be a beautiful and memorable event. Just be sure to include these kinds of details in your advance information so guests can make informed decisions and plan ahead.

Restaurants

Many restaurants have private meeting rooms they will reserve for a semiprivate meeting space. This is a great alternative for entertaining vendors, clients, or out-of-town executives. It could also work for small private events, such as a birthday, anniversary, or retirement celebration.

Check each restaurant's policy on bringing in decorations and outside food, such as a birthday cake. Depending on the size of your party, a restaurant may ask you to order from a special menu with a few of their most popular options instead of from their larger regular menu. Be prepared for the fact that they will always automatically add a standard gratuity to your final bill.

Outdoor Venues

Bugs. Wind. Rain. Heat. Cold. Noise. Scheduling an outdoor event can bring all kinds of special challenges. But the great outdoors can also be a beautiful setting for weddings, reunions, concerts, and fundraisers, and of course for golf outings, street fairs, and picnics.

Once you've decided that an outdoor venue is the right choice for your event, make sure that the one you select is appropriate. Schedule your site visit on the same day of the week and same time as the event you are planning. Spend some time on site, paying particular attention to anything that will affect your guests' experience: Could the noise from nearby roads or airports negatively impact your event? Where are the nearest restrooms? Is there enough parking? When will you lose daylight? What about access to electricity or refrigeration? Will you need to budget for additional equipment rentals, water for volunteers in case of extreme heat, or additional tents or shelters in case of heavy rain or cold?

If you will be coordinating an outdoor occasion, you must come up with a contingency plan. If there's a 75 percent chance of rain on the day of your event, will you continue on, cancel, or postpone? How will you communicate a postponement or cancellation to the attendees? How will you protect your participants in the case of severe weather? Once you have answers to these questions, you can concentrate on your other event planning basics. Remember—plan what you can, and anticipate the rest!

Unusual Venues

It's time to think outside the banquet room! Although many public and private facilities were originally designed for a completely different purpose, plenty of sites have the parking, facilities, and space necessary to host all sorts of affairs. I've attended events in the visitor's center of a state park, in the showroom of a home-theater store, on a riverboat, at a ballpark, at a racetrack, at an aquarium, and at the tasting room of a winery. So look around: your perfect venue may be right under your nose!

Consider some of these less commonly used sites when planning your next meeting or event:

- Museums
- Theaters
- Churches
- Wineries
- Bars and breweries
- Zoos
- Barns
- Universities
- Career centers
- Trade schools
- Funeral homes (Yes, that's right—funeral homes!)
- Government facilities (City halls or public libraries may also be available for use and for free!)

VENUE VISITS

Once you've narrowed down your choices with your online research, take the time to visit each venue to meet the sales team and experience the space in person. If traveling to a venue is cost prohibitive or otherwise impractical, most venues can provide a virtual tour to help you experience the property. Prior to scheduling your tour, prepare an RFP (see the template in the appendix) that includes all of the questions for which you need answers; having these questions written down will ensure that you come away with everything you need to know to compare and contrast venues and make the very best decision for your event. Best of all, the sales manager at the venue will love you for being so organized.

If you can't provide the basic information about your event, you will make it much more difficult for the venue to help you accomplish your goals. Meetings and events professional Tracy Zglinicki tells the story of a time when she was contacted by the administrative assistant of a corporate CEO to book a venue for an event. "She wasn't able to provide even the most basic of details—not a date, an approximate headcount, or even an outline of the agenda," said Tracy. "I'm always surprised when I am contacted by event organizers who have no idea about the basics of their event or even know the right questions to ask. It happens more often than you think."

Take care to evaluate the meeting spaces, and be sure that they have more than enough room to handle each of your activities comfortably and efficiently. Also check out the parking lot, restrooms, sleeping rooms, and amenities such as the pool, bar, or spa.

Review your event space for accessibility for those participants with disabilities. If every guest doesn't have reasonable access, you run the risk of not only violating the Americans with Disabilities Act but also damaging your organization's reputation.

CREATING AN RFP

The best way to organize your thoughts before contacting potential venues is to gather all of the known information and create a *request for proposal*, or RFP. The sales staff can use this information to prepare a detailed quote that will help you make a more informed decision. At a minimum, the RFP should contain the following pieces of information:

- Organization name
- Contact name
- Date(s) and whether your dates are flexible
- Time(s)—start and stop times for each day of your event

- Event name
- Type of event
- Goal(s) for the event
- Who the audience is and how many attendees are anticipated (using past numbers if it's a recurring event)
- Event agenda
- Type of sessions—presentations, training, labs, workshops, networking, etc.
- A/V and technology needs
- Internet access required, both Wi-Fi and hardwired
- Number of rooms needed and configuration of each room
- Other spaces required—exhibit hall, storage, presenter lounge, registration area, bookstore, outdoor spaces, etc.
- Food and beverage needs
- Sleeping room requirements, if any, and types of rooms needed
- Evening events and entertainment
- Special needs—rentals, transportation, traffic control, etc.

ATTENTION TO DETAIL

As you evaluate venues, spend some time with the staff, and get specific about your needs and what is and is not included in the quote they will provide. It is important that you read and understand everything contained in any contractual agreement before you sign. (A more in-depth discussion regarding contract terms is found in chapter 19.) Ask the venue to document any additional policies or guidelines that are not stated in the actual contract.

You'll want to pay special attention to a few particular details, specified in the following sections.

Remembering Your Audience and Your Purpose

As an event planner, you must understand and consider the demographics of your audience when selecting a location and venue. Perhaps your attendees are looking for events that incorporate lots of technology; if so, they are going to expect a secure Wi-Fi network and plenty of charging stations. Are they are looking for unique experiences and organizations that care about sustainability? Will they be open to venues in a metropolitan area, with access to public transportation and close proximity to entertainment districts? Will they be okay with navigating enormous venues that require miles of walking every day, or should you focus on smaller venues with good accessibility? No matter what demographic you serve, everyone will expect good food, great service, safety, and cleanliness above all.

Food and Beverage Clause

Most contracts will include a minimum purchase of food and beverages, which will often be accompanied by a reduced rate or waiver of fees for banquet rooms, meeting rooms, and other facility rentals. Review this clause carefully, and consider whether you can easily achieve this minimum based on the number of expected attendees and the number of meals you intend to serve.

"Be sure you understand when head counts are due for food or the cutoff date for the hotel room block," says events and meetings professional Erin Thomas. "I know from experience that it is very frustrating when you are trying to reach a client as their food head count is due and they don't know or won't call you back. Understand the guarantees you are making for the number of hotel rooms or meal counts. If you book a meeting room and meal for one hundred people and then only have twenty people RSVP, it shouldn't come as a surprise to learn that you will still have to pay the amount guaranteed in your contract."

Cancellation Policies

You can be on the hook for a lot of money if you have to cancel your event. Be aware of the venue's policies and deadlines and what you'll have to pay in case your event must be cancelled.

Additional Fees

Pay special attention to additional fees that aren't included in the contract—like for items such as microphones, projectors and screens, staging, lighting, and so on. Most venues will provide a menu of technology options clearly stating associated fees. Don't be afraid to negotiate a reduced charge for these items, especially if your event will be generating significant revenue for the venue from sleeping rooms or banquet fees.

"If you're planning an event at a large convention center," Erin reminds us, "don't assume that one contract will take care of all the components of your event. I once planned a big one-day event that required exhibit space, A/V, food—the works. Only by asking lots of questions through the contract negotiations with the venue did I discover that I would need to contract with separate providers for audiovisual, banquet services, phone lines, security, etc."

Cleanliness and Safety

In a post-COVID-19 world, event venues must be prepared to describe the measures they have in place to ensure the health and safety of your participants. Be sure to include questions in your RFP about their cleaning and disinfection practices, their availability of hand-sanitizing stations and other safety equipment, what safety measures have been incorporated into their food-service operations, and how room configurations can be modified if social-distancing protocols are required at your event.

HERE'S YOUR SIGN

Taking the time to research and select the perfect venue is crucial to your success. When you can stand in a space and visualize your participants having a great time and your goals being recognized, you'll know that you've found the perfect home for your event. I've been fortunate enough to work with many fantastic venues, but one in particular stands out in my mind when I think of top-notch hospitality and service.

Imagine that you have been working with an out-of-town venue for months primarily via telephone and e-mail to plan a three-day conference. You arrive on setup day to attend a precon meeting with your event manager. She invites you into a conference room to go over the details of the event one final time and discuss any last-minute changes. When you open the door, you stop dead in your tracks; there appears to be a meeting already in progress. You quickly take a step back, thinking there's been some mistake—that the room has been double-booked. But your event manager says, "No, this is for you!"

That's when you see a placard at the front of the table with your name on it as well as the names of the other members of your event planning team. As you take your seat, you notice the array of beverages on the side table and the yummy-looking dessert at each place setting. As you scan the table, you see people in suits and others wearing logoed polo shirts and khakis. One is even wearing an honest-to-goodness chef's hat!

Your event manager asks each person to introduce themselves; that's when you finally understand that these people will all play key roles in your event and that you were a genius for selecting this venue to host everything. You meet the general manager of the venue, the director and assistant director of sales, the beverage manager, the banquet manager, the head chef, the floor manager, the sleeping room coordinator, and several other people critical to the success of your event.

After your team has introduced themselves, you get down to business. As a group, the event order sheets are reviewed, day by day, hour by hour, room by room. Questions are asked, notes are made, and at the end of the meeting you are completely confident that the entire staff is on the same page about what you need in order for your event to be successful.

At the conclusion of the meeting, each of your core team members is presented with a lapel pin to wear throughout the event, indicating to the entire staff that these are the decision makers for the event and that nothing gets added to or changed on the approved banquet event orders without their approval.

This was my recent experience at Kalahari Resorts and Conventions—and my sign that we had chosen our venue wisely. Their mission is clear: to provide a world-class experience for the event planning organizers that choose Kalahari so that they'll want to come back again and again. This commitment to excellence carries through the entire organization, from buffet-line workers and bartenders to janitorial and housekeeping. They all strive to provide a fantastic experience for every client; they're the kind of partner I want to work with every time.

I'm sorry to say that you won't get this kind of reception at every venue you choose. The only way to know for sure that you're working with a great venue is to ask lots of questions during your site visits and interview staff to get a feel for their dedication to providing great customer service.

A CUT ABOVE

I recently had the privilege of spending some time talking shop with a couple of members of the Kalahari team. Jerry Simon, director of sales, and Leslie Meyer, director of catering and conference services, shared their best advice for planners looking for the perfect location for their event.

When asked how Kalahari sets themselves apart from their competitors, Jerry said it's their staff, their location, and their unique combination of entertainment and conference space. Kalahari is indeed a somewhat unconventional conference facility. The authentically African-themed decor includes textiles and artwork sourced from Africa, creating a dramatic and stunning environment. The resorts not only boast some of the largest indoor waterparks in the United States but also provide many other amenities, including a spa, exercise facility, game center, and several premium restaurants and shops. When helping potential clients compare their facility to other options, Jerry points out several differentiators: "Many of our competitors are in urban locations and may have higher bed taxes, parking garage fees, etc. We have the advantage of geography, with easy accessibility, whether flying or driving. We are also all highly trained and prepared to provide full service when it comes to traffic control, security, and crowd management."

Jerry and Leslie agree that the best thing event planners can do when evaluating venues is to look beyond price and really evaluate what each venue offers. "Take into the consideration the amenities," Leslie says. "Do the they have the ability to customize their offerings for your event and ensure that your attendees leave happy? Evaluate the quality of A/V, the meeting rooms, and the equipment. Is there soft seating in the lobby areas, or is it antiseptic? Also, is there reliable Wi-Fi accessibility throughout the facility that can support a large crowd?" The Kalahari team looks for ways to go above and beyond to create something extraordinary for their clients and help them exploit the unique attributes of the venue. They've customized rooms, created themed menus, designed after-hours spa events and lounge takeovers, and more.

Leslie's best recommendation for meeting planners is to "be open-minded to new ideas. The ideal client is one that has a vision, knows their attendees, and lets me offer suggestions and ideas of things that have worked well in the past. We know what works and what doesn't in our space, so we encourage clients to leave some of the details to us, because we know what works best. When they've lost trust because they were let down by another venue, it makes our job harder. Our job is to earn their trust and create happy customers who will come back again and again."

GETTING SOME HELP

If a venue search is something that seems like it will take more time than you could possibly devote to it, or if you're trying to find a venue in a location you aren't familiar with, then it may be time to enlist help. Luckily, there are partners that can take care of this part of your action plan so you can focus on the rest.

Margie Nolting is a meetings and events professional for HelmsBriscoe, a world leader in hotel and site selection and contract negotiations. In this business model, the procurement firm is compensated not by the event organizer but by the service providers (the hotels, resorts, and convention centers) in exchange for matching clients to their venue.

"If I could go back to the beginning of my career in event planning, the first thing I would do is find a third-party meetings planner," says Margie. "I like to say it's like using the services of a realtor to buy a home. A third-party partner like HelmsBriscoe is valuable because we understand that the hospitality business is changing every day, and we understand that it can be daunting when you don't understand the options and the cost factors."

A procurement specialist gathers as much history and information about your event as possible, including budget and goals, and then uses their knowledge in the field to find the best locations, properties, and venues to meet your event needs. They have the knowledge and contacts to bring in other third parties to see to food, A/V needs, and entertainment. Their procurement staff thoroughly vets each facility before adding them to their preferred list, so you can be confident that you will be connected with a venue that has the ability to produce the experience you desire.

"Many companies have professional planners on staff," says Margie, "but in some cases they're planning two hundred–plus events a year. They need to focus on speakers, volunteers, and dozens of other event elements. We can help them by negotiating contracts with the venue and other third-party partners, especially when that negotiation involves multiple meetings per year. It's also important to fully understand what you are agreeing to in areas such as attrition, cutoff dates, permission to extend, cancellation clauses, etc."

For example, she says, "Does your contract describe what remedies are available if agreed-upon services aren't provided (i.e., sleeping room isn't available)? Will the venue negotiate with their third-party A/V company, or will you have to do that? What about Internet availability and usage?" She finds that "oftentimes these issues don't get addressed until after the initial contract is signed, but we make sure it is negotiated and put in writing right from the beginning. It is another area where we can provide value."

If finding a venue for your event is stressing you out, consider partnering with a procurement specialist to help cross this essential item off your list.

Refer to the appendix for a Venue Evaluation worksheet and an RFP template.

8

Assembling Your Team

"Never doubt a small group of committed people can change the world," said American cultural anthropologist Margaret Mead. "Indeed, it is the only thing that ever has."[1] This particularly applies to the world of event planning. I have been fortunate to be a part of some extraordinary teams of people who've made extraordinary things happen with nothing more than a shoestring budget and a profound desire to make a positive difference in their corner of the world.

Once you've created a written action plan for your event, you should be able to easily identify the aspects of the plan that will involve commitments from others that are vital to your event's success. Once identified, those are the first things you need to focus on. Getting them moved to the Completed column on your list is your first priority. If key tasks are assigned to others, make sure your team members are checking in early and often with you on their progress.

STAFF

Your team is by far your most valuable resource. You can have access to all the money you could possibly need, but without a trained, dedicated, and motivated staff, your event and your goals will suffer. When you can look to your left and your right and see people you can trust with any and every part of your event, whom you know for certain will have your back and will support you every step of the way . . . that's when you know you have a great team.

Allison McKnight is an event operations and project management expert who has planned events all over the world and understands how crucial it is to assemble an effective team. In one of her previous gigs, she was director of entertainment for a huge expo that attracted thousands of people loving all things anime. She had been brought in after several key individuals had abandoned their roles, and when she walked in the door, she found a hostile and distrustful staff in total disarray.

No one on this team knew her, and she had no documentation to work with, so they all had to start from scratch. "I had sit-downs with the remaining team and created a spreadsheet that captured information about the previous year's event—budget information and how the budget was spent, what rooms were used at the convention center, etc.," Allison told me. "Then I created a separate spreadsheet that contained everything the staff thought we should consider changing for the next event. They provided input on where resources could best be spent, how they could repurpose spaces for better effect, and other concerns they had about how the event had been managed in the past. This information was used to create a new action plan."

"I understood that in order to get my newly appointed managers on board with this new plan, I had to involve them in the decision-making process and work to create some emotional investment in the project," Allison says. "Then we all made sure that everyone knew exactly what we wanted and how to make it happen." The end result was quite successful; that year they added several concerts and masquerade parties to the event, as well as a library where people could read and relax with friends.

By valuing her team members' contributions, communicating clearly with them, and clarifying an action plan, Allison was able to leverage her team into an invaluable resource that pulled off a memorable event building on past successes.

VOLUNTEERS

Finding and keeping volunteers can be a crucial component of your event's success. If the occasion you're planning recurs annually, look to those who have helped in the past; anyone who's previously invested time into a project should have a vested interest in its continued success and will most likely say yes if asked to help. They likewise have valuable insight into how the event is structured and what attendees expect of the experience. These past team members are also the best people to recruit additional volunteers for you, because many times they have coworkers, friends, and acquaintances with similar interests.

There are many places where you can begin your search for volunteers. Here are a few.

Internally

If it's a company event you're planning, look to other teams in the organization for volunteers. Create a shift schedule, and see whether you can convince upper management to have each team or department to commit to filling a certain number of shifts. Even if they may not be willing at first, the fact is that these people will be most familiar with your mission, your goals, your products and services, and your clients and guests.

Allison McKnight remembers a time when the event planning firm where she worked had a team with a reputation for acting like snooty divas because they often worked with celebrities. "But when one of our events failed an inspection by the fire marshal because he didn't like the room configuration, they were asked to jump in to help the other departments to correct the situation," she said. "Before long, everyone was laughing and working together to accomplish a common goal, and the 'cool frat house' team played a big part in making it happen." Enlisting the help of other departments that don't have regular event planning duties is an effective team-building strategy: when there is something important to be accomplished, it's always better when it can be accomplished together.

At Schools and Universities

Are you holding your event in a location with a school or university nearby? Students, including members of fraternal organizations or clubs, are always looking for community service opportunities. This may be especially relevant to you if you're organizing a nonprofit event, such as a community fair, a charity walk or run, or a fundraising gala.

If the school has a degree program in hospitality or travel and tourism, you've hit the jackpot! These students will be craving opportunities to help create any event that will provide them real-world experience in their chosen field, either as a volunteer or as a paid or unpaid intern.

Young people are so open to contributing that they should never be counted out as a valuable resource. They can bring enthusiasm and energy that will inject new life into your events.

In the Community

Regions with active convention and visitor's bureaus or chambers of commerce may have rosters of volunteers that you can draw from.

Senior adults can be recruited for a variety of roles. They can be quite useful as goodwill ambassadors at arrival points, registration desks, information kiosks, and so much more. Connect with senior-living facilities or activity centers in your area, and you may find that you have a whole new source of volunteers ready and willing to lend a hand.

Online

Check out volunteer-matching services online. Sites like Volunteer-Match specifically match qualified volunteers to nonprofit causes in larger metropolitan areas all over the United States working in a variety of categories, including human rights, arts and culture, children and youth, computers and technology, and health and medicine. Other sites to check out include Catchafire and Create the Good.

Among the Event Participants

Don't forget to draw from your participants. Can you offer a discount on registration or other perks in exchange for them to introduce speakers, help with setup or teardown, or stuff conference bags for a few hours? You'd be surprised how many of your guests would jump at the chance to help behind-the-scenes in exchange for free or reduced-price admission.

Take advantage of event websites and newsletters, online bulletin boards, e-mail lists, and social media sites. This will get the word out, but don't expect people to line up after simply reading about volunteer opportunities. Many people won't "volunteer to volunteer" without being approached personally; face-to-face recruiting is one of the best ways to get positive results. Some people are not inherently joiners but have a lot to contribute. Be open to reaching out to ask people to help you make your event a success.

TAKING CARE OF YOUR VOLUNTEERS

Adding volunteers to your team creates additional responsibilities and budget items that you need to plan for. They may need transportation, lodging, meals, apparel, and security credentials. But most important, they will require appropriate training. Make sure your volunteers understand the goals and objectives of the event and thoroughly explain the roles and responsibilities you expect them to fulfill. Be sure schedules are easily accessible and that your volunteers know what to do in case of an emergency, such as an unruly attendee, a suspicious package, or a safety issue.

One of the biggest mistakes you can make according to Allison McKnight is to not take care of your volunteers by providing substandard sleeping arrangements, inconvenient travel or shuttle buses that aren't on time, and poor food choices. "You have to treat your volunteers with respect, not as second-class citizens," she says. "They are your friends, and you must treat them the way that you would want to be treated." She recalls one year running through the convention center during an event in full swing, when she suddenly got a whiff of cooking meat. She entered a conference room and, to her surprise, found a group of volunteers in the corner, cooking hot dogs and hamburgers on a miniature grill! They had pooled their small stipends together, as well as some of their own money, to purchase the grill and buy food so they could prepare an inexpensive meal for themselves. It became quite clear to Allison that this event needed to reevaluate its budget for volunteers and adjust it so that meals would be provided, or so that the volunteers would at least be adequately compensated to buy their own food.

THE HEART OF A VOLUNTEER

Have you ever paid attention to the volunteers that are working an event? Stop and take a good, hard look: These people have jobs, families, and a lot of other responsibilities. But they made a choice to attend meetings, make phone calls, get dirty, work hard, lose sleep, and devote some of their precious time to make the event a success.

Why do they do it? Is it for the free snazzy green staff shirt? No—they do it because it's fun! Because it's for the greater good. Because they believe in the mission and the goals of the event. Their time and their effort are the gifts that they give to the people who attend and to the people who will ultimately benefit. Jay Samit, digital-marketing expert, author, and self-proclaimed "serial disrupter," says, "There is no better feeling than doing well while you are doing good. If you want to meet the nicest, most caring people in your field, get involved in charity work. The thankless hours that go into planning charity dinners, running a carnival, or gathering donations for silent auctions are noticed and appreciated." This is something I have witnessed time and again.

I have met some wonderful people through event planning. I think about Bob, a volunteer at an event I helped to organize. For many years, Bob volunteered for that event, quietly doing his part in his corner of the world to raise money for local civic organizations and to provide scholarships for local high school students. When Parkinson's disease affected his ability to walk, Bob had to give up many of his duties, but he still showed up, and many attendees made a point of seeking him out and saying hello. He was an inspiration to everyone who met him. Why did he continue to show up, you might ask. It's quite simple: This was his posse, his crew, his community. Despite his limitations, Bob still wanted to be a part of this community of volunteers devoted to making a difference—and having a ton of fun in the process. He wanted one more mountaintop moment to add to his long, long list, and we were all inspired by his presence and dedication.

SIX DEGREES

Six Degrees of Kevin Bacon is a pop-culture game where one tries to link the actor to anyone else in the entertainment industry in six steps or fewer. For instance, James Van Der Beek (1) starred with Katie Holmes in the television show *Dawson's Creek*. Katie was once married to (2) Tom Cruise, who starred with Kevin Bacon in *A Few Good Men*. Only two degrees' separation between James Van Der Beek and Kevin Bacon!

Apply this kind of thinking to your event planning: consider past events, relationships, and experiences that you've had, and see whether you can uncover a resource or contact you can use in the future. I can't tell you how many times I've attended an event and discovered something new or met someone who was able to help me up my event planning game. Through an industry seminar I once discovered a mobile survey tool that I was able to use at my next customer event. Another time, while enjoying a retreat experience, I found a mentor who taught me how to improve my marketing skills by adding compelling images to my social media posts. Years later I had the opportunity to write a couple of guest blog posts on her website and recommend her event planning skills to others.

Many of the experts interviewed for this book were generous enough to connect me with others who were instrumental in its evolution.

Likewise, I'm constantly looking for opportunities to pay it forward, by arranging introductions and recommending facilities and vendors that have impressed me with their services. It's the right thing to do.

LONNIE

I had the pleasure of working side by side with my friend Lonnie on the core planning team for the Ohio Sauerkraut Festival in Waynesville for more than twenty years. This festival had started out as a hometown event back in early October 1970 with about a thousand visitors and has since grown into one of the top two hundred festivals in the nation, attracting more than 250,000 visitors annually over the span of a weekend. I have served in various capacities on the core planning team over the years and even stepped away a couple of times to take a break from organizing the massive event to tend to other commitments. But Lonnie never wavered.

Year after year, Lonnie showed up. Year-round, he made himself available to this team and this event, offering his time and attention to whatever needed to be done. There were the meetings that went late into the evening as we pored over third-party contracts and vendor applications; weekends when booths needed repairing or budget reports needed to be assembled for the board of directors; endless rounds of committee meetings, council meetings, and meetings with attorneys, insurance representatives, and security personnel. Lonnie was in the middle of it all. On the weekend of the event, he was invariably the first to show up and the last to leave. He always had a smile on his face, even when I knew his feet were throbbing from walking miles up and down the festival boundaries, dealing with one issue or another.

Lonnie demonstrated kindness, compassion, integrity, and strength in everything he did. He didn't back down when times got tough, and he worked tirelessly to uphold the vision and mission of the festival, no matter the obstacle thrown in his way. He was smart and funny and pragmatic, and everyone on the planning team looked to him as a leader and mentor. Tragically, we lost Lonnie in 2020. Our town and our festival will never be the same. But I know his legacy will be honored by the thoughts, words, and actions of the amazing volunteers who will carry on in his place.

As you assemble your team, look for the Lonnies in the crowd. These are the solid-gold people you want with you in the arena—the people who will work with you and stand beside you until your goals have been achieved.

9

Designing Your
Action Plan

You are already well on your way to developing a firm foundation for your event. If you've followed the steps in previous chapters, you've identified your goals, developed a budget, found your perfect venue, and started assembling a team. Now it's time to build a framework on that foundation, to gather the tools and equipment and the skill to construct an event plan that is solid, one that will help you execute your event to its successful conclusion.

Once you've completed each step detailed above, you will be able to identify the action points required to achieve your goals, including who owns each action and the due date for completion. Your plan will describe the scope of work required and the critical path your team needs to follow. After you've been able to articulate your objectives, you can focus on each goal and start identifying the people and the resources that will be required in order to achieve success.

If you're planning a training event, your action plan will focus on providing solid content presented by knowledgeable speakers and using state-of-the-art technology. You will work to make sure that the environment is conducive to learning—effective meeting room configurations, presentation screens that are large enough to be easily read, content that is provided online ahead of time or recorded for reviewing after the event has concluded. You will create a schedule that reserves your most interactive sessions for the hour or two after the attendees have had lunch to counteract the inevitable afternoon "food coma" when people struggle to maintain concentration. And most important, you will work with your presenters to ensure that they are well prepared and that the information they are providing is accurate and relevant to all attendees.

If your goal is to motivate your guests to buy your product, change their behavior, or take some other action, you will ensure that the speakers and staff members directly interacting with your attendees understand and *believe* in the mission of your organization and can effectively communicate it to your audience. You will create a program that is innovative and full of life by injecting some excitement and outside-the-box activities. Your team will be tasked with finding lively entertainment, selecting a menu that will keep energy levels high, and incorporating lots of free time for networking opportunities and mindful reflection.

If you're not familiar with your potential audience, conduct a pre-survey and ask what they would most like to see on the agenda. This information can go a long way toward helping you select relevant topics, speakers, and activities.

SELECTING A DATE

As you work on selecting a date to hold your event, there are lots of things to consider. If you have a guest of honor or a featured speaker who will be the focus of your event, confirm their availability. If you've got your heart set on a particular venue, get it booked early. Do some research about other events occurring near your date to make sure there aren't so many conflicts that it would jeopardize attendance at your event. You may want to remain flexible with your dates until these essentials are confirmed.

If you will rely heavily on third-party vendors for food, entertainment, equipment rentals, or technology needs, get your contracts signed and deposits paid early in the planning process. Don't jeopardize your event by waiting too late to reserve your third-party resources. Always assume that the best vendors are booking their goods and services for events that are eighteen to twenty-four months away.

BUILDING THE PLAN

David Allen, productivity consultant and author of *Getting Things Done*, teaches us that "You don't actually *do* a project at all! You can only do action steps *related* to it. When enough of the right action steps have been taken, some situation will have been created that matches your initial picture of the outcome closely enough that you can call it 'done.'"[1]

Assign a target date for each item on your action plan, as well as a level of urgency (critical path, high, medium, and low). This enables you to sort your tasks by these criteria and gives you a clear picture of what you should be tackling first.

Critical-path items are those foundational in nature and have a hard deadline. For instance, your registration website must go live a minimum of twelve weeks prior to the event in order to offer an early-bird registration window. Or your conference program must be ready to go to print no fewer than two weeks prior to the event to provide enough time for printing and shipping.

Be sure to incorporate enough time in your planning schedule to allow for delivery of any imprinted or specialty items. Finalize your order, and schedule the delivery a month earlier than you actually need it; this should allow time for a rerun in case of a misprint or shipping delays.

Create a time line, and work your way backward from the date of your event. Use a project management tool, a spreadsheet, a notebook, or a giant desk or wall calendar—something that allows you to view your entire time line at a glance. Insert the date of your event, and then start adding each item that must be completed.

WORKING BY THE NUMBERS

The earlier you know your head count, the easier your planning will be. If your event is an invitation-only event, make sure the invite includes a deadline for RSVP. There's nothing more detrimental to the planning process than not knowing your final head count until the last minute.

If the event you're planning requires registration, offer a significant discount for early registration so you can start estimating your attendance and begin ordering supplies, planning room sizes and configurations, and calculating realistic meal counts. If it's a recurring event, after a year or two's experience working on it, you'll be able to accurately gauge your final head count based on the percentage of your total audience that reserves their spot before the early-bird deadline.

BOOSTING ATTENDANCE AT A RECURRING EVENT

If attendance at your recurring event is starting to wane, you may need to get creative to boost interest. Here are a few ways to guarantee return participants to your conference, gala, seminar, or summit:

- *Create an awards system.* If you are planning an event that happens annually, recognize individuals or organizations for certain accomplishments. For instance, incorporate a recognition for the companies that have belonged to the organization (or attended the event) for ten, fifteen, twenty, or twenty-five years, and send out a special invitation asking them to attend. Create a framed certificate, plaque, or engraved award, and have a photographer on standby to take photos of the recipients that can be used on their social media accounts and your own. Not many people will turn down an opportunity to be recognized in this manner.
- *Honor past participants.* If you're hosting an event for an association, have an honors ceremony for all past presidents or board members in attendance. Create a recognition program, such as Innovator of the Year, Company of the Year, or Distinguished Service Award, where companies or individuals must apply or be nominated. Announce the finalists, but don't announce the winner until the ceremony. All of the

finalists and their colleagues (and perhaps family) will want to attend. If you create an award based on nominations, have prior winners nominate new candidates, and be sure they are in attendance to read their nomination application or introduce the nominees.

- *Reward repeat attendees.* Offer a small registration discount for award winners to attend the event. For instance, offer a discount on their meal if they buy an entire table of eight or more people; this gesture could dramatically increase your attendance list.
- *Ask previous participants to engage.* They may make excellent guest speakers, panel members, facilitators, or volunteers.
- *Be first.* Send out a save-the-date announcement as soon as your dates are set. Your potential participants are busy and have many obligations vying for a spot on their calendar. Be sure you include a little sizzle in the announcement, such as the introduction of your keynote or a mention of some new entertainment element you have planned.
- *Make it easy.* Be sure that all your e-mails and social media posts include the basic who, what, when, and where information, as well as clickable links to the information and registration website.
- *Create a sense of urgency.* Provide an early-bird rate that has a clear expiration date.
- *Create a media kit or newsroom page on your conference website.* Make sure it contains the history of your event, a fact sheet, and an overview of the entire event, including the complete agenda and the can't-miss keynotes or special events. The media kit should also include photos of previous events, frequently asked questions, and a complete list of contacts, contact info, directions, and social media sites.

DOCUMENTATION

To ensure that nothing critical slips through the cracks, it is essential that you maintain clear and orderly documentation of the decisions made in planning your event, the action steps to be taken, and the postevent review.

Planning Documents

If you're planning a recurring event, work with each committee or chairperson to create a thorough description of their roles and responsibilities. I can't stress enough how important it is to completely document everything required to execute your event. Give each committee chair a notebook or a spreadsheet so they can document their tasks, time line, contact names, and numbers. Make sure they also provide copies of any budgets, schedules, contracts, and instructions or checklists they've created for their team.

Every event planning team will eventually experience the loss of key personnel for one reason or another. Sometimes you'll receive sufficient advance notice to train someone to take their place. Other times an abrupt exit will change your plans. In these cases, you must have the information you need to carry on and make sure the tasks assigned to the departing team member are quickly reassigned.

Contracts

Be sure you have a complete set of signed contracts related to your event and that you are familiar with the terms of each contract. File each contract by expiration date, with the nearest dates at the top. These are the contracts that will demand your immediate attention. Be sure to schedule a time prior to the contract expiration date to sit down and negotiate for the next contract period. You can't assume that each contract negotiation will be successful, so make sure you're leaving enough time to find another vendor if negotiations start to deteriorate.

Agendas and Meeting Minutes

Every event planning process will involve regular meetings where progress will be reported, issues discussed, and new action steps developed. It's important to document these meetings and decisions and to incorporate them into your action plan. See chapter 24 for a more detailed discussion of how to develop an effective meeting strategy.

Debrief Binder

Have a notebook or binder at your command center or registration desk where discussion topics can be written down throughout the event and then discussed at the debrief meeting. Three days after your event's wrapped, it's going to be very hard to remember the idea you had on day one of your event for better registration flow. Write ideas down as they occur to you—right then and there—in the debrief binder so you don't lose those valuable insights.

CREATING A SCRIPT

Creating a day-by-day, hour-by-hour, minute-by-minute script not only helps draw out forgotten details during the planning process but also is an essential tool during the actual event. Your ability to write a comprehensive event script is evidence that you have fully developed your action plan and left absolutely nothing to chance. It is a separate, more detailed document that will help you and your team execute your vision with accuracy and precision.

I usually create my scripts in a spreadsheet tool such as Microsoft Excel. This is a living document that will be continually updated; using a spreadsheet makes it easy to insert rows in the middle of the schedule as additional tasks are identified during the planning process. The rows represent dates and times, and the columns contain at the very least (1) a description of each task or event, (2) what resources are needed, (3) the name of the person responsible for seeing the task through, and (4) any special instructions. I make sure that the spreadsheet is configured so that it can be easily reproduced and handed out to the entire team.

The beginning of your script shouldn't start on the opening day of your event. Instead, use it to track to-do items starting a week or two before the event to be sure that no last-minute details are overlooked. Below are a couple of examples that illustrate the level of detail you will include in your event script (also see the Event Script template in the appendix).

1. *Conference.* Let's say you're scripting the keynote address taking place at 9 a.m. on the first day of a regional conference. Tasks that will show up on your action plan in the weeks prior to the event will include finalizing any contractual agreements related to speaker fees and expenses, obtaining a biography and headshot of each speaker for promotional spots and the conference program, and getting a copy of speaker introductions, presentations, videos, or any handouts they want to provide to the audience. Your script will need to include tasks such as making speaker travel and lodging arrangements, printing their name badges, and adding them to meal counts. In addition, you will need to assign someone to communicate regularly with speakers so they are informed of every detail and obtaining confirmation numbers for flights or sleeping rooms, schedule details, and instructions and deadlines for submitting documentation, including invoices, presentations, and the like.

The day-before tasks on your script might consist of setting up and testing the technology and other A/V required for speaker presentations (be sure to include the room name and number on your script), confirming that the room is configured correctly, picking up speakers from the airport, placing a welcome gift in their hotel rooms, and perhaps meeting them for dinner.

On the morning of the presentation, tasks will involve making sure your facilitator has a copy of the introduction they'll be reading for the speakers and confirming that they've reviewed it to be sure there are no pronunciation issues. You'll also want to place a copy of the intro on the lectern just in case your facilitator forgets their copy. Your script will state who is assigned to welcome your speaker when they arrive at the function area and direct them to the speaker lounge, restrooms, and refreshment stations. You will schedule a time for your speaker to test the audio and familiarize themselves with the presentation equipment they'll be using, making sure their handouts are ready and ensuring they have easy access to drinking water from the stage. Finally, you'll want to appoint someone to distribute handouts during the session, be available in the room in case technical difficulties or other issues arise, and make any closing hospitality announcements before the audience proceeds to their next destination.

2. *Silent auction or fundraiser.* You have been tasked with organizing a silent auction to raise money for a nonprofit organization. Entries in your action plan in the months prior to the event will consist of tasks like printing tickets and marketing material, assigning a team to solicit donations, tracking ticket sales, finalizing banquet orders, selecting and purchasing decor, and filling in volunteer slots for auction setup, registration, auctioneering, cashiering, and teardown.

In the final days leading up to the event, tasks on your event script will include calling in final head counts for food and beverage, printing the bid sheets and event program, collecting and preparing donations for the bid tables, touching base with the auctioneer to review the schedule of events, and making sure that cashiers have what they need to process payments, including start-up cash for making change and credit card processors.

The day-of tasks will include assigning someone to supervise the setup at the venue, setting up auction items, establishing a time for greeters to be in place to welcome guests and assign bid numbers, setting up cashier stations and testing equipment, having a team ready to collect and tally bid sheets once the bidding stops, and so on.

These examples demonstrate the level of detailed, advanced preparation necessary for each activity related to your event—no matter the type of event—if you want to be confident that nothing is going to fall through the cracks.

As you begin to fill out the script for each hour of your event, you can assess your staffing needs, identify any missing components, and alert your venue to any additional details or equipment needs you may have failed to identify in your earlier planning meetings. Once your script is complete, distribute copies to each of your volunteers and staff members so they can refer to it throughout the conference and identify their specific roles and responsibilities. If your script is complex, try color-coding it by name to make it easier to read: Jill's tasks are in green, Jack's tasks are in blue, and Jane's in yellow.

FAILURE? *WHAT* FAILURE??

In 2013, the Baltimore Ravens were beating the San Francisco 49ers in the second half of Super Bowl XLVII when the power went out inside the Louisiana Superdome. For thirty-four minutes, the escalators and ATM machines were shut down, and the only lights came from auxiliary power.

Some say that the power outage was a huge black mark on the event that changed the momentum of the game. Some say it just provided a little more time for fans to grab another beer. But in my opinion, the "Blackout Bowl" was actually a huge success. After all, it only took thirty-four minutes to get the power back on. The game resumed, and a winner was declared. The only reason the game could continue was because the action plan created in advance by the event management team included having the tools, equipment, staff, and expertise on the premises to handle any situation. I would venture to say that this was probably a scenario that they had talked about or perhaps even practiced so that if and when it occurred, they would know exactly how to methodically track down the issue and fix it as quickly as possible.

AN EXPENSIVE LESSON

I once had a fantastic idea for a new event—a ladies' weekend retreat that was to be one part artistic and creative, one part spiritual, and one part entrepreneurial and personal development. I'd felt inspired from the very beginning that this mix and match "create-your-own-retreat" concept could really be something special. I selected a date and used my network of contacts to begin developing three tracks full of truly incredible speakers, teachers, artists, and friends who would conduct sessions on everything from spiritual yoga and stress management strategies to time management and wellness topics to art journaling and watercolor basics. I selected and booked a venue that I had successfully used in the past. I put together a budget that would rely solely on registration fees, created a website, and began to promote the heck out of the retreat on social media and through the social networks of the various speakers on the agenda. The whole process was so organic, and everyone I talked to was just as enamored with the idea of the event as I was, so I was convinced that it would be a real hit.

Unfortunately, I was wrong. As wonderful as my idea was, no one showed up to the party. It could have been that the cost was too steep or that the weekend I'd selected was too close to the holidays or competed with other, better-established events. It could have been that the location wasn't right, or perhaps it was just that people weren't willing to take a chance with their time and money and invest an entire weekend in an unproven event with a somewhat confusing message and no name recognition. Whatever the reasons, I was forced to cancel the event due to lack of signups.

What wasn't cancelled was my contractual agreement with the venue and the expenses for promotional materials and website hosting fees. I ended up forfeiting a lot of my own money to pay off the debts I had incurred (although the venue was extremely generous and discounted my cancellation fee, which is not normal and a gesture for which I will be forever grateful).

In hindsight, it's clear that I had a few flaws in my action plan. In one sentence, I let my vision override my common sense. My unbridled enthusiasm blinded me to some critical issues. I didn't thoroughly vet the date I selected to make sure there weren't other local events that would take away from my potential audience (there were many). I selected a date that didn't allow enough time for appropriate planning. I started with an aggressive forty-eight-hour agenda that included two overnight stays instead of starting with a shorter event that would have been less expensive to produce and would have acted as a proving ground for the larger concept. I selected the venue that was convenient for me but probably a little too far from home for the region I was promoting to. And most of all, I didn't take the time to seek sponsorships, which could have not only offset some of the overhead costs but also brought with them a built-in audience. It was as if I were trying to bake a loaf of bread but forgot the yeast; I had left out some essential ingredients, so the whole thing fell flat.

It may seem odd that I'm confessing to what many would call a failure. But one thing I've learned in my years of project planning is that the only real failure is failing to try. I understand that my worth is not reflected in the number of times that I fail; it is reflected in the number of times that I try, fail, learn, and try again. I would have regretted not trying. If I hadn't tried, I wouldn't have learned how to use the Wix platform to create a website. I wouldn't have reconnected with colleagues whose paths I hadn't crossed in a very long time. I wouldn't have been introduced to many new friends—women who are funny, smart, and generous, all of whom subsequently pledged their support if and when I decide to resurrect the retreat and try again, and whom I will support in any way I can when the opportunity arises.

This particular event may not have been a success, but I now possess many things in my toolkit that I will incorporate into future events. And who knows—under the right circumstances (and with a bullet-proof action plan!) this retreat may become a reality somewhere down the road.

III

DESIGNING AN EVENT TO REMEMBER

This section addresses all of the elements that will define the look and feel of the event. These are the things that attendees will hear, see, feel, and taste—the things that they'll be talking about long after the event is over.

Your goal should be to create an event so compelling that it becomes a can't-miss opportunity, when the tickets are so highly prized that they quickly sell out, when it becomes so big that you have to explore finding a larger venue, and when your goals are not simply met but exceeded in a way that goes above and beyond anyone's expectations. This is often called a "signature event," one that highlights your brand, builds and delivers great content, and guarantees consistent attendance. It is visually appealing, has extraordinary attention to detail, and creates tremendous value to your attendees. Over time, it becomes synonymous with your organization and your mission; it becomes part of your DNA.

Think about all of the events and conferences you've attended, both personal and professional. What are the things you remember most, the elements that stand out to you as impressive or noteworthy? What highlights did you share with your friends and colleagues when you returned? What ideas do you want to replicate at your next event? And

most important, which events have you already added to next year's calendar? The elements that come to mind as you answer these questions
are the building blocks of effective event design and those that help to
create a signature event.

Let's explore further.

10

Working with Your Venue

Once you've found the perfect venue and negotiated a contract (see chapter 19 for more on contract negotiation), you will be assigned a meeting manager or event coordinator who will serve as your primary contact throughout the planning process. Treat this important resource as your new best friend; they are the key to making sure that you receive a first-class experience.

Many of the logistical details of your event will be documented as part of the contract negotiation. But inevitably, as you work through your action plan, other details and questions will arise. Don't be shy about reaching out to the representative assigned to you with your questions. As long as you are reasonable and respectful of their time, I've found that these professionals are quite willing to keep the communication flowing throughout the planning process.

BANQUET EVENT ORDERS

As your event nears, your manager will prepare detailed *banquet event orders*—or BEOs—that, once approved by you, will be shared with every staff member responsible for any part of your event's success. From the setup crew to kitchen staff, each team will use your event orders as the blueprint to create your vision.

Event managers will start preparing the BEOs a few weeks in advance of your event. These documents will outline each and every detail the venue will be responsible for. You will be expected to verify the details, including the headcount for each separate meal and activity. Once you have signed the event orders, the venue can start preparing food orders, planning room configurations, assembling equipment, and scheduling staff.

Approximately five to seven days before your event, you will need to provide a final headcount and sign off on every page of the final BEO; those numbers will be used to calculate your final bill.

For a multiday event, a detailed BEO could be dozens or even hundreds of pages long. Be sure to allot enough time to thoroughly review the document before signing off so you don't have any surprises on your big day.

A BEO should contain the following information:

- Start and end times for the event and for each space that will be used
- A detailed time line, especially if there will be actions required to be taken by the staff at certain times—namely, resetting a room midway through the program for a different activity or changing text on message boards to coincide with the program schedule
- Configuration for each room and each space, including diagrams
- Equipment and furnishings—tables, chairs, linens, staging, bar setups, etc.
- Table setting and decor—how tables will be set for each meal, including centerpieces
- Audiovisual equipment and setup for each event and each space—this section must be detailed down to the last mic stand; if you don't see it on the BEO, assume it will not be provided
- Detailed food and beverage orders, including menu, setup, and a time line for service—if you've asked for meals to accommodate special needs, be sure the quantities and type of meal are noted

- Special requests—for example, "Hold final clearing of tables until keynote speaker has concluded their presentation"
- Contact names and numbers of all third-party vendors, as well as their arrival times and any special requirements they have—access to loading dock, A/V equipment, etc.
- Pricing for all of the above, including taxes, gratuities, and service fees

MORE TIPS AND TRICKS FOR WORKING WITH YOUR VENUE

Keep Security Top of Mind

"The safety of your attendees should be a top priority," says meetings and events professional Tracy Zglinicki. "Know where the nearest exits are at your venue, and ask them if there are any special emergency procedures that your core team needs to be aware of. Ask if your venue allows concealed-carry permit holders to carry their weapons inside the facility." Tracy describes a time when a corporation booked one of the largest rooms at their facility for the sole purpose of announcing a mass layoff. When she learned the purpose of the meeting, she knew there would be many angry people in the audience, so she required the company to pay for additional security. If there is a component to your event that you think will require a more secure environment, let your event manager know so they can help you meet the challenge.

You Don't Know Until You Ask

"Our motto has always been that there wasn't anything we wouldn't do for a client," says Tracy. "We have had to run out to get cough drops for a planner who was suffering from an uncontrollable cough, clear snow from cars after an unexpected snowfall, drive a client to the airport when their taxi didn't arrive, and help at their registration table because they were short-staffed." If you checked references for the venue, those former clients should be able to tell you whether the management team was willing to go above and beyond for them.

Leverage the Expertise in the Room

If your event manager makes a recommendation or cautions against a decision you've made, pay attention! "A light soup-and-salad lunch for a group of men is probably a no-no," says event and meetings professional Erin Thomas. "The same goes for serving beef on a Friday during Lent." Erin recalls working with a very money-conscious bride who had invited 150 people to her reception. The bride insisted on only ordering 150 appetizers, one for each person: fifty crackers with cheese, fifty meatballs, and fifty chicken wings. Erin advised her to order more, knowing that the reception would quickly run out of food, but the bride wouldn't budge. So Erin did the only thing she could: she put the kitchen on standby with additional items ready to serve. Of course, the obvious happened, and Erin and her staff were prepared when they were asked to serve more food. "As a company, you have to stand out from the competition by going the extra mile and ensuring a positive experience for your client," she says.

Stay True to Your Vision (and Your Budget)

"If you decide to hire a professional event planner, don't allow them to overrun your event with their vision," says Tracy. "We once hosted an event where a well-known planner wasted an obscene amount of her client's money on elements that were totally unnecessary. It was a weekend-long retirement event for the company's CEO that included a seventies theme party, a reception, and a formal dinner event on Saturday night for three hundred people. There were water walls, celebrity hosts—you name it. The carpet in the venue wasn't good enough, in the event planner's opinion, so special carpeting was purchased to overlay the entire banquet area. The hotel banquet tables and chairs didn't make the grade, so clear glass tables and chairs were rented."

On the night of the formal dinner, the banquet room was prepared, and the glass tables were laden with formal place settings, including multiple pieces of stemware, while the three hundred guests enjoyed a cocktail reception in an adjacent room. When dinner was announced and the doors were opened, the guests started streaming in. "Because the room was dimly lit," Tracy recalled, "and because all of the furnishings were clear, guests started running into the corners of the virtually invisible tables. Several attendees—some of whom were company retirees—started to trip and fall, and the stemware was tipping over and breaking everywhere. We had to think fast, because the stream of people just kept coming. My team jumped into action, spreading out over the room and moving chairs to the corner of each table to prevent people from crashing into them. It was a costly and completely avoidable situation."

Maintain Two-Way Communication

"Communication with your event manager is key. If your manager isn't returning your phone calls or e-mails on the same business day, it says a lot about them and their organization," Tracy says. "Likewise, be sure that you are prompt and consistent with your communication. Try to designate one or two people on your team as the main communicators of the group with the venue. There is nothing more confusing than getting multiple separate e-mails or phone calls from every member of the planning committee." She advises planners to never assume that the venue knows what they need: be very specific about setup needs, audiovisual and speaker needs, agenda changes, Internet access, menus, and dietary requests. "More information is always better than not enough," says Tracy.

SUSTAINABILITY

There are a lot of things you can do to create a sustainable event, one that doesn't leave a large footprint of careless waste. Here are a few suggestions that you should discuss with your venue:

- *Talk about your venue's sustainability efforts.* Do they provide recycling at their venue? Do they use recycled paper products? Do they limit single-use plastics? Will they provide pitchers of fruit-infused water and reusable glasses during refreshment breaks instead of plastic water bottles? Eliminating bottled water is both good for the environment and a great money-saving tactic for your budget.

- *Opt for a plated meal.* A plated meal will create less food waste than a buffet meal. Chefs will typically prepare a bit more than needed at a buffet table (3 to 5 percent) to be sure they don't run out of food. Most experienced chefs will have this down to a science; they know their menu intimately and will do their best to create as little waste as possible. But a plated meal allows the chef to order a more exact quantity, eliminating a lot of food waste.
- *Donate the excess.* If you do decide to opt for a buffet meal, ask your venue whether they have arrangements with local nonprofit organizations to accept unused food. The Bill Emerson Good Samaritan Act of 1996 provides liability protections for donation of food as long as certain cooking and handling standards are met.
- *Ticket meals.* Depending on the type of event you're planning, it might make sense to ticket each meal separately. This will make it more likely that participants will actually attend the meal, thereby reducing food waste.
- *Adopt a BYOB policy.* If your venue has water stations where reusable water bottles can be refilled, advise attendees to bring their own bottles, or else provide a bottle in each swag bag.

Other sustainability ideas include the following:

- *Ditch the paper handouts.* Instead, make them available online or on your event app. This will be good not only for the environment but also for your bottom line. You can save hundreds (if not thousands) of dollars in labor and copying costs by eliminating printed handouts at all of your events. You might even be able to lower your registration fees as a result!
- *Make sure your swag can be repurposed or is made of all recycled or sustainable materials.* Think bamboo or cotton canvas tote bags, stainless steel water bottles, and notepads made of recycled paper.

- *Repurpose decor.* Invest in some basic items that can be used again and again. A simple glass cylinder vase can be used for a floral arrangement, but the next time around you could fill it with silver and gold beads, a pillar candle sitting atop a bed of sand or polished stones, seashells, a small succulent plant, fresh limes or lemons, or a string of mini lights wrapped around holiday ornaments.
- *Use potted plants or flower arrangements.* These centerpieces can be purchased or given away to attendees and enjoyed after the event is over.
- *Stay local, or go virtual.* More and more meetings are studying ways to reduce their carbon footprints by opting out of exotic locations and choosing venues closer to their audiences, creating virtual-registration options, or shifting to hybrid or virtual events to reduce travel emissions.

THE GOLDEN RULE

This is a true story told to me by an event coordinator at a popular venue. A corporation was holding an all-day retreat in a beautiful renovated barn located on the property. The venue's event coordinator made an appearance every half hour throughout the morning to make sure the group's needs were being met. Everything seemed to be going smoothly but quickly turned sour when, in between her walk-throughs, some fast-thinking person in the meeting yanked a rented white linen tablecloth off a table and nailed it to the gorgeous knotty pine paneling of the meeting space to use as a projection screen!

To be clear, the group had never requested a screen either during the planning process or at any time during setup. Needless to say, their deposit was not returned so the rental company could be reimbursed for the ruined table linen and the walls could be repaired. If they were ever to dare trying to book that facility again, I'd think the venue scheduler would have a difficult time finding an open date for them.

Any manager of an event venue will tell you that one of the most important things their customers can do to guarantee a successful event is think through their needs regarding equipment, decorations, and display areas and make them known to the venue prior to the event.

If you expect to be welcomed back to a venue for repeat events (or even if you're using it only once), the golden rule applies: treat the venue as if it were a property that you own. When it comes to decorations, never use a stapler, staple gun, tacks, glue gun, duct tape, nails, or anything of a permanent nature. Floral wire, string, or residue-free painter's tape will usually be okay, but you should always ask first.

11

Food and Beverage

Food is often the main attraction at a special event (think food festivals, wine tastings, or cooking contests). As you start to consider what you plan to serve, take a moment to revisit your action plan and your budget. Food costs can vary wildly depending on the type of menu you plan and the location of your event. The menu prices at a chain hotel in the suburbs are one thing, but check out the offerings with the same hotel group in a downtown city center, and the cost could double. When you review the banquet menu at the same hotel group in an exotic location, you'll find that the price just went up four or five times than that of the suburban location. These price swings will probably be representative of most of your expenses depending on the location of your event.

If you've ever wondered why a convention or training event at a destination location has such a high registration cost, you don't have to look much further than the banquet menu. If you're providing three meals a day, break food, beverages, and a cocktail reception with appetizers, you'll spend literally hundreds of dollars per person per day, especially once you add taxes, gratuities, and service fees.

If you have any plans to bring in your own food or beverages to a venue, be sure your contract doesn't prohibit it. Many contracts restrict any outside food from being brought into their facility, even something as simple as a birthday cake. And don't even think about bringing in alcohol of any kind to a rented meeting space; you could jeopardize the venue's liquor license if it is discovered.

TYPES OF FOOD SERVICE

Finger foods, buffets, plated meals, or cake and ice cream. Soft drinks, host bar, cash bar, or a champagne toast. Build-your-own food bars, smoothie bowls, and candy stations. There are as many food and beverage options as there are events to plan.

Hot or Cold Appetizers and Finger Foods

This is a perfect menu for a networking event or happy hour where guests are talking, mingling, or visiting exhibit booths or vendors. Depending on how heavy the hors d'oeuvres are, they can serve as a replacement for a meal if you don't plan to host a sit-down dinner. Heavy hors d'oeuvres include items such as sliders, meatballs, antipasti platters, or other protein-heavy items, coupled with some vegetable and starch choices. Light hors d'oeuvres might include platters of crudité, cheese cubes and crackers, or a fruit plate.

Plated Meals

Plated meals are served at the table by service staff, one course at a time. This method of service is great when you want to have a leisurely meal with lots of talking and interaction between guests at the beginning of the meal, perhaps followed by a speech or presentation. It's also a more sanitary option than a buffet line, where everyone files past open food trays and handles the same serving utensils. You must allow time for each course to be placed and removed, hopefully before your planned programming begins, to eliminate any noisy plate and silverware removal during the presentation.

Buffets

This is one of the preferred methods to feed a large crowd quickly. Buffet lines can typically be set up double-sided so people can serve themselves from both sides for even faster service. The head count you provide will determine the quantity of food prepared. Most chefs will prepare enough food for a little more than your final number in a buffet setup. This is typically a self-serve situation where folks are free to take as much of each item as they wish, so the chef will want to be sure there is no chance of running out of anything. Another option is to have servers stationed at your buffet to serve up portions, thereby controlling portion sizes and eliminating the handling of serving utensils by each guest.

Boxed Meals

A large crowd can be served and fed quickly if the meals are boxed or bagged and ready to go ahead of time. Boxed meals are quickly becoming a fan favorite, because each meal is safely secured in its own container. Many times a boxed meal includes a sandwich or wrap, a side like pasta salad, chips, a piece of fruit, a bottle of water, and perhaps a sweet treat like a cookie or brownie. These meals have typically been prepared well ahead of time, chilled, and stored until time of service. Banquet menus are starting to get more inventive and inclusive with their boxed selections, now offering some nice grilled veggie wraps and artisanal salads. Boxed lunches are also a great option if you're hosting a working lunch and want something simple to eat in a conference room or a classroom setting.

Snack Breaks

Break food can bring a ton of variety and fun to your menu. It can provide a much-needed lift to a long afternoon of training or lectures when attention spans start to wane.

Most banquet menus include a wide array of themed food and beverage choices for a midmorning or midafternoon break. It's not unusual to see selections such as a ballpark break (peanuts, popcorn, soft pretzels with cheese or mustard), a savory break (grilled flatbreads with hummus, roasted red peppers, olive tapenade, and crumbled feta), a sweet-tooth break (cookies, brownies, chocolate-covered strawber-ries, and chocolate mousse shooters), or something healthier (like a juice bar, make-your-own trail mix bar, fresh fruit with yogurt dip, or smoothie shots).

If you are providing a full-on break food display in either the morning or the afternoon, you can probably go lighter on your meal choices and perhaps skip the desserts. After all, you don't want to put your participants into a food coma! It's also important to note that adding break food can be a budget-buster; be prepared to add anywhere from $10 to $40 per person per day to your budget (or more, depending on how elaborate your choices are). More budget-friendly options for break foods include granola bars, ice cream sandwiches, cups of yogurt, or assorted cookie trays.

Break food will probably be expected if you have scheduled lunch and dinner more than five to six hours apart from each other. Snack breaks are also a great way to add one more themed element into your plan, but be sure you incorporate the cost of this additional item into your budget.

Build-Your-Own Food Bars

This option is becoming more and more popular for all sorts of events. Guests have the opportunity to get creative by selecting from an assortment of ingredients to build their own masterpiece. This could be anything from a waffle bar with a variety of toppings, berries, and assorted syrups to a pasta bar with several types of pasta noodles, sauces, and add-ins like sun-dried tomatoes or grilled veggies.

The sky's the limit here. Start with a base of your choice (crostini, tortilla chips, mac and cheese, baked potatoes, slider buns, etc.), and then think of every possible topping or add-on that would be appealing with your primary ingredient. This option is friendly for attendees who have very specific food preferences or allergies, because they have the ability to select only the ingredients that work for them.

The biggest drawback to this option is the time it takes each person to assemble their own creation. If you plan on doing this for a large crowd, you'll need multiple food stations and lots of help to keep the ingredients well stocked throughout the entire time of service.

Innovations in Food Service

Many venues are providing new options for food service. They include anything from food trucks and themed food stations to snack carts and family-style meals. For a more hands-on experience, create an opportunity for participants to cook all or part of their meal, such as a create-your-own pasta or pizza dough. Or bring in a mixologist to demonstrate how the event's signature drink is made.

Bar Foods

Any time you're hosting an open bar, or even a cash bar, be sure to provide some snacks to offset the alcohol intake and slow down consumption, especially if your guests will be driving after the event is over. Provide some crunchy snacks, such as popcorn or peanuts, or something more filling, like soft pretzels or trail mix.

Dietary Considerations

Consider your audience when choosing your menu. Is there a specific age range or demographic that you can identify? If so, consider that some may prefer a more traditional, mildly flavored menu, while a different demographic may be more adventurous with meal choices and spice levels. There are those who would prefer a light, plant-based lunch, while others will expect a full meat-and-potatoes meal. In any case, it's good practice to automatically provide a vegetarian choice when planning any menu.

Allergies have become a huge consideration when menu planning— and one that most reputable caterers and banquet staff should be ready to accommodate. Ask questions during your invitation process that give each guest the opportunity to disclose nut or gluten allergies, vegetarianism or veganism, or restrictions based on religious practices. Make sure to provide the banquet team with these details well in advance so they can prepare accordingly.

Allergies are becoming more and more commonplace, and it can become a liability issue if someone is exposed through hidden ingredients or cross contamination. The best way to avoid this issue is to eliminate these ingredients from your menu altogether. But if you do decide to serve anything that contains common allergens (peanuts or shellfish, for instance), be sure it is prominently disclosed; provide a menu card at each place setting or signage at the beginning of the buffet line.

CONTROLLING COSTS

There are lots of ways to control food and beverage costs:

- Schedule your event at a time when a meal isn't expected to be served—a midafternoon birthday party or a late-night reception.
- Banquet-menu pricing is typically lower per person for a breakfast or lunch than for an evening meal; consider holding your event earlier in the day.
- Ask your caterer or banquet manager whether the dessert provided with lunch can be held over and served as a midafternoon snack as opposed to having to pay for separate afternoon break food. Many venues allow this, although there may be an additional service fee.
- To control costs when serving alcohol, provide a limited number of drink tickets to each guest; guests must pay for subsequent drinks.
- Talk to your caterer about your budget concerns, and see whether they will work with you to prepare a customized menu that is both satisfying and affordable.

FEEDING A CROWD IN A SMALL WINDOW OF TIME

There are several ways to reduce the amount of time it takes to feed your guests:

- Have your salad, condiments, desserts, and tea and water glasses already set at the table when your guests arrive. You can save fifteen to twenty minutes by eliminating table service and having folks walk through a buffet line.
- Provide prepackaged boxed lunches, and arrange them by type, with highly visible signage so attendees can just grab and go. One downside of this kind of meal service is the amount of waste it can generate, so be sure that your vendor is using recycled products and that plenty of trash receptacles are available.
- Don't select a menu that includes a choice involving a lot of assembly. Avoid menus that include a baked potato bar, taco bar, or salad bar if you're crunched for time; this kind of menu item will slow down your buffet line and cause a lot of frustration to your attendees if the staff can't keep everything well stocked.
- It's always a good idea to offer a longer window of time for breakfast on the final day of a multiday event. Many times, it's been preceded by a night of fun, excitement, and sleep deprivation, so allowing some grace for people to sleep an extra hour or check out of their hotel room is a great idea. If you have an open window of time for your breakfast buffet, don't set the table with full place settings. Instead, provide rolled silverware on the buffet line and cups and glasses at the coffee and juice station. This ensures that late arrivals won't have to hunt for a spot with an unused place setting.

Your food and beverage choices can be the element that firmly establishes your event theme. It can also become one of the things that your attendees look forward to most.

12

Room Configurations

The seating you provide for your attendees can enhance or diminish the effectiveness of your event. If you've ever been at a conference and tried to take copious notes while seated in a tight row of chairs configured theater-style or seated at a banquet table set for ten when it was only large enough for eight, you know what I mean.

All venues will provide a chart on their website that shows how many people each of their rooms will hold based on the room configuration. Get familiar with the available seating capacity of these spaces before you make a final venue selection. I've learned that the capacity stated on these charts can be a little generous. If social distancing is a concern, venues and event planners will have to adjust standard room configurations, and capacity estimates will have to be recalculated.

When evaluating spaces, always assume you will need more room than you think. It can be quite deceiving to stand in a grand ballroom devoid of tables, chairs, people, staging, and other necessary equipment and believe that it has more than enough square footage to host your event. It's always best to visit a venue when it is set up for another event so you can see what it really looks like when arranged at their stated maximum capacity. If their literature says that the ballroom can seat seven hundred people, that setup may not allow for a stage, dance floor,

band, and bar. Ask the sales manager to prepare a diagram of your desired setup so you can see how or if it will work. If you want people to be
able to navigate the space when everyone is seated, and not be literally
elbow-to-elbow, don't select a space that can barely manage the size of
your crowd. Check out photos on the venue's website, or ask whether
they can provide photos of each space that is set up in the configuration
you desire.

I once received a conference registration packet for a large national
conference, and after reading the breakout descriptions and speaker
biographies, I knew I had to attend. The topics were perfectly tailored
for my current career path, and I knew I would be able to pick up a lot
of great information that would benefit both me and my organization. I
got permission to go, registered for the sessions I planned to attend, and
invested over $2,000 of my company's money (conference fees, airfare,
hotel stay, food, etc.) in order to participate in this valuable educational
experience.

What I found when I arrived at my first breakout session was a
room packed to overflowing. Every seat was occupied, and people were
sprawled on the floor and spilling out into the hallway. There were
dozens of others who'd been turned away and left to wade through the
program to find another session or to camp out in the hallway in front
of their next breakout so they would be assured a seat!

The venue you select must have the capacity to accommodate your
audience, as well as a contingency plan if your attendance exceeds your
original estimates. Have stacks of overflow chairs in each room, offer a
repeat of an especially popular topic, or locate the breakout in a space
that has the ability to open an air wall to expand. Better yet, use a registration tool that allows attendees to select which sessions they plan
to attend. While you may not necessarily hold them to their original
selection, you'll quickly be able to see which sessions are popular and
may require a larger space than what you might have originally thought
when making room assignments.

COMMON ROOM CONFIGURATIONS

Consider the pros and cons of the following room configurations when deciding which would be best for your event.

Theater or Auditorium

This configuration is made up of rows of chairs facing a stage or podium. These can be set in straight rows, curved rows, or a chevron pattern, with one or more aisles depending on the size of the room. Many conference centers have chairs that can be linked together to provide maximum capacity. A better, more comfortable option is to allow a little space between chairs and provide enough room between rows to allow those in the center of the row to move in and out with minimal disruption to the other guests. Break up long rows by adding more aisles for added ease of movement. The benefit of a theater-style configuration is that it can accommodate a very large crowd in a small space. This is the ideal setup for an introductory session, a general assembly, or a keynote. The downside is that it can be uncomfortable for your attendees if the session lasts for more than an hour.

Banquet Seating

This typically involves round (or sometimes rectangular) tables with six to ten chairs, depending on the size of the table. Banquet rounds are the gold standard for any event that involves serving a meal—weddings, parties, luncheons, and galas, in addition to conventions and conferences. Banquet rounds are also ideal for small-group networking events when you want to encourage people to brainstorm and collaborate.

Crescent Rounds

This is the same configuration as banquet seating but removing the three or four chairs that would normally face away from the focal point of the room, such as a stage or podium. This is a comfortable option for an event that starts with a meal and concludes with a keynote speaker or awards presentation. This setup ensures that everyone will be able to watch the proceedings without having to adjust their chairs in the middle of the program.

Classroom

This layout uses narrow tables accommodating three to four chairs that can be configured in straight rows or angled to face the front of the room. Classroom seating is the most desired configuration when attendees must take notes, work from a computer, or reference a workbook or binder for any length of time. All eyes are forward, and attention is focused on the presenter. The downside of this configuration is that the total capacity of a room is reduced by the addition of tables. But whenever possible, it is much preferred over a theater setup, where people are reduced to having to balance laptops or notebooks on their laps.

U Shape

Rectangular tables are arranged in a U shape, with chairs arranged around the outside—great for small-group meetings and all-day strategizing when you want everyone to be able to directly address one another throughout the event. The top of the U will be at the front of the room, where a projection screen or facilitator might stand.

Hollow Square, Circle, or Rectangle

Tables are arranged in a closed square or rectangle, or chairs are arranged in a circle. This setup is a great option for small-group meetings or strategic planning sessions.

360-Degree Stage

A stage is set in the center of the room, with seats set on every side. In this setup, the presenter must continually move around so that they spend an equal time addressing every side of the room. While this setup is not typical, it can be quite intimate. A centered stage can be a perfect setup for unique entertainment events and concerts.

Unconventional Seating

As event design evolves, many participants are looking for unconventional room configurations. Some sessions might be more impactful if the seating were super casual; think beanbag chairs, soft cubes, or floor cushions. Certain networking opportunities could take advantage of the soft seating found in the common areas of your venue or by setting up rows of small café tables with two people seated face-to-face.

TABLE DESIGN

When it comes to the banquet table, the possibilities for place setting, linen, chair, and centerpiece design are endless. Most venues will provide the standard neutral tablecloths and napkins as well as a basic centerpiece, such as a lantern or glass vase. But if you really want to transform your dining space, spend some time developing a clever table design.

Banquet tables are the perfect place to really play up the theme of your event:

- *Sports-themed event (team awards banquet, golf outing, conference).* Place a square of artificial grass in the center of each table, and pile it high with pom-poms, sports stress balls, pennants, and a regulation football that can be donated to a local charity after the event is over.
- *Formal evening (anniversary, gala, holiday party).* Gold-rimmed glassware, satin table toppers, and tall chandelier-style crystal candleholders add just the right touch to a formal affair.
- *Rustic outdoor event (wedding reception, birthday, company-sponsored family event).* Use birchbark logs with holes drilled in them to hold tea-light candles, random glass bottles and jugs filled with wildflowers and eucalyptus stems, and burlap table runners and linen napkins tied with a bow made of twine.

This is where a great rental company can come in handy to help you make your vision a reality (see chapter 18 for more information on selecting appropriate service vendors). Most rental companies will have showrooms where you can view sample table designs to gain some inspiration. For the budget-conscious, Pinterest is also a great resource to get ideas for DIY tablescapes that won't break the bank.

OTHER ROOM CONSIDERATIONS

Depending on the type of event you are planning, you may have additional needs from your venue.

Business Meetings

If you're hosting a business meeting of senior staff, the board of directors, or prospective business partners, a professional table setting is a must, especially if your meeting will last several hours. Take some time to make sure the room is spotlessly clean and that chairs, window shades, conference phones, and A/V and all other equipment are in perfect working order. Prepare each place setting with a new pad of paper and a pen (with your company logo for an extra touch), and have a beverage station either on the table within easy reach or on a side table or cart elsewhere in the room. If you're really trying to impress your guests, consider adding a leather placemat, a bottle of sparkling water next to each glass, a piece of fruit, or a sweet snack.

Conference Rooms

Pens, paper, mints, water pitchers, glasses, and other table paraphernalia can look inviting in the initial room setup typically provided by a conference venue. But in fact they can be a nuisance, especially if different people will be moving in and out of the room throughout the day. These extras take up valuable space and make tables look messy and unkempt as the day goes on. Instead, ask the venue to place these items on a table in the back of the room so people can access them, leaving the tables empty for people to place their own drinks, portfolio, and laptop without having to work around the additional clutter.

Room Temperature

Always keep room temperatures relatively cool. A room that is too warm is a recipe for inattentive, sleepy, and unengaged attendees. Encourage your guests to dress in layers when you send out the pre-conference information packet so they can be ready for fluctuating temperatures.

Consider Your Goals

It's time to refer again to the goal statement you prepared for your event and use it to help guide your decisions about room configurations. If it's a small group that needs to collaborate all day, use a U-shape or rectangle configuration so everyone can see who's speaking at any given time without twisting and turning. If you want to break up a large gathering into smaller groups for collaborative conversation, use banquet seating. If it's a training session at which handouts will be provided or notes will be taken, utilize a classroom-style setup in which each person has a writing surface for computers or notebooks. If you have a keynote speaker and you want everyone's eyes up front, then by all means darken the room and utilize that theater seating. Do everything you can to select a room setup conducive to achieving your objectives.

13

Selecting a Theme

Selecting a theme for your event will set the tone for everything else, from speakers and entertainment to food, colors, and decor. This can be very helpful when planning not only association meetings and conferences but also weddings and parties.

Start by brainstorming some ideas, and you'll quickly see how easily the details start to fall into place. If Mardi Gras comes to mind, it's time to pull out the purple, green, and gold; add lots of beads, masks and feathers, jambalaya, red beans and rice, some Cajun music, and you've got yourself a party! When you think about a carnival theme, the vision instantly goes toward a primary color palette of blue, red, and yellow and to clowns and balloons, popcorn, peanuts and cotton candy, games of chance, caricature artists, magicians, and other similar performers. If a tailgate or sports theme is more your style, put on your favorite team jersey, and go for it; think megaphones, marching bands, stadium backdrops, and a keynote speaker from the sports world.

FINDING INSPIRATION FOR YOUR THEME

Many people find that creating a theme can be the hardest part of planning an event. You may be an organizational genius but lack the creative mindset to dream up a great theme. The good news is that, with a few simple keystrokes, you can find a world of inspiration online to help you create a theme for your event. Using search tools and websites, all you have to do is type a few words to get thousands of images and ideas that you can incorporate into your theme.

A Google search on "corporate conference themes" yields over 110,000,000 results! Narrow down your search by typing in "medical conference themes" or "retirement party themes" or "basket raffle ideas," and you'll find more specific examples that can direct your event planning. Type in the same search criteria on Pinterest, and you'll find page after page of incredible images, including links, that you can use as creative inspiration to design a special experience for your guests.

EXAMPLES OF CORPORATE THEMES

Software Solutions, Inc., is a software company that provides accounting, human capital management, and utility billing solutions for public agencies in the United States. As their administrator and events coordinator, I am responsible for organizing a three-day conference for our clients each year, providing a robust agenda full of training and advanced-education sessions. It's also an opportunity to strengthen relationships with our clients and give them the opportunity to network with their peers. This event grows more popular every year because of the value it delivers. Here are few examples of themes used in a few of the events I've planned for Software Solutions that have really impacted the success of the conference:

- *Making a Splash.* This theme was used for a conference we held at a venue with an indoor water park. This theme also fell right in line with our efforts to "make a splash" with a new product announcement. A facility with a water park can be a great location for a corporate conference; just be sure your event isn't scheduled during school breaks, when attendance of families with children is at its highest. Try to negotiate with the venue to waive the water park fee for your attendees during the conference, most of whom will not visit the water park but will spend the majority of their time in the conference center. I've even been able to negotiate reduced room rates for the weekend adjacent to the conference dates for those who want to enjoy the water park with their families after the conference has concluded.

- *Be Prepared.* We concentrated on disaster preparedness at this conference. Our keynote speaker was an expert on disaster planning; one of the giveaway items was a sling pack perfect for hiking or backpacking. Entertainment included a team-building event at which the participants' various readiness skills were put to the test.

- *Putting You in the Winner's Circle.* This theme was centered on setting and achieving goals and included a bus trip to the local racetrack. One of the races was dedicated to our group, and we were all able to go down to the winner's circle for a picture with the winning horse and jockey.

- *Highway to Health.* At this event we spent a lot of time focusing on topics surrounding physical health, mental health, employee health, and fiscal health. In addition to typical training and educational sessions, we offered sessions on stress reduction, beginner's yoga, conflict resolution, and how to start an employee wellness program.

- *Passport to Success.* This conference was held at a resort known for its international decor and menu, so we picked a travel theme; the agenda was fashioned after an actual passport (which, by the way, fit nicely into a standard name-badge holder). Attendees earned stamps in their passports when they attended certain events or visited vendor booths, making them eligible for a prize drawing each day. We also hosted an international food fest, where participants had the opportunity to try delicacies from around the globe.

Pick a theme and have fun with it! Work with your team, your speakers, your entertainers, and the sales manager at your venue to find ways to incorporate your theme in every aspect of your event.

REPRESENT YOUR BRAND

While you may want to keep things fresh by creating a unique theme at each of your events, use a consistent name and a recognizable brand logo in all of your collateral. Consistency builds trust, so be sure that your logo and your brand name shine through whatever theme you choose and demonstrate your unique identity, one that you want your attendees to remember. Create merchandise and giveaway items that include links to your website and other online platforms. Finally, make sure your staff and volunteers are properly trained to be your brand ambassadors and are ready and willing to serve.

THEMES FOR OTHER TYPES OF EVENTS

You've been tasked with creating a party for a group of coworkers or neighbors or family, and you want to create a fun theme that will set the tone. Here are some suggestions to get those creative juices flowing:

- *Decade party.* If you're celebrating a birthday, anniversary, retirement, or some other milestone celebration, pick the decade when it all began, and re-create it. Or pick any decade just for the fun of it, and make that your theme. Incorporate it into the food, activities, and suggested dress code for your guests (bell bottoms, anyone?). Perhaps you or someone you know has some memorabilia or photos that you can incorporate into your decor. Create a playlist of popular music from that decade, and have a dance contest.
- *Viewing party.* You don't have to look too far ahead on the calendar to find a reason to throw a party. It starts with New Year's Eve and watching the ball drop in Times Square. After that, it's the Super Bowl, the Oscars, March Madness, the Kentucky Derby, the Summer Olympics, and on and on. A viewing party starts with great audiovisual equipment, lots of drinks and snacks, and some games for the commercial breaks that require people to team up and work together (trivia, minute-to-win-it, puzzle challenges, etc.).

- *Foodies unite.* Time to play with your food! Host a chili cook-off, a wine and cheese party, a taco bar party, or a grilled cheese party. Provide the ingredients to make your own pasta or salsa or salad-in-a-jar. A food-themed party is best when it's participatory. It's also easy on your budget. Have all the guests participate by bringing a theme-based item to share with the rest of the guests.

MATCH YOUR THEME TO YOUR AUDIENCE

As you start to consider possible themes for your event, one of the most important considerations will be how it aligns with your goals. But just as important is how your audience will embrace your theme. It's certainly a great idea to shake things up by creating some unexpected elements at your event; many times those are the things that will end up being fan favorites. However, I suggest that if you're not sure how a theme will be accepted, you start slow.

For instance, at the Highway to Health conference described above, we decided to incorporate the theme into our menu by serving lighter, healthier breakfasts instead of the typical bacon-and-eggs buffet. However, we stuck with more standard fare for lunches and dinners. In the end, we were glad we took this approach. When we sent out the conference surveys, we got plenty of feedback from people who did not enjoy the steel-cut oatmeal with yogurt and granola.

If your theme will involve significant changes to a format that is well known to your guests, give them a heads-up ahead of time in your registration materials so they know what to expect.

14

Creating a Program

Spend some time with your team reviewing the goals for your event and developing ways to further that mission by developing an engaging and relevant program.

Put yourself in the shoes of your guests. Create a persona or multiple personas that represent the different groups of people you plan to attract to your event. Envision them participating in your program: Is there something relevant for them throughout the event? Is there any point in time where your offerings are weak, where your guests might be tempted to leave early because there's nothing of interest or value for them? Experience coordinator Alexandria Tomayko says, "Your audience will definitely have an experience. What kind of experience will it be?"

The ability to promote an agenda that has been thoughtfully crafted is the key to helping your attendees choose your event above the others. Your potential participants have a lot of choices as they decide whether to register for your event. Every organization and association affiliated with their industry or area of interest is vying for their attention by marketing to them via print, social media, and e-mail. Most of your prospective clients have a limit to the time they can take away from their regular lives. They probably have a limited travel budget, and they have to select events that will provide them with the best value. Your task is to create a program that stands out from the crowd.

LET THE IDEAS FLOW

There is no idea too crazy or too out of reach at this stage; get creative, get inspired, and make sure all of your team's suggestions make it to the table. This is the time to let your thought process venture far outside of the box and allow your innovative side to take control. Once you have identified all possibilities, work together to narrow the scope. Are there specific skills or assets that are readily available that make some ideas more attractive than others, such as a great venue or sought-after speaker or entertainer? Are there known constraints that make certain types of suggestions impractical, such as lack of budget or cultural considerations?

CREATE A THOUGHTFUL SCHEDULE OF EVENTS

If you are planning an event that has a complex agenda, with several tracks or sessions offered simultaneously, you have a lot to consider. When you start giving your guests options on how to spend their time, you'll need to assess what activities or speakers or topics will compete with one another for their attention. This is where creating those personas really starts to pay off. For instance, you're creating a program for a marketing conference, and "Joe" is attending as a professional who specializes in digital media. Will he find two competing digital media sessions at the same time? If so, you've made it very hard for him to plan his day. He will have to make a difficult choice to attend one or the other, and he'll probably suffer a fear of missing out on something important when he's unable to benefit from both sessions. Instead, look at your agenda from Joe's point of view, and see whether there are relevant sessions for him during every segment of your event. Then move on to the next persona, and complete the exercise again.

WEIGH THE ADVANTAGES OF WORKSHOPS VERSUS LECTURES

The very best way to create an unforgettable experience is to transition your guests from observers to active participants.

If you want to liven up your educational tracks, consider scheduling more workshops and fewer presentations. You know the presentations I'm talking about—the sessions that have a single lecturer with a slide deck full of charts and bullet points. Be honest; at one point or another we've all struggled to stay focused (or even awake) during this type of presentation. Most speakers are quite knowledgeable about the topic they've been asked to present, but not every speaker has acquired effective presentation skills. Too often they simply read their words directly from the slides in a monotone. In cases such as these, the retention rate for the information delivered is very low.

The primary difference between focusing on workshops rather than on traditional lecture is that workshops provide an active experience rather than a passive experience. In a workshop, you're going to "show" instead of "tell." Many people learn more quickly and retain information longer through experiential learning, and recent surveys have shown that participatory sessions are preferred over a straight lecture format.

A workshop format can involve something as simple as a handout that requires the audience to fill in the blank or answer questions, a series of small-group discussions as different topics are brought forward, or administering an on-the-spot group survey using voting paddles, colored flags, or a phone app. A longer workshop could include a demonstration of a technique or skill, a hands-on computer exercise, a tactile learning experience, or longer interactions with other attendees via team activities or role-play.

There are a few adjustments you will need to consider if you're going to shift more toward a workshop format in your program. Workshops may need different space requirements, different equipment, and different supplies and materials. This could mean an adjustment in your budget to account for these items. Workshops can last longer than regular presentations (up to three to four hours), so you may need to incorporate time for breaks, as well as time for shifting from one exercise to another. Be aware that if your workshop involves breaking your group into smaller-group discussions, it will take more than a minute to bring a halt to the discussion and bring their attention back to the front of the room. This is what you hoped for; just be sure to compensate by incorporating time for transitions.

Take a look at your agenda and see whether you can find ways to change things up and make it more interesting and interactive by adding more workshops and fewer lectures. If you do, chances are that your survey results and your attendance retention will improve.

Make Presentations Count

In some cases a presentation or lecture format is the best way to share information with your audience members. In these cases, do everything you can to select presenters who have some experience with not only their topic but also presenting it effectively. It's perfectly okay to provide some guidelines on effective PowerPoint presentations (don't read from the slides, use more images and fewer words, keep the number of slides to a minimum, be sure that background and text are in contrasting colors so the slides are readable, avoid red and green tones since they may not be easily seen by those who are color-blind, and so on).

Consider these other ways to make a presentation session more digestible and less one-note:

- *Turn it into a panel discussion.* This breaks up a monotone presentation and provides many points of view. Do everything you can to create a diverse panel, one that your audience members can relate to.
- *Consider a debate format.* Offer two or more points of view on the same topic, and encourage audience participation.
- *Present information in bite-sized chunks.* Break up the presentation with a story, a video, or an online poll.
- *Use technology to your advantage.* Consider presentation tools such as Canva or Prezi; these tools provide lots of theme, design, animation,

and transition options that can really make for a more compelling presentation.

CREATE MEANINGFUL EXPERIENCES

What kinds of activities can you provide that will make participants set down their phones and connect in the moment? It's time to get creative! Design events that will encourage your audience members to stay engaged and get the most out of their investment.

Provide a Tactile Experience

Offer a maker space that allows attendees to participate in a hands-on activity, such as experimenting with new technology, creating a vision board, participating in a software-development hackathon, enjoying a food or wine tasting, or experiencing a virtual-reality adventure.

Leverage Outdoor Spaces

After a long day spent in artificially lit rooms, moving things outdoors can be a welcome respite. A happy hour set up in a hotel courtyard, an after-hours dance party on a rooftop bar, or a patio party complete with a barbecue feast and lawn games are all things to consider for events held at a location and time that will permit outdoor activities.

Plan Offsite Events

Try to incorporate a relevant offsite event into your schedule. If you're hosting a conference for academics, connect with a local university for a visit to campus for a tour, lecture, or knowledge exchange. If you're hosting a conference for medical professionals, schedule a tour at a local teaching hospital to meet with program directors and staff.

These local resources can also help you fill your speaker roster. Do some research, and make some contacts to see whether these organizations can provide speakers to your event or participate in a panel discussion on a relevant topic.

PROGRAM A CONSIDERATE EVENT

You can go above and beyond as an event planner by considering the particular needs of your guests. Take a minute to consider what tweaks you can make to your event that would make it more enjoyable for them.

Offer Orientation for First-Time Guests

If you have a multiday event in a destination city and a significant number of guests who are attending your event for the first time, it's a really good idea to provide a virtual orientation session prior to the event. You could also offer a precon session the day before everyone else arrives or an early-bird session on the first full day of your program. This is a chance for new participants to learn more about the structure of the program and ask questions about anything and everything, from logistics to free-time options.

Schedule Thoughtfully

On the last day of the conference, provide at least one extended break in the morning to allow time for people to vacate their room and get their luggage secured before checkout time. Otherwise they're going to miss a session or perhaps bail on it altogether because the logistics just make things too difficult for them to attend.

Provide a Quiet Zone

Most people need breaks throughout the day to catch their breath and decompress a bit. Create a quiet zone where attendees can check e-mails, catch up on the news, charge their phones, or just put in their earbuds, close their eyes, and listen to some music. Scatter a few hospitality items around your quiet zone, such as individually wrapped breath mints and hard candy, tissues, Post-it Notes and pens, hand sanitizer, and hand lotion. This might be a good spot to have a monitor replaying a keynote at low volume or showing the event's Twitter activity in real time.

Schedule Time to Move

One of the most popular activities I've added in recent years to a corporate conference was an early-morning yoga session. Some participants were regular yoga practitioners, and others were trying it for the first time. We also offered a "chair yoga" session, with the instructor providing some moves that could be incorporated into the workday using nothing but an office chair. What other kinds of programming can you think of to promote movement?

Shopping? Yes, Please!

I attended an event last year at a large venue that had several different conferences going on at once. As I wandered down the concourse during a break, I came upon an association event that had lined its part of the venue with vendor tables containing a dazzling and colorful collection of purses, jewelry, hats, and clothing. It was clear that these event organizers knew their audience and had provided unique products and services to entertain and inspire. Think about what kinds of offerings you could provide for your guests that would add to their event experience.

Create Instagram-Worthy Moments

Create a space where guests can snap a selfie, take a group photo, or create a video that is shareable. In addition to a few fun hats, glasses, and other accessories in keeping with your theme, be sure to provide backdrops or props that include your event name, logo, and hashtag to take advantage of your participants' reach on social media. Locate the selfie station in an area that will get heavy traffic. If you opt to rent a photo or video booth, select a vendor that can provide social media integration for sharing images in real time.

Include Significant Others

Many times, conference-goers will bring along their spouses, partners, or even entire families, especially if the event is being held in a locale that has lots of entertainment options and points of interest. Consider adding a schedule of planned events for these family members during the time when their loved ones will be in training sessions or other mandatory activities.

Work with the local convention and visitor's bureau or concierge service to obtain discount tickets for amusement parks, museums, restaurants, shopping centers, and other local attractions. Provide as much information as possible on your registration website, along with links to sign up in advance for bus tours or to get tickets to your after-hours events where spouses or partners are welcome.

Create a welcome kit with local information about public transportation, shopping, and dining options within easy walking distance of the event venue and lodging. This kind of attention to detail will generate a lot of goodwill and perhaps boost attendance.

Plan the Registration Area

Here's your best chance to make a great first impression on your attendees: if your registration setup is highly visible, inviting, and efficiently run, it's a sign to your guests that the rest of the event will be the same.

I recently attended a conference where we were decidedly *not* greeted in this way. Attendees had to walk a long distance to get from the parking garage to the convention concourse, and there wasn't a directional sign to be found. When we finally made our way to the registration area, there was a single line so long that we couldn't even see the registration counter from the back of the line. It did not bode well for the rest of the conference.

If you know you're going to have long lines at registration, at least make it interesting. Hire entertainers to keep people occupied along the way, or create signposts with interesting facts, jokes, or riddles. Create a registration space that matches the theme of your event to give attendees something interesting to look at. Does your event have a sports theme? Create a stadium-themed arrival gate, complete with cheerleaders, foam footballs to toss around, and fight songs piped in the background.

Make Your Name Badges Count

Make sure you use the biggest font possible for the name on your name badges, especially the first name. There's nothing worse than having to lean in and squint at another person's midsection, trying to read a name hanging off of a lanyard. And speaking of lanyards, look for the double bulldog clip style; it will make it less likely that the badge will swivel backward, ensuring that the badge can always be seen. Be sure to reserve room on the badge for preferred pronouns.

Badge ribbons make an informative addition easily seen across the room. Ribbon color can indicate which attendees are speakers, sponsors, exhibitors, and first-time attendees. You can also create custom ribbons and have a little fun: how about Rock Star, Princess, or Dreamer?

At the Writer's Digest Annual Conference in New York City, aspiring authors meet for several days to pitch their ideas to agents, hear from industry experts about everything from plot to publicity, and get inspired by authors who have already achieved success in the industry. Another great advantage of attending this conference is the opportunity to meet members of your writing community, like-minded professionals who understand the unique challenges of the writing life.

The WD team helps conference attendees discover their community by providing the opportunity to add ribbons to their name badges indicating their writing focus: romance, young adult, nonfiction, mystery, and so on. The simple addition of a ribbon on a name badge can create an instant connection between participants with similar interests and pursuits.

CREATE OPPORTUNITIES FOR NETWORKING

Almost every business conference I've ever attended kicks off their event with a welcome reception or meet and greet, but one stands out in my mind because it was especially frustrating.

Two thousand of us had come from all over the country to attend a large technology conference in New Orleans. We had arranged our schedules and flights in order to get settled in our hotels, change out of our travel clothes, make ourselves presentable, and make our way to the venue in time for this important networking opportunity.

After I checked in at the registration desk to receive my name badge and conference materials, I proceeded down the hall to the reception. When I arrived, I saw multiple beverage bars and food stations scattered throughout the large hall, a live band playing in the corner, and hundreds of people milling about. As I got closer, I realized that it was happening again.

I approached the bar and was handed a drink in a plastic cup along with a cocktail napkin. I progressed to one of the food tables and took a plastic plate, a napkin, and a fork—because the finger food wasn't finger food at all; it required a utensil to eat it. There I stood with my conference tote bag, purse, drink, food plate, napkins, and utensils, and . . . not a single solitary seat or even a flat surface to set anything down! A very few high-top café tables dotted the space but had already been snagged by the first arrivals, leaving several hundred of us out of luck—no way to shake hands, make introductions, exchange business cards, or interact comfortably.

I am sure that this international corporation spent a fortune on those lovely avocado boats stuffed with shrimp salad, but their poor planning made it impossible to achieve any of the goals they had set for the networking event. This failure was evident as droves of people left the reception shortly after it began, headed for their hotels and their room-service menus. Thinking through these kinds of logistics will help you achieve your goals and exceed your participants' expectations instead of sabotaging yourself with poor planning.

Not every organization gets this wrong: the trick is to provide your guests with somewhere to sit, something to watch, or something to talk about. Have your networking event in the exhibitor hall, where attendees can at least wander through and preview the vendors they'll want to chat with later. Or schedule the event at a museum or aquarium, with food and drink stations scattered throughout (and plenty of trash cans!), allowing guests to make a natural progression through the exhibits. Provide a good number of banquet tables and chairs around the perimeter so people can sit and chat. And if you decide to provide background music, make sure it's not so loud that people can't hold a conversation; an acoustic group or single musician is usually more than sufficient to provide a pleasant atmosphere.

If you're thinking about creating a networking event as part of your next conference or at any event attended by people who are meeting for the first time, think about ways to make it easier for people to actually network with each other. Here are a few ideas I've used in the past:

- *Coffeehouse.* Instead of a typical networking setup, create a coffeehouse atmosphere. Get lots of soft seating (sofas and chairs), and arrange them in small groupings; provide a coffee bar where people can get their favorite flavored coffee drinks and some biscotti or shortbread cookies. Have an acoustic guitar player create some soft background music that people can talk over without shouting.
- *Roundtable experience.* Provide an opportunity to talk in small groups on a particular topic, kind of like speed dating. Everyone spends ten to fifteen minutes at a table of their choice; when the bell rings, everyone gets up a travel to another table to talk to five different people about a different topic. Inevitably everyone learns a few tips and tricks and ends up exchanging business cards and finding peers whom they stay in touch with long after the event. It's hard to get them to switch tables sometimes because the conversation is going so well!
- *Team-building activities.* Create teams of people who don't know each other or work together on a daily basis, and have them complete small challenges with a prize for the team who completes their challenges first. Because people with many different physical abilities will be in attendance, make sure that some of the challenges are mental rather than physical—assembling a puzzle, solving a riddle, answering trivia

questions, and so on. Search online for team-building activities that can be undertaken in an office or conference setting. Relay races, scavenger hunts, poster contests, name that tune, and putt-putt golf competitions are a few examples of fun ways help attendees meet someone new or exchange ideas.

- *Table-topics activities.* If you're in a setting where people will be sitting at a table, have a tent card at the table with a list of conversation starters—they can be business or personal, depending on your event goals. Fill a fishbowl with questions written on slips of paper, and have people draw a random question. Use "Would You Rather?" questions (Google it) to generate some lively discussion. Or create a snowball game: Have everyone write down a question or topic on a white piece of paper, wad it up, and throw it across the room. Everyone then picks up a paper that is not their own, reads it aloud, and kicks off the discussion with their thoughts on the topic written on the paper.

DELIVER VALUE WITH A TWIST

I recently attended a state conference that included the dynamic keynote speaker and author Jon Petz. His presentation began with a video that showed his frantic ("wink-wink") attempt to arrive to the venue on time. The video showed him sleeping through his alarm clock, racing through the airport, and running past local landmarks, ending with his crashing through the doors at the rear of the auditorium and running up to the podium, trying valiantly to catch his breath. Before he'd uttered a single word, the entire audience was already riveted, and his subsequent talk was extremely entertaining, memorable, and, most of all, relevant to everyone in the crowd.

I have attended this annual event multiple times, and it is firmly etched into my schedule every year. Their planning team delivers an agenda packed with compelling content and gift-wrapped with a unique twist—so much so that they've had to change venues to accommodate their growing attendance. Their proven track record guarantees the word-of-mouth that is increasing their numbers.

MAKE TIME FOR FUN!

Adding a few entertainment components throughout the day can help set the tone for your entire event. It not only provides a welcome relief from the important work being done by your participants but also can elevate the fun and excitement.

This is an area where recommendations can really come in handy. Ask around for ideas from friends and colleagues for entertainment companies and individuals that brought the fun to their events. When choosing off-site tours and experiences, look to locals for recommendations. Online reviews can help as well, but you can't beat the information provided by the staff members of your venue or the local convention and visitor's bureau.

Offer Downtime

Think about the things you can do to make free time more enjoyable for your attendees. This is the time between sessions, the extended breaks, or the extra hour between lunch and the start of the afternoon schedule. There are only so many times your guests can wander through the exhibit hall or check their e-mails. During a multiday conference, they're going to be ready for some other options.

A colleague of mine recently flew across the country to attend a weeklong training event. A week is a long time to be away from home, so the organizers came up with some pretty innovative activities that attendees could enjoy during their downtime. There was a zone where guests who were missing their own pets back home got the chance to play and snuggle with a pack of adorable pups. Air hockey, foosball, and other games were set up for attendees to play. Lounges were furnished with massage chairs and charging stations, and appointments were available for head-and-neck massages. So many options, so little time!

This is the kind of added value that people will be talking about long after the event is over. If budget is a concern, seek out sponsors that might be willing to foot the bill for these kinds of extras.

One of the most popular downtime activities I incorporate into almost every conference I plan is a jigsaw puzzle. I purchase a one thousand–piece puzzle that matches the theme of my event and set it out on a table in the main concourse for people to work on as time allows. People visit the table all day long, stopping by for a few minutes to check progress and work with others to place a few pieces before moving on to their next session. This is a seemingly small but immensely satisfying activity for many participants, and at this point I would be in big trouble if that puzzle weren't waiting for them when they arrived!

Don't Forget After Hours

As you try to create the perfect after-hours schedule, first go back to your original goals. If one of your goals is to have your attendees network and get to know each other, for example, hosting a friendly tournament at an upscale bowling alley is a better choice than renting out a movie theater where everyone is sitting quietly in the dark, staring at a screen. An acoustic music ensemble is probably a better choice at your patio party than a full-on band blasting in the background so no one can be heard. A murder-mystery night where people are working together to solve the crime is better than putting a comedian onstage with little audience interaction.

There are hundreds of other experiences to explore. Here are a few to consider:

- Scavenger hunt
- Escape room
- Cooking class or demonstration by a local celebrity chef
- Painting class
- Wine tasting or brewery tour
- Casino night

- Drum circle
- Maker stations—arts and crafts, journals, vision boards, etc.
- Team-building or television game shows
- Karaoke party
- Tailgate party
- Entertainers—caricature artists, magicians, tarot card readers
- Talent show/open-mic night—poetry, music, etc.
- Field trip—to a casino, comedy club, museum, aquarium, zoo, racetrack, or other nearby attraction

Connect with local officials to see whether there are any volunteer opportunities that your attendees can participate in during their free time. Perhaps some of your attendees would be excited by the chance to use their free time volunteering at a food bank, a homeless shelter, or a Habit for Humanity build site.

GO, BUCKS!

One of the most successful after-hours events I've ever organized for a group of corporate clients was a tour of Ohio Stadium, otherwise known as the "the Shoe." This renowned football stadium is located in the heart of The Ohio State University campus. For just $10 per person, we were able to receive a guided tour of the beautifully appointed Yassenoff Recruit Center lined with team pictures and memorabilia, explore the enormous press box, and get a bird's-eye view of the field from one of eighty-one luxury suites. A highlight for me was being given front-row seats to a practice session of the award-winning drum line and an impromptu serenade by the sousaphone section from "the Best Damn Band in the Land." But the best part of the tour was the chance to stand in the middle of the field on the fifty-yard line and experience the perspective that the Buckeye team has when they take the field. This is a perfect example of how you can provide an outstanding experience while allowing your guests to sample a little local flavor, all without spending a lot of money.

LEARN FROM THE SUCCESSES

One of the best ways to shape your event into a meaningful, impactful, enjoyable experience for your attendees is to pay attention to the organizers who've done it right. We can learn a few things from them.

Sweat the Small Stuff

The Midwest Writers Workshop is a conference that has been around for over four decades. They have a sellout crowd every year, and for good reason. The team that organizes this event has an incredible eye for detail, from the registration process to the finale. Here are six examples of little things they do that make a huge difference:

- *Website.* It's evident that the organizers of the MWW have learned a lot in their decades of planning the event when you navigate their website to register for the event and research the details. They do an excellent job of anticipating every question a registrant could possibly have about fees, speakers, session options, transportation, lodging— you name it!
- *Daily newsletter.* A copy of *Shop Talk*, MWW's daily newsletter, is distributed to conference attendees each day upon arrival. It includes photos and highlights from the day before as well as schedule reminders, announcements, contest deadlines, and open slots still available for agent pitches, social media coaching, and manuscript evaluations. To pull this off, there must be several people assigned each day and night to create content and then print and copy the newsletter for the next morning.
- *Social media.* As writers, those who attend MWW are very active on social media, and the conference hashtag #MWW gets heavy use year-round. During the event, tweets are displayed in real time on monitors in the venue's common areas.
- *One-on-one sessions.* MWW's conference is held on a college campus, and many of the volunteers are college students. One of the highlights of the event is a chance to schedule an appointment with

social media experts from the university. Those who take advantage of this opportunity walk away with some great tips and advice from these young experts for making a bigger impact with their own social media accounts.

- *Buttonhole sessions.* These twenty-minute roundtable sessions allow attendees to speak in small groups (no more than six or seven people) with agents, publishers, published authors, and other writing industry experts on a variety of topics. Attendees can peruse the options in advance and grab a seat at the tables that interest them most, rotating every twenty minutes to a new table until the two-hour session has concluded. I once snagged a seat at a buttonhole session featuring renowned author Roxane Gay, who patiently answered questions from our tiny group of aspiring authors in her own pragmatic style. What an amazing opportunity! While I thoroughly enjoyed the keynotes and other presentations at this event, the buttonhole sessions alone were worth the price of admission.

- *Temperature control (or, if you can't beat 'em, join 'em).* The venue for the MWW conference has an HVAC system that keeps rooms pretty cool. The event planners are told in advance that the temperature cannot be adjusted, so they make it very clear in their registration information that participants should dress in layers. For those who don't heed the warnings, a table of MWW logo fleece jackets are made available for sale. The event organizers know that sweating the small stuff is the difference between a good and great conference; they also know a money-making opportunity when they see one!

Make It an Event to Remember

I was once fortunate enough to attend a one-day women's-health event that developed a program devoted to educating participants on how to take charge of their own health and well-being. In addition to booking doctors, pharmacists, and other relevant speakers on topics such as diabetes, cancer, aging, stress, and nutrition, the event organizers had set up a whole host of stations where attendees could receive complimentary bone-density screenings, blood-pressure checks, body-fat measurements, vision and hearing exams, blood-sugar tests, and head-and-neck massages. Every person attending the conference received a themed tote bag containing some great take-home information, including full-length books on a variety of health topics.

But the real treat came at lunchtime. When everyone arrived at their table, their place setting and chair were absolutely covered with some delightful gifts, all provided by a variety of generous sponsors. We're talking an overwhelming array: umbrellas, makeup brushes, an insulated lunch tote, full-size product samples, stationery, and so on. A healthy lunch was followed by a recognition program for rising stars in the world of women's health. As attendees filed out of the afternoon sessions, volunteers were stationed at each exit with baskets of chocolates for them to enjoy. At the end of the day, women could be seen leaving with their mothers, sisters, daughters, and friends, laughing as they tried to wrangle their tote bags now filled to overflowing with fun freebies and important information that could help them make better health choices moving forward.

The organizers had spent a great amount of time creating an event that had immeasurable impact and value. They accomplished this by establishing close relationships with dozens of sponsors. This meant that every attendee left the event feeling pampered, valued, educated, and empowered. This is a perfect example of an occasion that was planned down to the last detail and designed to further the mission—in this case, to provide women with important health information in a fun and entertaining way. I've never forgotten how that event made me feel, and I always try emulating it by incorporating at least one special element into my programming that will give my participants something unexpected, something to remember with joy and enthusiasm.

15

Trade Shows and Expos

Whether you call it a convention, an exhibition, an exposition, or a trade show, many of the events you plan may involve creating a space where those who are promoting their businesses, products, or services can connect with potential customers. Put in the most basic terms, a trade show is a way to connect buyers and sellers. Your primary goal should be to create an event that is effective for both the exhibitor and the attendees, including multiple ways for them to interact and connect. Offering exhibit space is also an opportunity for you to generate revenue for your event and help you cover many of your overhead costs through booth-rental fees and the additional sponsorship dollars.

Exhibiting at a trade show is an investment. Between travel, registration, booth rentals, shipping, giveaways, and personnel costs exhibitors must invest in attending your event, you must be able to demonstrate a potential return on their investment. After all, businesses already have a website that provides lots of information about their products or services. As an event organizer, your job is to provide opportunities for exhibitors to find new and different ways to connect with their prospects that go beyond their website and demo videos, to turn your audience from passive spectators into active participants. Exhibitors will be looking for ways to create a notable interaction, incorporate sensory experiences, offer continuing education, develop personal connections, and offer participants the chance to experience their brand.

If your event includes a space for exhibitors, do everything you can to communicate the demographics of your audience so potential exhibitors can evaluate whether it's beneficial for them to participate. Most exhibitors will prefer to interact with attendees who are decision makers for their organizations.

USE THE BINGO CARD

Anyone who has ever attended a conference has probably seen this common tool used by event organizers to entice every attendee to visit every exhibitor booth in the show. Each participant receives a stamp on their card at each booth; once it's completely filled out, they turn it in to be entered into a prize drawing. While this tactic generates lots of booth traffic and is an honest attempt by event organizers to encourage interaction, some exhibitors believe that it doesn't translate into qualified leads. In fact, if your show has a large attendance, each exhibitor may have to assign an additional team member to stamp cards instead of talking to truly interested prospects. Many attendees use this as an opportunity for some adult trick-or-treating, grabbing up the promotional items offered at each booth. This may not be the most effective way to encourage relevant interactions; survey your exhibitors to get their opinions on whether the bingo card is effective in helping them achieve their goals.

TRY THESE ALTERNATIVES TO DRIVE BOOTH TRAFFIC

Instead of the bingo card, try these strategies to create meaningful interactions between exhibitors and attendees:

- *Create an education pavilion.* Here exhibitors can present a spotlight talk or product demonstration. Make sure your education schedule is clearly displayed on message boards, event apps, and websites.
- *Offer exhibitor appointments.* Give attendees the opportunity to spend a few minutes conversing with exhibitors about their products and

services. Explore apps and websites that provide an opportunity for exhibitors and attendees to schedule one-on-one meetups. Provide a space for them away from the main exhibit floor.

- *Drive traffic to the trade-show floor.* Providing other experiences in the same area—like a bookstore, photo or video booth, VIP lounge, break area, food and beverage stations, and so on.

ASK HOW YOU CAN IMPROVE

Survey your exhibitors and, if possible, your audience members to find out how you can improve your show in the future. In talking to dozens of exhibitors who travel from show to show throughout the year, I learned that one of their biggest pet peeves is the confusing or sparse communication they receive from conference organizers. In one instance, a team of exhibitors had gone all out and dressed in costume to match the theme of the event. They said that leading up to the conference they had received three different messages about when the exhibit hall would be open—one time in an e-mail, another on the website, and a different time on the event app. In the end, they ended up sitting in their booth, in full costume, for four hours prior to the time the exhibit hall doors were even opened.

PRIORITIZE YOUR EVENT ORGANIZATION

Use these tips to go the extra mile to attract exhibitors whose participation will be most meaningful to your attendees.

- *Prepare attractive invitations to sponsors and exhibitors.* Send it out to all prospects as early as possible. Talk about all of the benefits your event offers them, as well as the spaces and packages available and the costs for each. Provide an early-bird rate to encourage registration.
- *Consider your exhibitors' needs.* Exhibitors will experience your venue and your location just as your participants will. Be sure they receive all of the same information regarding hotels, transportation, dress code, average temperature, area attractions, and other FAQs.

- *Thank your exhibitors.* Explore all of the ways to recognize exhibitors and promote their contributions to the event. As one trade show exhibitor told me, "I wish the organizers would do more to recognize the exhibitors and help attendees understand and appreciate the fact that our dollars help keep their registration costs low."
- *Connect your exhibitors with your participants.* Decide how you will provide your participants' contact information to your trade show exhibitors. Be aware that most will expect to receive a list both before and after the event. Most exhibitors will want e-mail addresses and mailing addresses along with name, company name, and title. Some event organizers simply send a spreadsheet via e-mail, while others provide preprinted mailing labels for a fee.
- *Include your exhibitors.* Will you display their logos on monitors in the general session? Will you offer speaking opportunities? Will they be permitted to participate in sessions and activities? How about after-hours activities? How many meals will you provide in the exhibitor base price, if any?
- *Display exhibitor information.* Make sure all printed materials given to your audience members make it easy for them to find and interact with your exhibitors. Include a floor map that helps participants find the exhibitors they want to visit.
- *Announce winners of exhibitors' contests.* Many exhibitors will offer a raffle or contest during the trade show. Create time in your agenda to announce those raffle winners in a public way, or, if there are too many to announce, scroll the winners on a monitor near the exhibit floor, along with instructions on how to claim prizes.
- *Provide spaces for your exhibitors to rest.* Give them a chance to sit, take a moment, and converse with one another off of the main floor.
- *Conduct exhibitor contests.* If you've selected a theme for your event, hold a contest for the booth that best represents the event theme. To encourage participation, award the winner a free booth registration the following year.

- *Help your attendees find your exhibitors.* If your show becomes so big that you have to branch out into multiple rooms, hallways, or even buildings, it becomes more important than ever that you provide information in advance so attendees can map out their plan of attack. If you select a theme for your event, create subthemed areas to make navigation a little easier for your attendees.
- *Don't forget your exhibitors just because you've gone virtual.* If you've decided to conduct a virtual event, choose a platform that provides opportunities for exhibitors to purchase banner ads, insert videos and marketing collateral, and set up a virtual booth where they can create livestream sessions, chat rooms, and one-on-one meetups.

ASK FOR HELP

If organizing the trade show portion of your event is getting too big for you to manage on your own, it's time to contract with an exhibition-management company. These firms provide expertise in everything from creating an initial budget and action plan to selecting contractors, managing registration, coordinating logistics—including preshow and postshow shipping, storage, and setup/teardown—assisting exhibitors with equipment and display rentals, and managing the floor throughout the event.

One of the biggest advantages in contracting with a reputable exhibition management company is that they will take charge of all exhibitor communications and booth services. They will create an information packet for exhibitors, explaining all of the event details, including the pricing for exhibit space, technology and furniture rentals, labor rates, and shipping and handling fees. They will communicate all dates and deadlines as well as detailed instructions for move-in and move-out of the displays. Best of all, their staff will orchestrate all exhibit hall activities and troubleshoot any problems that arise. When their fork-truck driver impales a box containing a wall monitor (because sometimes these things happen), they will be the ones who will acquire another monitor for the show, manage the claim, and reimburse the exhibitor.

Most large convention centers and conference venues have preferred vendors they can recommend to manage your trade show activities. As with any third-party vendor selection, take the time to check references and talk to others who have used their services. Be sure to discuss your goals and ask what they will do to help you host a successful show. And most important, get everything in writing: create a detailed list of your responsibilities and theirs when it comes to the exhibit hall, leaving nothing to chance.

Choosing Speakers and Presenters

SPEAKERS AND KEYNOTES

A thoughtfully planned roster of relevant and captivating speakers is the key to creating content that will keep people signing up for your events again and again. If you're involved in conference planning for your business or organization, you are probably searching for one or more keynote speakers to set the tone and round out your agenda.

I once attended an annual statewide conference for several hundred finance professionals. It was a mandatory training event in the state's capital. The luncheon keynote speaker chosen by the organizers was a long-time color commentator for a popular college football team. Although the speaker was very knowledgeable about his subject, his stories about obscure players and events from seasons past were lost on the majority of his audience.

As the speaker continued to regale the crowd with personal anecdotes, people started quietly (and some not so quietly) gathering their things and leaving the banquet room. Singles and pairs eventually grew to tables full of people exiting the large banquet room at the same time, leaving only a scant one-third of the group by the time the speaker concluded his remarks. I was embarrassed for the speaker, for the event planners, and for the audience who clearly didn't want to listen to one more football story.

Now, don't get me wrong—people from the sports world can be extremely engaging and relevant speakers for a variety of audiences. I heard Peyton Manning, former quarterback for the Indianapolis Colts and the Denver Broncos, speak a couple of years ago (at an HR conference, of all things), and he held the crowd's attention throughout his entire presentation, telling stories about teammates, mentors, and coaches from his high school and college days all the way through to his professional football career. What made his talk so memorable was that he included beautiful little jewels of insight on motivation, leadership, and overcoming challenges ("Leaders must have the audacity to believe there is something more out there to strive for . . .") that I wrote down and reference to this day. He took the time to understand his crowd and used that knowledge to provide some inspiring insights that people could apply in their own lives.

Here are a few questions to ask yourself when planning for a keynote presentation:

- Is the speakers' topic appropriate for your crowd?
- Will their presentation add to your guests' experience?
- Is the topic relevant to the goals you've set for your event?
- Does the speaker understand your goals, your audience, and your time limitations?
- Is the speaker available and within budget?
- Should you schedule a speaker during a meal? Have you provided enough time for your attendees to network with each other and discuss what they've experienced throughout the day? If not, don't program mealtimes. Just add some soft music in the background; a great table conversation may just be what your audience members need.

WHAT SPEAKERS NEED

It's just as important that you consider your speakers' needs when preparing for your event.

Communication

Professional speakers expect to receive timely and thorough communication from your team. Where will the session be held? Where should they park? What kind of A/V equipment is available to them? And most important, what can the speaker do to tailor their talk to the event and provide the best value to the participants?

Phil Mershon maintains a private Facebook page for speakers participating in the Social Media Marketing World event. "We're all about helping our speakers make their topic relevant and help them accomplish their goals," says Phil. "We have a party just for our speakers at the event; we are very relational in how we approach them."

Introduction

Every speaker should be introduced, whether by the master of ceremonies or emcee, a session facilitator, a volunteer, or some other team member. Ask the speaker to provide a short biography, and make sure your facilitator is familiar with the text and can correctly pronounce the name of the speaker as well as everything in the biography.

Referrals

It also is extremely helpful to a professional speaker when you can recommend them to decision makers at other organizations who could use their services. Be sure that someone is assigned to take pictures of them presenting, and then uses relevant hashtags to post these pictures on your (and their) social media outlets immediately afterward.

WHEN ORGANIZERS GET IT WRONG

Scott Warrick, an attorney and professional speaker who specializes in human resources and employment law, recounts his worst experience ever as an event speaker. It happened to be for an association he belonged to. He'd been asked by the incoming president to give a one-hour talk at a lunch, which would be followed by an afternoon seminar.

Scott negotiated his fee with the president and then waited to hear from the programming director to hone in on a topic. Unfortunately, all he heard was crickets—no communication of any kind, even though he reached out multiple times. His presentation eventually had to be postponed a month because of the lack of communication, but again his e-mails to the programming director went largely unanswered.

"When I showed up to the meeting, no one was there to assist me," says Scott. "I found the venue's IT person near the stage, and we got everything ready. No one from the core team came to see if I needed anything; they all sat huddled together, away from the attendees, in their own little clique. I did my presentation and even provided a pass code to access an additional webinar at no charge—with advance approval from the president."

Scott continues, "Afterward the programming director sent an e-mail to the attendees telling them that the free webinar I provided was my own doing and was not supported by the organization. I wrote the president and told him that there needed to be a serious discussion regarding the programming director and that no speaker should ever be treated this way. He wrote back and said he felt I overcharged the association for the presentation and didn't want any further conversation. The whole thing was a nightmare."

Wow. Just . . . wow. There is never an excuse for a speaker or presenter to be treated this way; it is the height of unprofessionalism and disorganization. In my conversations with dozens of professional speakers, I've been amazed at the stories they tell about organizations that have selected them to make a presentation and then undervalued or frustrated them from beginning to end.

Consider these other speaker pet peeves:

- Miscommunication or lack of information
- A disorganized event
- A poorly designed room with bad audiovisual equipment

- Lack of directions or assistance upon arrival (Where is my room, where are my handouts, when can I test my setup . . .)
- Getting "squeezed" on agenda time when the prior session has run long and they're asked to cut their carefully prepared forty-five-minute presentation into a twenty-minute time slot in order to keep the event running on schedule

WHEN ORGANIZERS GET IT RIGHT
However, many organizations get it right. Lori Firsdon, professional organizer, speaker, and author, explains that several things make her feel respected and valued as a speaker. "I work very hard at getting everything planned ahead of time, so I really appreciate it when I walk in and the room is set up and ready to go," says Lori. "Handouts are printed and passed out to each attendee, and the IT staff is on hand in case anything goes wrong. I also appreciate it when I am provided audience feedback after the program."

Greg Hawks, keynote speaker and corporate culture specialist, talks about a great experience he had at one speaking engagement. "Upon arrival, someone went over the entire schedule of the conference," he said. "How it was going and how excited they were for me to be there. They walked me to the speaker's room. Offered coffee, water, soda, etc. They were upbeat and positive. It was run like a clock and very smooth. They were generous in preparing the audience to receive my message. It was incredibly delightful!"

CONSIDER THESE ARRANGEMENTS FOR SPEAKERS
It is imperative that you address these details when preparing for your event speakers.

- Do you have your speaker's bio and photo, and have you included it on your website, in your program, and along with other promotional materials?

- If the speaker is making their own travel arrangements, do they have accurate directions to the venue?
- If you're providing transportation from the airport to the venue and back, who will see to it and when?
- Is there a place for your speakers to view information about your conference and get updates (such as a private Facebook page, a private page on your website, a Slack channel, etc.)?
- Do they have a copy of the event agenda?
- Do they know what room they'll be presenting in?
- Do they have adequate time to set up and practice in the presentation room?
- Have they been invited to attend meals or other event activities?
- Do they have a name badge?
- If you're providing your speaker a sleeping room, have reservations been made? Does the speaker have a confirmation number?
- Will you prepare a welcome or thank-you gift for your speaker? Will it be placed in their room or presented some other way?
- Who will introduce speaker, and when will they meet? Will the speaker provide the text, and do you have it?
- Will the speaker have handouts? Who will print and distribute them?
- Does the speaker know what time they'll present? Have you confirmed this with the speaker?
- How will payment be handled? Has a check been prepared? Who has it, and who will give it to the speaker? If you will be invoiced, arrange the payment terms well in advance.
- If the speaker agrees to speak for free, can you at least provide a small honorarium to help cover their cost to participate?

SEND OUT A CALL FOR SPEAKERS

Your speaker track could make the difference between a so-so attendance and a sellout crowd. Your job is to create a "call for speakers," a page on your website or social media that describes the content you're looking for and the criteria you will use to select the presenters who will appear on your agenda. Prepare submission guidelines that require potential speakers to provide not only a biography and basic contact information but also details on their proposed topics and the credentials that make them the right person to deliver the content. Ask for details on the presentation format they use and what kind of room setup and equipment needs they will have. If your event is virtual, ask your prospective speakers about their experience in delivering their content in an online format and how they adapt their presentations to engage a virtual audience.

One of the ways you can be sure your speakers will resonate with your audience is to view presentations they've done in the past. Many speakers can address a variety of topics, so take a look at their website and promotional materials to see what topic might be most appropriate for your attendees. Spend some time familiarizing your speaker with your audience—what they do, what they care about, their challenges and goals. Any speaker worth their salt should be willing to customize their talks for your audience for maximum impact.

If you're using professional speakers, those who speak to groups for a living, their fees may not be as flexible as those who speak occasionally to promote their primary business or their services or their book. In addition to the professional speaker's fee, there may be other costs associated with their presentation, including technology needs, copies of handouts, props, lodging, food, and travel. They are most likely worth every penny; just be sure you understand all of the expenses involved in bringing them to your event.

THE NO-SHOW

Author and keynote speaker Andy Masters has literally seen it all in his years of speaking around the world. He provides some great advice for meeting planners who are faced with a no-show or with a keynote speaker or presenter who has fallen ill or whose flight is cancelled or delayed.

"First, contact the other speakers on the agenda, and see if they can swap and present in the morning rather than the afternoon, in the hopes the original speaker can make it later in the day," says Andy. "Second, many professional speakers who are members of the National Speakers Association have a vast network of colleagues to call on in every local area to fill in, in case of emergency. Ask the speaker if they can make arrangements or have a recommendation of another speaker on short notice."

Andy further advises that "if you are completely stuck, rather than having an audience with no speaker stare at each other for an hour, have a backup plan ready to go. Engage the group in a roundtable or group discussion for an hour, with questions such as 'What is your biggest challenge this year?' or 'What ideas do you have to make it a more fun or positive work environment this year?' Whatever, you do, don't panic."

IV

LOGISTICS

It's time to start getting down to the nitty-gritty of event planning—the infrastructure that represents the backbone of your event. These are the logistics that your attendees will pay absolutely no attention to . . . until something goes wrong. Whether your plan fails or whether you fail to plan, a misstep in any of these areas can turn an otherwise awesome event into something less than what you'd hoped for. When people are wandering aimlessly trying to find the registration area or the keynote speaker's presentation won't advance from one slide to the next or the trash cans are overflowing or half of your attendees miss the opening session because they're still trying find a parking space or are waiting in a long line in the restroom, you will wish you'd spent a little more time thinking though these important details.

DEVELOPING YOUR LOGISTICAL PROWESS

I have to say that when it comes to handling logistics, The Ohio State University is hands-down the best I've ever seen. If you've ever experienced move-in day on a college campus, you know it can be chaos. But not in Buckeye territory! They have a proven system that can get more than ten thousand students moved and settled in an extraordinarily organized way.

The key to running an operation of this magnitude with such finesse is anticipating the needs of the students and their families well ahead of move-in day. On the day we moved our freshman into the dorms, from the time we pulled onto campus until the time we drove away, OSU had anticipated every question we could have asked about traffic patterns, parking, check-in, what to bring, where to eat, textbook pickup, and many more questions we hadn't even thought to ask!

Take a leaf from OSU's playbook, and try this tactic the next time you're planning your event: Put yourself in the shoes of your participants, and anticipate every question they might have. First make sure you've developed an answer for each of those questions, and then use every method at your disposal to communicate the answers before they're ever asked.

17

Nuts and Bolts

Planning a successful event includes making sure you've done everything you can to keep your attendees informed, comfortable, and safe. In this chapter, we consider a few logistics to think through when planning your event.

GETTING FROM POINT A TO POINT B

Transportation

The road from home to your registration kiosk can be long and stressful. Your participants will potentially use several modes of transportation to travel to your event; anything you can do to make their journey less traumatic will be appreciated.

- *Airports.* As you consider event locations, evaluate the airport that will be used by your guests. Selecting a locale that has a quality airport with a reputation for on-time departures and arrivals, great amenities, and above-average customer service ratings will help elevate your attendee's total experience. If you're hosting a large event with a high percentage of air travelers, work with the airport's customer service department to establish an on-premise presence for your event. This could include signage, print collateral, and even a welcome station with staff members standing by to greet folks as they arrive to answer any questions.

- *Shuttle buses.* If you're planning a large event and have several hotels housing your attendees, be sure to confirm any transportation options the hotel may have to the closest airport as well as to the event venue. Your attendees will have lots of questions about their options, so interview each facility ahead of time and prepare your team to be able to answer questions.
- *Public transportation.* Provide information on the bus, train, and subway systems that provide direct service to your location. Be sure to include links to websites that provide details on routes, fees, and other information that someone new to the area would need to know.

Maps and Directions

My tiny hometown shares a zip code with two other nearby towns, all of which have a "Main Street." Can you imagine what happens when you put a Main Street address and our zip code into a GPS? It can be chaos. I vividly remember the time we ordered a street sweeper to come in after a two-day event on Main Street to clean the last of the debris from the festival area, and the equipment ended up be delivered to the wrong location—twice! Believe me when I tell you that this is the last thing you want to hear late on a Sunday night after working several fifteen-hour days on your feet. What a relief when that sweeper finally came rolling into town and we were able to check our last task off the list!

When communicating the location of your event to participants, make sure the address you provide is 100 percent accurate, and confirm that your address pops up correctly on all popular online driving apps and mapping tools, including Waze and Google Maps. If your search doesn't yield consistent results, your pre-event collateral should include turn-by-turn directions from every direction.

Parking

Think through where your attendees will park and how they will get from the parking lot to the event area. Will they be within walking distance, or will shuttles be required? Is there an adequate amount of handicapped parking? Will you provide reserved parking for guests of honor, speakers, VIPs, or volunteers? If the answer is yes, you need to determine how will you designate those areas separately from attendee parking and what you will provide to those VIPs so they can identify themselves with minimal effort when they arrive. This could include sending them a hangtag for their car's rearview mirror or providing them with a letter to present to the parking attendant.

Will normal traffic patterns need to be adjusted to accommodate the influx of traffic created by your event? If so, you'll need to coordinate with the local police department so they can be prepared to handle volume and plan for appropriate staffing levels. They may work with you to manage the traffic signals in the vicinity of your venue to provide smoother flow. Will you need to assign a staff of volunteers to direct traffic, or will additional signage be enough to keep things organized?

Keep an eye on the weather forecast, and develop some contingencies—especially if you're unable to provide paved parking for all of your guests. I once reserved a corporate cabana for the opening day of a large air show. The rain had been relentless in the twenty-four hours leading up to the show, and the grassy areas around the airfield designated for parking had become muddy swamps. After the show was over and people made their way to their vehicles, it became clear that many cars were going to need some help getting back onto a paved surface. People were losing shoes in the muck and getting sprayed with watery mud when they tried to help each other push cars out, and a few quick-thinking folks with trucks and tow chains made a few bucks pulling people out of the sloppy mess.

We learned later on that the organizers were able to come up with an alternative plan for day two of the air show, making arrangements with nearby manufacturing plants to use their paved parking lots and arranging for shuttle buses to get guests to the show grounds. But the big question is this: Why didn't they have that plan in place from the beginning that included arrangements for day one?? The weather forecast had been very consistent in the days leading up to the event; a large swath of rain had been steadily moving from west to east all week long. Their attendees would have been much better served had the organizers heeded the weather warnings and been ready with their backup plan from the very beginning.

Signage

I can't count the number of times I've shown up for a meeting or conference only to walk into the venue and see nothing that points me in the right direction. Your attendees should never have to ask how to find their way to parking, entrances and exits, registration, restrooms, meal spaces, meeting spaces, the entertainment stage, or shuttle drop-off and pickup. Any instructions you can provide in advance of your attendees' arrival will help, but signage at the event site is a key component to a smooth, stress-free arrival experience. Whether it's carpet decals, electronic signboards, or fun way-finding signposts, there should be directional signs for everything. Add a map of the venue in the registration packet and event app for good measure. This is a budget item that can't be ignored; it can eliminate a lot of frustration for your attendees and provide a nice, relaxed vibe.

Navigating the Venue

How will your attendees travel through the event? Are there any bottlenecks or congested areas that need to be rerouted or reconfigured? Consider the timing of your schedule: Have you incorporated enough time between events for attendees to comfortably manage the transition from one end of your venue to the other, including bathroom or coffee breaks?

Do you have adequate seating in the common areas of your event space for people to rest, read, check messages, review the program, chat with one another, and otherwise just get off of their feet for a moment?

Lining a hallway with exhibitor booths or tables on both sides can be difficult to navigate for people who want to stop and chat with the vendors. Those who are just trying to walk through may feel like they're navigating a gauntlet. Instead, try staggering the exhibitor spaces or lining them up on one side of the aisle so traffic flow is unrestricted.

EQUIPMENT

As you start to identify the unique equipment needs for your event, begin by having a discussion with the event manager at your venue. They may be able to provide the items you need—although you will likely have to pay an extra fee to rent it. Typically, they can provide items such as projectors, screens, monitors, sound systems, flip charts, and white boards. If you require items such as laptops, video walls, or crowd-control equipment, you will probably need to reach out to a third-party provider.

What systems and equipment are crucial to your event? What would you do if it failed? Do you have backup equipment and staff on standby to troubleshoot and resolve issues as needed? Having a strong contingency plan that is reviewed and practiced regularly can go a long way toward ensuring that your event is successful no matter what happens.

RESTROOM FACILITIES

Most of us have probably experienced the frustration of attending an event at a venue where the restrooms were inadequate for the size of the crowd or of finally getting into the restroom only to find that they aren't being serviced frequently enough and the paper dispensers are empty. This kind of unpleasant experience can quickly turn an enjoyable occasion into a real disappointment.

When selecting a venue, take into consideration the number of restroom facilities available in the general proximity of the space you'll be using for your event and whether they are adequate for the size of your crowd. Take some time to talk to your sales manager about the housekeeping staff that will be scheduled during your event and how you will be able to communicate with them should the facilities need servicing in a hurry.

Outdoor Restroom Facilities

If you're hosting an outdoor festival or any event that does not have easy access to adequate toilet facilities, you will need to rent portable restrooms. If you've been to an event recently where portable facilities were used, you may have noticed that there are lots of options these days in the world of porta-potties! ADA–compliant units, high-rise VIP units, hand-sanitizing or hand-wash stations, and infant-care stations are all options now available to keep your guests comfortable—which means they'll stay at your event longer. Make sure you have a line item in your budget for these facilities; high-end units, while quite luxurious compared to the typical unit, will come with a high-end price tag.

The number of units you should reserve depends primarily on the size of the crowd you expect. The rental company will be able to help you make these calculations. It's better to have too many units than not enough so that your guests won't have to wait in long lines. Increase the number of units if you're serving beverages—especially alcohol. For multiday events, you will have to consider the placement of the units; make sure they're in an area where they can be easily serviced multiple times each day and most definitely upwind from where your crowd will congregate.

ELECTRICITY

Assess your electricity needs for lighting, sound, cooking, and A/V and other technology. This is especially important if you're organizing an outdoor event. If electricity access is limited, or if the local regulations restrict the use of extension cords, make sure your vendors and other participants are aware of the limitation before they arrive so they can plan accordingly. For instance, if you're using a giant tent to serve an outdoor meal (on a golf course, for instance), you may need to stage the food prep in or near the clubhouse and transport the food to the area of service after it's been cooked.

If you're outside and must resort to the use of generators to power speakers, lighting, or an entertainment stage, it's important to realize the extraordinary amount of noise generators can make. Sitting a generator next to a performance stage can be problematic; at the very least, start it up ahead of time so you can experience the noise it creates and determine whether it's an acceptable source of power.

The use of a generator may require a special permit from local authorities. This may involve an inspection to be sure it's been installed safely and is properly ventilated.

A Different Kind of Hero

My friend Bill was an electrician who for years took responsibility for setting up temporary electric service for over 450 art vendors and food vendors at a local festival. Over the years he perfected the grid so that everyone would have solid, reliable electric service throughout the event. Of course, there were moments when someone overloaded a circuit or weather caused an issue, and Bill would then be called to the location to troubleshoot and fix the problem. Bill was always ready with an inventory of all of the parts and equipment he could possibly need to fix any situation.

Here's a shout-out to the people who are responsible for developing an alternate plan in advance so that when plan A starts to crumble they're ready to go. You are my kind of hero!

TRASH

You should be able to stand at any position in your venue and be in clear sight of a trash receptacle. If you have too few containers, you and your team will spend a lot of time collecting trash from every surface, especially the ground. If your event will generate a lot of trash, you will need to make sure the venue has adequate personnel available to empty trash cans at regular intervals. For instance, a box lunch, while a safe and expedient way to serve hundreds of attendees quickly, will generate mountains of trash within a short period of time; you must be prepared with extra trash containers wherever this type of lunch will be consumed.

If you're hosting a fair or festival, you'll have to create your own sanitation crew to manage waste and put a system into place to constantly monitor and empty trash cans. Ask your trash removal company about recycling options—especially if you're selling or providing beverages in plastic bottles or aluminum cans.

PREPARING FOR THE UNEXPECTED

I love the movie *The Wedding Planner*, starring Jennifer Lopez. In the movie, Jennifer plays Mary Fiore, San Francisco's premier wedding planner, sought after by the most discerning brides and their families. Her organization and planning skills are legendary; she actually sports a custom tool belt under her designer jacket that holds everything from breath spray to super glue, and she wears an earphone that keeps her in constant contact with her planning team (be still, my heart!). That woman is ready for anything!

I've planned dozens of events over the years, and if there's one thing I've learned, it's to expect the unexpected. Someone will show up who didn't register in advance. More directional signage will be needed. The radios being used for staff communications will run out of battery life. An exhibitor will ask to borrow an electrical strip or a container to collect business cards from attendees in their booth. A staff member will wear the wrong shoes and complain of a massive blister on their foot. A speaker will walk in with two hundred copies of a ten-page handout that they didn't have time to collate or staple (or will walk in with their original copy and expect you to have a way to make the two hundred copies!).

Basic Event Emergency Kit

One way to prepare for the unexpected is to have an emergency kit available with items that might be needed during the event. I have accessed my emergency kit many times over the years, and I can relax knowing that I'll be prepared for almost anything. Before my event, I pack a plastic tub full of items that might be helpful and keep it close at hand.

The following is a list of the items I find helpful to have on hand no matter what type of event I'm planning: scissors, a spool of florist wire, poster adhesive putty or blue painter's tape (which won't leave residue on painted or papered walls), safety pins, paper clips, a stapler and box of staples, stain remover wipes, rubber bands, trash bags, transparent tape, large and small black magic markers, several pieces of card stock and poster board, a couple of portable tripods or sign stands, pens, index cards, static spray, a box of tissues, extra batteries, phone chargers, and a small manicure set. You'll also want to include a basic tool kit and a simple first aid kit that includes pain reliever, bandages, cough drops, antibiotic ointment, chewable antacid tablets, eye drops, and so on.

Seeing to these foundational issues is often where mistakes or miscalculations can be avoided—the kind of mistakes that can sabotage your entire event. Make sure you have team members dedicated to ensuring that these logistical tasks and others unique to your event are carefully planned and that a risk assessment and contingency plan has been prepared.

18

Selecting Service Providers

There will be many times when the size or scope of your event will require that you bring in one or more third-party vendors to help you achieve your goals.

Don't get me wrong—I've been a part of some fantastic DIY events, and they were simply beautiful. But if you're organizing anything much larger than a low-key home party, you'll need to start thinking about your partners in crime, the experts who can help you achieve the experience you want to create. Rental companies that provide tents, tables, linens, and decor. Procurement specialists to help you find your ideal location. Venues that offer a variety of equipment and services. Audio-visual teams to create the perfect combination of light, sound, staging, and technical equipment and expertise. Caterers, florists, entertainers, deejays, staffing and security firms, transportation providers . . . the list goes on and on.

If you're working with a venue, ask them about their preferred vendor list. Most sales managers will typically keep a roster of the vendors they've worked with before, those who've been successful at producing events within the venue's layout and guidelines. Remember, they work with caterers, florists, photographers, lighting and sound technicians, equipment rental companies, and security firms every single day. They will only want to work with the best, so if you trust the venue, you should be able to trust their recommendations.

THE SELECTION PROCESS

When talking to prospective vendors, ask them about their willingness to get to know your event and to come up with a custom plan that will help you achieve your goals. Ask to see their portfolio, a collection of their previous work that demonstrates their range and creativity.

An experienced vendor will take the time to get to know you, your preferences, and your event from start to finish. The only way they can give a complete and detailed quote for their services is to have a clear understanding of your needs and expectations. But don't leave anything to chance. After you've scheduled a meeting with a prospective vendor, sit down and create a list of topics you want to cover and questions you need answered before you enter into a contract.

If you're meeting with a caterer, you'll need to have an approximate head count and budget and some idea of the type of food you hope to serve to your guests, down to the last appetizer and signature drink. If you're meeting with the sales manager of a venue, you'll need to know ahead of time all of the spaces you'll need to reserve, from the hospitality rooms and registration space to meeting rooms and storage areas. If you're meeting with a rental company to help create your vision for style and decor, be prepared to hand them a portfolio that defines your theme—color samples, fabric swatches, and ideas cut from magazines or found on Pinterest or Instagram.

If you have the luxury of time, talk to two or three vendors that provide similar services. While you may fall in love with the first one you meet, taking the time to meet with others will give you some perspective: Are you really getting the best quality and service available? Is your preferred vendor more or less expensive than comparable vendors? If their prices are way off one way or the other, make sure you're entirely clear on what is included in their quotes.

UNDERSTANDING THE DIFFERENCE BETWEEN
A CONTRACTOR AND A VENDOR-PARTNER

I believe that there is a huge difference between a contractor and vendor-partner. A contractor is a someone who doesn't take much interest in learning about you or your event. Their online reviews are mostly mediocre, and they don't show up on your venue's preferred vendor list. They have zero flexibility in their contract terms to accommodate your special circumstances. They aren't willing to provide any emergency or after-hours contact information and are more interested in getting your deposit than in understanding your unique needs.

A vendor-partner can be pretty easy to spot if you know what to look for. They are willing to invest the time it takes to understand your vision and your specific requirements before creating and entering into a written agreement. They are interested in creating a relationship and can explain in detail how their team will work alongside you to deliver their products or services. They have great references and reviews and will introduce you early in the process to the team members that will be in charge of your event.

Kosins Tents and Events is a great example of what a vendor-partner looks like. They are a full-service rental company in Dayton, Ohio, that provides supplies and equipment for events of all kinds—concession machines and bouncy houses for kid's birthday parties, tents for outdoor festivals and events, red carpets and equipment for corporate conferences and expos, and gorgeous table decor and linens for weddings and galas of every description.

The Kosins team doesn't like to think of themselves as simply as a contractor; they pride themselves on being a partner in helping you achieve your goals. Every team member at Kosins is skilled in event planning. They have years of experience in handling detailed logistics. They are constantly studying trends in fashion, colors, home decor, and design, all in an effort to keep their inventory fresh and relevant. The first client of the day may be seeking rustic country chic all in white, and the next client wants over-the-top shine and sparkle using deep jewel tones. The team at Kosins must be prepared to equip all sorts of events for a wide variety of clients, styles, and cultures. To demonstrate their capabilities, Kosins creates an assortment of styled event landscapes and tablescapes both in their showroom and on social media. These examples help their clients envision what is possible.

Lysa Kosins, event designer for Kosins, recommends Pinterest as a place to explore styles and design elements when trying to decide on an overall theme for your event. But she also warns that walking in the door with too many diverse ideas can hinder the planning process: "Communicating ideas can be difficult. I love it when a client can walk in the door with a clear direction. But even when they come in with a jumbled mess of ideas, we hone in on what is most important to them and use that to create the vision they have in their mind."

Often clients can be unyielding in their ideas or have a difficult time accepting that their budget doesn't match their vision. Lysa says that is where her team can help: "The rental service is the foundation of what we do, but our primary focus is on building a relationship. We are the ones who will be there from the very beginning of the event, and we'll be there for them until the very end. We provide a hands-on customer experience, and we'll be there to help no matter what. That is what sets us apart from our competition."

When selecting a vendor-partner for your event, discuss how you will communicate with them before, during, and after the occasion. A lot of the events planned by Kosins are held on weekends, but make no mistake—this team is always available. After regular office hours, their main office number rings to an emergency phone to ensure that staff will be accessible at a moment's notice if anything needs attention during the event, no matter the day or time.

Kosins provides tents for every kind of outdoor occasion. Since one can't assume that the day of the event is going to be seventy-two degrees and sunny with a light breeze, these outdoor occasions can be a little tricky to manage. Planners must be prepared for the fact that they may be visited by some unwelcome weather, such as rain, heat, or high winds. Lysa says that when it comes to outdoor events, Kosins automatically puts a plan B in place from the very beginning so they're prepared to pivot quickly if necessary. If a bride is enamored of the current trend of a no-tent wedding in a meadow or on the lush grounds of golf course or grand estate, they recommend erecting a bare tent frame and embellishing it with filmy drapery, twinkle lights, or greenery in keeping with the general decor. The frame provides some definition to the event space, and, if the weather takes a turn for the worse, they can quickly add a tent topper to protect the guests from a soaking rain or unbearable heat.

Lysa recommends sticking with the advice of the experts to avoid unnecessary stress and drama at your event. She recalls one time when the Kosins team had erected a one-hundred-by-forty-foot tent for an outdoor wedding. The weather turned ugly, with hurricane-force winds and rain. "Even though we had provided instructions against it, their coordinator thought it would be a good idea to tie down the sides of the tent when the wind kicked up. This created a hot-air-balloon situation inside the tent," said Lysa. "The wind was trapped inside, and the tent anchors started lifting out of the ground; that's when we were called." Using equipment improperly or ignoring safety precautions is never a good idea and can have devastating consequences. It is imperative that you select partners who are diligent about permitting, inspections, and safety and who use that expertise to your advantage.

COMMUNICATING AND CONFIRMING

Even when you're planning something as simple as a catered lunch, the vendor you choose can either help you accomplish your goals or create a mini crisis that you will have to overcome.

I once used an online catering site to order food for a thirty-five-person luncheon to be held prior to a quarterly meeting. Their ordering system was user-friendly, and there were lots of great choices that would provide a satisfying but healthy lunch for people with a wide variety of food preferences. I immediately received an e-mail confirming the date and time I would pick up my order and receipt of my payment. I confidently checked that item off of my planning list and moved on to other logistics for the day—meeting agenda, handouts, audiovisual, and so on.

On the day of the event, I arrived early at the restaurant to pick up my order, allowing plenty of time to secure it all in my car and get back to the meeting location with time to spare. When I gave my name and presented my e-mail confirmation, I immediately knew there was a problem when I saw the deer-in-headlights look on the manager's face. She began to explain that she had no record of the order and that there was no food ready for my event. As she was explaining this to me, another employee walked toward a printer on the back counter that had a long piece of paper sticking out of it. She tore it off, walked up behind the manager, and quietly handed her the slip of paper that apparently contained the details of my order; no one had bothered to check the machine for online orders for the day.

As the manager started to apologize profusely, offering me not only a complete refund but also a free lunch for my entire group (albeit for some other day), my mind started racing. I needed a solution, and I needed it now! Then it came to me: LaRosa's, a Cincinnati-based pizza chain that we'd used many times in the past for casual team lunches and other occasions. Their phone number was embedded into my subconscious thanks to their catchy television commercials, so I just grabbed my phone and dialed. Standing in the middle of the other restaurant, I spoke with the LaRosa's order dispatcher and explained my dilemma, and she walked me through ordering enough pasta, salad, and pizza for a crowd. They confirmed that their closest location could deliver the goods, and in the end we served a delicious lunch to the attendees with only a twenty-minute delay to the original schedule.

Have you spotted the one thing that could have been done to completely avoid this situation? If I had just picked up the phone early on the morning of my event to talk to the catering restaurant to confirm that my order was in the process of being prepared, and reviewed the entire order, including the pickup time and other important details, this entire crisis could have been averted. I'd gotten complacent. After all, I had the confirmation e-mail in hand, and my credit card had already been charged; that should have been enough. But, unfortunately, neither of those things confirmed that there were *actual* people preparing *actual* food at the appointed time. True confirmation requires a person-to-person conversation with the people responsible for completing the order, and in the flurry of my other day-of event planning tasks, I'd overlooked that small but important step.

When selecting a vendor, start by asking for recommendations from people you know and trust. Ask about their experiences with the vendor—if they were reasonably priced, easy to work with, and delivered as promised. And most important, ask whether they would work with them again. This kind of input will help you be more confident that you're selecting a vendor-partner that you can trust.

Contract Negotiations

If the services provided by third-party vendors and contractors are essential to your event's success, you must agree on terms and put them into a written, binding contract.

Contracts protect both parties. If a vendor values their reputation, they will do everything within their power to deliver the agreed-upon products and services in a professional and timely manner. After all, most providers associated with event planning get their business through referrals, recommendations, reviews, and repeat business, and they don't want to jeopardize their standing in the event planning community. You know you're on the right track if your vendor-partner is committed to ensuring that all agreed-upon deliverables are clearly stated in a written contract.

Of course, when you sign a contract, you're also making a promise. You are guaranteeing payment for use of a facility or reserving a vendor's products or services and will pay the agreed-upon amount in full on a timely basis. These kinds of contracts should never be signed unless and until your event is definitely going to take place and you have a rock-solid plan to meet your commitments to the other party.

Patrick Wartan chairs the Food and Beverage Practice Group at the law firm of Taft Stettinius & Hollister, LLP. When it comes to initiating contracts, "start as early as possible," Patrick suggests. "When negotiating a contract for a venue or catering, leverage goes out the window when you are short on time. You're probably going to pay a premium and won't be able to bargain for a better price if you're out of options and out of time." He also recommends that you always negotiate for a fixed price, especially if you're signing an agreement for multiple years. "Whether it's catering, venue, or transportation, lock in the current rate; don't sign anything that includes a floating rate."

If your planning efforts begin too late and you're trying to book the hottest venue in town, the place that everyone wants to be, you're going to lose some ability to negotiate. At that point, you'll have to either accept their terms or move on to a different venue.

COMMON CONTRACT TERMS

Before signing on the dotted line, you should make sure your contract clearly states deliverables and remedies in case of nonperformance or some other breach of contract. Some of the most common terms found in an event contract include the following:

1. *Services.* This is a detailed description of the scope of work. Patrick says that one of the biggest mistakes an event planner can make is not being clear about what they want. Make sure every detail is included—who, what, when, where, and how the products or services will be delivered. If the contract is for an event venue, be sure that this clause includes each room space you are reserving, including dates, times, and cost per room per day. Never assume a service or a space is included if it's not expressly stated in the contract.

2. *Sleeping rooms.* There are many elements that should be clearly stated when it comes to contracting for sleeping rooms, such as additional fees beyond the stated room rate, like resort fees, check-in and check-out times, cutoff date for reservations, and a detailed reservation process including a unique event code to ensure the attendee received the negotiated room rate.

3. *Payment terms.* This section will include not only the total amount you will pay the vendor but also a schedule of payments. Is a deposit required? Are interim payments required, and, if so, when? When is the final payment due? Many larger contracts will include a schedule of payments in order to provide the cash flow they need to plan the event.

4. *Types of payment*

   - *Direct bill.* This is the ability to pay your unpaid fees via invoice after the event has concluded and all charges have been tallied. In order to qualify for direct billing as a method of payment, you may be required to complete an application to establish a master account, which will involve undergoing a credit check and providing references from other vendors you have worked with in the past.

   - *Credit card.* A credit card number is provided to pay for all services. A deposit may be charged to the credit card when the contract is initiated and the balance charged to the card just prior to or on the first day of the event. Watch for credit card fees that may be assessed in addition to the quoted charge if you opt for this method of payment.

   - *Deposit.* This is an amount determined to be paid when the contract is initiated. There may be subsequent payments required throughout the planning process. Be aware that work may not commence by the vendor until the deposit has been paid in full. Watch for language that states that advance payments will be non-refundable. This is not necessarily an unreasonable request; the service provider may have completed significant work and should be entitled to be compensated for that work should you have to cancel your event.

5. *Labor rates.* If you see this clause in a contract, pay special attention. This may mean that the service provider plans to charge you a "time and material" rate that can't be stated at the time of signing the contract. This is a red flag, because you can't be sure what your final rate will be.

6. *Damage and security.* These clauses are written to protect the venue or service provider, putting the responsibility squarely on your shoulders if equipment or facilities are damaged, lost, or stolen by your staff or guests. If your event has an element of risk to it—for instance, a controversial speaker who might attract some unrest—you may be required to provide or pay for additional security personnel.

7. *Equipment failure.* This often attempts to protect the venue or service provider and claims that they have no liability for loss or damage if their equipment doesn't work. It is reasonable to ask for language requiring the venue and the equipment to be in the same or better working order than it was when you signed the contract.

8. *Event cancellation.* This clause explains any penalties you will incur if you must cancel your event for any reason after you have signed the contract. This clause is the section where a lot of event planners can get into trouble.

"It's important to understand the mechanics of the cancellation policy," Patrick says. "Cancellation is usually where venues retain funds, so understand the risk you are taking. At a minimum, any deposit you provided when you executed the contract (a 10 percent to 50 percent deposit is customary) is in jeopardy."

Many times, you will see a tiered penalty depending on how far out from the event date you cancel. For instance, you may only be charged a penalty of 20 percent of the total value of the contract if you cancel more than 365 days prior to the event start date, but you may incur an 80 percent penalty or more if you cancel less than ninety days prior. If you cancel far enough out, there is an outside chance that the venue or service provider can fill the slot that was reserved for you with another revenue-generating event. But if you cancel at the last minute, there is an opportunity cost that they will never be able to recoup; this is why the cancellation rate is so much higher the closer you get to the event date.

9. *Indemnification.* This clause protects the venue or service provider from liability if the event organizer (you) gets sued for damages, injuries, or losses due to you or your staff's actions or inactions.

10. *Force majeure.* This is a termination clause that excuses either or both parties from fulfilling their obligations in the case of an unexpected disaster. Examples include a weather event like a hurricane or tornado, a fire, a water main break, a labor stoppage, a terrorist attack, or a government action such as a declaration of war or a travel ban. It explains who has the power to terminate and what will happen if any of the stated circumstances occur and make it impossible to proceed.

    In 2020, the World Health Organization declared a worldwide pandemic as the COVID-19 virus spread around the globe. Thousands of events were cancelled as government entities announced shelter-in-place orders and travel bans and urged social distancing. Many generic force majeure clauses didn't have "epidemic" or "pandemic" specifically listed as a condition for invoking the clause, and even if they did, the applicability and impact of such clause was often questionable. But typically parties were able to come to a reasonable agreement regarding the amendment, postponement, or cancellation of these contracts due to the extraordinary circumstances. Moving forward, parties to event contracts can expect to see more detail added to the force majeure section and should pay special attention to any language that excludes certain types of occurrences from being covered by the clause.

11. *Minimums and commitments.* This is the section where you make assurances to a venue that you will spend a certain dollar amount in food and beverage and/or guarantee that a certain number of sleeping rooms will be reserved and paid for at the stated rate. If your attendance is unexpectedly low or you decide to go offsite for one or more meals and these minimum amounts aren't met by the time your event has concluded, you're still on the hook for the

minimums you agreed to in your contract. Be sure that you understand exactly what you're agreeing to in this section before signing
your contract, and keep it in mind as you plan your agenda. Minimum food and beverage amounts do not typically include service
fees, taxes, or gratuities when they are calculated.

12. *Attrition.* This is typically related to a sleeping room minimum
guarantee. A contract that includes sleeping rooms will stipulate
that the venue will hold a certain number of rooms for your group
until a certain date (for instance, they'll hold the rooms until thirty
days prior to your event). The attrition clause sets the percentage
of total rooms that must be reserved by that date—typically 75 to
80 percent. At that point you will most likely have two choices: to
release the unreserved rooms back to the venue to be reserved by
the general public or to pay a percentage of the total cost of the
unbooked rooms to continue to hold them for exclusive use by
your group.

13. *Food and beverage/liquor license policies.* Be sure you understand
the restrictions for bringing in outside food and beverages or for
taking leftover food outside of the facility. Most venues will allow
small packaged consumables such as prewrapped candies to be
offered at exhibit booths. But allowing other food that has been
prepared elsewhere not only cuts into their profits but also exposes
them to potential liability. What if someone claims they contracted
food poisoning at your event and the venue allowed food in their
facility that had been prepared outside of their control? The same
applies to leftover food being removed from the venue that isn't
stored at the proper temperature and causes someone to fall ill.
These are risks that most vendors are not willing to take.

When it comes to liquor, venues are especially vulnerable. If it
has been discovered that you are either serving or drinking alcohol
that wasn't provided by the venue, it could mean the loss of the
venue's liquor license and possibly a large fine. It is imperative that

you communicate to your staff and your guests the serious ramifications of trying to bring in their own alcohol.

However, you should always ask for language that holds your organization harmless in the event of a liquor liability claim. The venue's team must be sure that they are doing their part to train their servers to verify age, refuse underage service, and refuse to serve anyone who appears to be intoxicated.

14. *Clauses that prohibit changes, additions, stipulations, or lining out.* "Lining out" refers to making last-minute changes to the written contract before signing by drawing a line through a word or a section and replacing it with different wording. At this point, you may have gone through several iterations of the contract and just don't want to go through it again, but this is bad practice. Your final signed contract should be free of any manual changes.

After you've signed your contract and you begin to meet with your vendors, it's easy to start discussing and agreeing to changes to the scope of the work. But as we all know, there are at least two sides to every conversation. You may think you've communicated what you want, but the vendor may walk away with a completely different impression of what you've agreed to. Take the time to get those change orders in writing so that nothing is open to interpretation. Assume nothing; you may be severely disappointed on the day of your event if you don't have any proof of the revised agreement. Generally, an e-mail should be sufficient as a change order unless the contract says otherwise. "If the contract has a 'no oral modification clause,'" says Patrick, "make sure it is modified to include language that states that change orders communicated and agreed to by both parties via e-mail are binding."

15. *Severability.* This clause typically states what will happen in the case any clause in the contract is declared to be unenforceable or unlawful and will affirm that the remainder of the contract will remain in full force and effect.

16. *Americans with Disabilities Act.* This clause should be standard in all US event contracts. If one of the attendees can't participate in any part of your event due to noncompliance with legally required ADA guidelines, that participant can sue not only the venue or service provider but your organization as well. Patrick advises that you examine every aspect of your program and facilities to be sure that every attendee has appropriate access and the ability to participate without restrictions.

Other clauses to look for in your event contracts include noise restrictions (in case of an outdoor event there may be time restrictions—no amplified music after 10:00 p.m., for example), nonsmoking facilities (are designated smoking areas available?), restrictions on use of materials (such as glitter, confetti, rice, or bird seed) or open flames (such as candles or torches), and a photo release that allows the service provider to take photos and/or video of your event and use it without restriction in their promotional campaigns (including social media).

OTHER CONSIDERATIONS BEFORE YOU SIGN

Not all contracts will contain each of the elements listed above. You may be presented with a one-page agreement from a speaker that basically says that you agree to pay them "x" dollars to deliver their "y" presentation on a particular date. It's not a problem to sign a simple agreement like this; just be aware that these simple documents are no less binding than twenty-page agreements drawn up by law firms for a premium event venue and that you will be expected to hold up your end of the bargain.

Don't hesitate to ask for a vendor's standard agreement to be modified before you sign if you find that there's an important element missing such as a cancellation clause or failure to perform.

If you are signing a contract as the representative of a corporation or an officer of a civic organization or association, Patrick suggests that, as long as the corporation or association is a registered, bona fide entity, you cannot be found personally liable in the case of nonperformance by the organization. If you're not sure that you are acting on behalf of a legitimate entity, never sign your name to any legally binding document.

DON'T ASK, DON'T GET

Patrick's final tip is this: "Remember that everything is technically negotiable, not just price. Look for comped rooms, suite upgrades, late checkout, or other perks that are important to your event." Don't be afraid to ask for what you want. Perhaps there is a discount available if you use one of the vendors on the venue's preferred list, or free access to a venue's transportation fleet to and from the airport. You never know what's possible until you ask.

The information provided in this chapter does not, and is not intended to, constitute legal advice; instead, all information is for general informational purposes only. Readers should contact their own attorney to obtain advice with respect to any particular legal matter. Patrick Wartan is only licensed to practice law in Illinois and California.

20

Technology

There aren't too many events these days that don't have a technology component to them. It could be as simple as creating a mood with subtle lighting or having a good sound system for playing music or equipment to play a short video retrospective. Or it could as complex as having multiple stages, complete with light and sound shows, or audience-response technology that can read facial expressions to give you an immediate response to the material being presented.

Every technology component you add to your event should be deliberate, a means to accomplishing your objectives. Does it engage your audience members or enhance their experience? Does it deliver a return on investment? Jon Petz, motivational speaker and author of *Boring Meetings Suck*, reminds us that "whatever technology you decide to implement, have fun with it, and have everyone be a part of it. Experiment. See what works and what doesn't, and keep everything that your meeting attendees respond to well. And always remember, the technology is not in charge, *you* are."[1]

SOUND

There's nothing worse than sitting in the back of a large banquet room or entertainment area and not being able to hear anything because the sound system is inadequate. Part of your planning must include a test of the sound system well in advance; stand in the back of your event space and make sure that the speakers, entertainers, and presenters will be able to be heard by everyone in attendance.

And speaking of sound, do some research before playing any copy-righted music at your event; you may have to obtain a license from a performing-rights agency such as ASCAP, BMI, or SESAC. Those who hold the copyrights to music and songs take their rights very seriously; it's best to not skip this important step.

LIGHTING

Uplights, twinkle lights, tree lights, marquees, chandeliers, LED strips, centerpiece lighting, stage and auditorium lighting, museum lighting, floodlights, and full-on light shows set to the music of your choice— innovative lighting solutions are becoming one of the best ways to transform a venue into a space that perfectly matches the theme and mood you wish to create.

Your venue will likely have basic lighting equipment available but will often contract with a preferred vendor if custom lighting is re-quired. It's always a good idea to consider the recommendations of the venue when selecting third-party vendors, as they have probably worked with them successfully in the past and know that they will get a professional result.

WI-FI

A reliable Wi-Fi network is no longer an option at any event; it's a ne-cessity. Your participants will expect immediate access to Wi-Fi from the moment they arrive at your event, so be sure to address this with your venue very early in the planning stages.

In this age of identity theft and other cyber threats, it is imperative that you provide a password-protected Wi-Fi connection throughout your event and provide the password in a location only available to your audience (on your online app or somewhere in the conference program).

I heard a story recently about a conference participant at a local venue who brought his laptop to get a little work done during the breaks. He logged into the free Wi-Fi offered by the conference center (no password needed), and within an hour he started getting e-mail alerts that his banking information was being used fraudulently. Someone had been phishing the area, looking for unsuspecting Wi-Fi users, capturing their information, and then using it to make online purchases! It happens more often than you'd think. Providing a secure Wi-Fi network at your event is essential. If you will incur a cost to create a password-protected Wi-Fi platform, try finding a sponsor to cover the price of this critical service.

Experience coordinator Alexandria Tomayko recalls a conference she organized that offered both live and virtual attendance. Her goal was to offer livestreaming for forty breakout sessions, but unfortunately the Wi-Fi available at the venue just wouldn't support it. "We adjusted by reducing the number of concurrent breakouts and lengthening the day to accommodate all of our scheduled speakers. Then we recorded each session and published the recordings to the audience with a twenty-four-hour delay. This involved swapping out memory cards during every fifteen-minute break, but we were able to make it work."

PRESENTATION NEEDS

If the presentation portion of your event includes a single keynote or speech, you may need nothing more than a lectern and a wireless microphone and perhaps a screen and projector. But if you're planning multiple breakout sessions complete with a wide assortment of visual presentations, workshops, and panel discussions, you might require multiples of everything from staging, tables, and chairs to flip charts, conference phones, and laptops in every room.

Beware of the additional costs involved in selecting your venue's presentation equipment. Most venues will have a menu of additional fees associated with utilizing their equipment. Don't assume that built-in projectors and screens are included in the quote you received for room rental. Very often this equipment will be priced out separately (although it might be negotiable if your total spend is high enough).

Many keynote speakers are incorporating technology into their presentations by playing video, inviting guests to access apps or answer polling questions on their smart devices, or displaying a web URL where the audience can access slides or presentation materials in real time. Be sure to talk to each of your speakers about their unique technology needs prior to the event so you can coordinate with your tech team to deliver the goods.

SELECTING A TECHNOLOGY PARTNER

Prestige AV and Creative Services is a single-source destination for all sorts of technology and design needs. They not only provide audiovisual equipment but also have a creative services team that can develop content, such as PowerPoint templates, training videos, sizzle reels, and openers. They can also provide scenic elements for the opening sessions, exhibitor areas, and trade shows. "At Prestige," says Brian Monahan, vice president of sales and development, "we pride ourselves on providing a professional experience. Our team members don't look like roadies; they are always professionally attired. We take a lot of consideration into how we skirt our equipment to make sure it aesthetically matches the room. We take a higher-level view and consider ourselves partners of the event, not just the service provider."

Finding the right technology partner is one of the most important decisions you will make as an event planner. Their ability to provide a highly trained staff that you can trust to understand your goals and manage this component of your project is important to your success and your peace of mind. As Brian says, "At some point, all technology will fail; the question is whether you have a solid relationship with your vendor, someone you can be sure you can call on and someone who will be there when you need them."

EVENT MANAGEMENT TECHNOLOGY

Technology choices start long before the actual event. You can incorporate tech into your marketing campaign, your registration and ticketing process, and even the actual planning process. If your event is so large in scope that you don't think you can effectively manage it without some tools that go beyond e-mails and spreadsheets, then it's time to investigate the wide variety of technology platforms and services available. There are tools specifically designed to handle the registration process, including badges and attendance tracking. There are apps for engaging your participants once they've registered. There are project management tools that will help you manage your budget and keep track of your planning tasks. Then there are the event management platforms that *claim* to do it all.

Only you will be able to evaluate the technology tools available and make a decision that is the right size for your event, the one that has the features you need and the pricing that's good for your budget.

Online Registration Tools

Many small events can be managed by e-mailing invitations and creating spreadsheets for tracking registrations. But if you need to promote your event, send invitations, sell tickets, collect payments, create discount codes, track multiple speakers and exhibitors, distribute agendas and presentation materials, provide a way for attendees to connect with each other, create name badges, and survey your attendees after the event is over, then it's time for you to get online!

Online registration tools have come a long way and can do a lot of the heavy lifting for a DIY event planner. And many have a pricing structure that won't break the bank. The best way to select the perfect online registration product for your event is to watch their marketing videos and then schedule a Web demo. Also read online reviews, and ask other event planners what works best for them.

Not all registration tools are the same; they will vary in their features, functionality, and ease of use. Before you start comparing tools, prepare a list of the things you need to be able to do on this platform. Do you want to offer a discounted price for early registration, have participants select which breakout sessions they plan to attend, offer optional events for an additional cost, survey each registrant on their dietary restrictions, and provide links to hotel reservation sites? Your registration software will need to be able to provide all of those capabilities and many more, so do your homework before you make your final decision.

The pricing structure for an online registration tool can vary. Most companies that provide registration software do a good job of explaining their pricing options right on their website. Some charge by the event, by the attendee, or by a percentage of each ticket sold or charge a monthly or annual fee for unlimited events. Think about your event calendar as you decide which option is right for you: unless you have several events in the queue, a price based on the tickets or the attendee may be a more economical choice than paying a large up-front or annual fee.

Using Technology to Improve the Registration Experience

Travis Tucker is president and CEO of GTR, an event technology firm that provides online registration, onsite badge printing, attendance tracking, and lead-retrieval hardware and software for the event industry. They ship their equipment to events around the globe and provide the expertise onsite to set it up and be a resource for the event from start to finish. The team at GTR understands that the one thing an event planner doesn't have is extra time, so they provide a full-service solution, building the registration site with input from their client.

Attendee tracking via technology such as badge scanning can be useful for certain types of events where attendance at certain sessions is required. Many industries require continuing-education credits to maintain certain certifications, such as in medical, legal, accounting, and HR professions, among others, and event planners must have a way to provide proof of attendance to those who request it. But in recent years, attendee tracking has taken on a new level of importance when it comes to event security. "Security has become such a growing piece of the attendee-tracking conversation. It really creates a level of confidence when you can say you know that all of the people in the room are actually supposed to be there," says Travis.

While his company is devoted to providing meaningful technology for the event industry, Travis cautions against adopting technology for no good reason: "I tell clients to be intentional about what they're doing. If you're providing a mobile app, understand your purpose, and make sure you're using the right tool. Use strategies around your technology that make sense to reach your goals."

21

Safety and Security

It was Tuesday, September 18, 2001, one week after the 9/11 terrorist attacks. I was acting as chairperson for a large outdoor arts and crafts show that drew hundreds of thousands of visitors each year. Our event had long been on the calendar, but after witnessing the devastation in New York, Virginia, and Pennsylvania, our team's focus changed. That evening at our regular planning meeting, our typical committee reports regarding the entertainment schedule and parking logistics were quickly replaced with conversations about more urgent issues. As our venue was a large, nationally recognized event held in an outdoor venue, many felt it could be a potential target for those seeking to do harm. The safety of our vendors, visitors, and volunteers was at risk. Words like *anthrax* had become part of our vocabulary. There were those among us who thought the festival shouldn't be held at all. But in the end, we made the decision to press on.

As we assessed our potential vulnerabilities, our primary concerns became (1) protecting the airspace above the event, (2) barricading side streets to prevent cars from entering into the crowd from adjacent roadways, and (3) working with emergency personnel to establish evacuation and quarantine procedures in the case of a suspicious package or other potential threat.

Our regular action plan changed dramatically during that meeting. Calls to local authorities were made, and multiple meetings were held; additional equipment was secured; radio procedures were modified. Even though the festival had been held on the same date and at the same time every year for the past thirty years, it wasn't until that moment that we completely understood the responsibility that we had as event managers to do everything in our power to ensure the safety of our invited guests. I had a team of volunteers in place that I trusted implicitly, and each and every one of them stepped up to the challenge. With some quick thinking and a lot of hard work, they did everything within their power to make sure the festival was fun, profitable, and, most of all, safe for everyone.

COMPLETING A RISK ASSESSMENT

When establishing security for the event you are planning, your action plan should include a complete risk assessment, a process that identifies all the potential threats to the safe execution of your event and methods for managing each scenario. The depth of your security plan will be dependent on factors such as the size and demographics of the crowd, your ability to control ingress and egress, and whether you are serving alcohol.

When completing a risk assessment, consider how likely each threat is to occur, what its impact would be, and what can be done in advance to prevent it or minimize the risk. Here are some considerations for your risk assessment:

- Gatekeeping and bag searches
- Crowd control
- Guarding of parking lots and nonpublic areas
- Tripping and other potential hazards
- Enforcement of opening and closing times
- Dealing with lost people and property

- Conflict management
- Security for VIPs and dignitaries
- Security for money handlers—and written policies for handling money to prevent theft
- Proper background checks and vetting of staff and volunteers
- Written safety procedures and proper training of all personnel
- Policy on concealed firearms inside the boundaries of your event
- Protestors and other threats
- Health emergencies
- Weather emergencies
- Ensuring the venue has no outstanding health violations, safety violations, or maintenance issues that could create a potential hazard
- Having an emergency communication plan to provide all your stakeholders the important information they need to know in case of an emergency

Make plans to contract with a security company or with local law enforcement if your event is being held in an area that cannot be completely secured. If someone is renting booth space from you or providing rental equipment, they will assume (and rightly so) that you will do everything in your power to secure their property and protect it from theft or vandalism.

Also make sure your staff knows where fire extinguishers and emergency exits are located, and discuss the evacuation procedures and policies established by you and your venue.

SAFETY IN SEVERE WEATHER

If your event is outdoors (like at a golf course or on fairgrounds), severe weather is a safety risk for you. Consider how long it will take to get participants out of harm's way. If there is a threat of lightning or damaging winds in the forecast, someone on your team should be in constant contact with the local weather authorities to monitor current conditions so you can make an informed decision regarding whether to move, postpone, or cancel your activities. Remember, if you can hear thunder, you are close enough to be struck by lightning; it can strike many miles away from the center of the storm!

There is no doubt that inclement weather can wreak havoc on an outdoor event. I experienced this when I once helped to organize an event that had hundreds of pop-up-style vendor tents set up on a narrow street in the center of town. Although the weather forecast had called for rain that day, what we weren't prepared for was a storm that brought with it some extremely high winds. Many of the tents were not sufficiently anchored with weights, and all of a sudden, during a savage gust of wind, one of the tents was swept up, and a tent pole went straight through the window of a residential structure. No one was injured, but we instantly made the call: the event was shut down, pedestrians were evacuated from the area, and we instructed vendors to immediately stop selling and dismantle their tents in preparation to pack up and go home. Depending on the type of event, having to make this kind of judgment call can cost thousands of dollars to everyone involved. But these are the hard decisions that must be made by event organizers. Safety of persons must always prevail over profit. And, yes, changes were immediately made to the vendor regulations requiring that each and every tent be properly anchored and inspected for safety prior to opening for business.

If you're having your event outdoors, consider obtaining event-cancellation insurance due to weather events, sometimes called "acts of God" in the insurance industry.

GETTING FRIENDLY WITH YOUR LOCAL AUTHORITIES

Be sure to share your risk assessment and security plan with local authorities, including police, fire, and EMT personnel. Let them know as much as possible about your event so they can be prepared in the event of an emergency. This also ensures that you are aware of any codes or regulations that may apply to your event so you can plan ahead to stay in complete compliance and eliminate the risk of being shut down.

Be sure your local police, fire, and EMT personnel are aware of any road closures or potential traffic issues that may occur; they will need to plan alternate routes in case of an emergency. It would also be helpful for them to know the expected number of attendees so they can schedule additional personnel to manage additional car and foot traffic, signal timing, road closures, and so on.

Check the local fire department and building department for regulations regarding tents and other temporary structures. Be sure you understand any required permits and code restrictions regarding the use of candles and other open flames such as propane or kerosene stoves and space heaters, as well as the sizes and types of fire extinguishers you will need to have on hand.

Many local law enforcement personnel would welcome the opportunity to meet with your staff to review the risk assessment plan and provide guidance on how to manage certain scenarios.

If you're serving food, you'll want to check with your local health department about required permits and food safety regulations (handwashing stations, food storage guidelines, and so on).

MEDICAL EMERGENCIES

Think about how you will deal with a medical emergency during your event. If someone passes out cold during one of your sessions, would you or your staff know what to do?

Talk to your venue about their preparedness in case of a medical emergency: Is there a first aid room or a first aid kit nearby? Do they have people on staff who are trained to use the AED machine or perform CPR? Does your staff know where the first aid facilities are located? What about access to emergency phones or contact numbers? Do you have adequate cell phone service throughout the venue in case you have to dial 911, or will you have access to a landline?

Do you ask for emergency contact information from your registered guests? At the very least, you should obtain a work number or an additional contact number that is different from the cell phone they're holding in their hand.

INSURANCE

A guest trips over a power cord and breaks their wrist. A presenter damages a rented projector while trying to connect an incompatible cord. A directional sign is blown over by the wind and damages several cars in your designated parking area. A member of the security team ejects an unruly guest and is accused of assault. A meeting has to be cancelled due to a widespread health emergency that causes travel restrictions.

All events come with some element of risk to you, your volunteers, and your guests. Completing a thorough risk assessment will help you determine the potential liability you have and the types and levels of insurance you will need to secure.

You need to consider what kinds of injuries, damages, or other losses could be incurred by your guests, your staff, your vendors, and other participants; you must have adequate coverage should a lawsuit be filed by any one of these parties. Conversely, you must be protected if the actions or inactions by your team members cause injury to someone else.

You also need to be protected from any damage that occurs to the venue you are using or equipment you are renting from third parties. You may be asked to provide a certificate of insurance as part of entering into a contract with third parties for equipment or services; as a matter of fact, you should count on it.

Many states have specific requirements for the types and amounts of insurance that must be secured, especially when planning a public event. Be sure you're using an insurance company that not only is familiar with insuring your type of event but also has a thorough knowledge of the pertinent laws in the state where your event will be held.

DEALING WITH PROTESTORS AND OTHER THREATS

I once had an encounter with an artist who ignored a long-standing show requirement that everything on display in their booth be hand-crafted by them. The jury team that was confirming the compliance of this rule reported that this particular vendor was unapologetically displaying items that were clearly commercially manufactured. When she refused to remove the items, it was my job to address the issue and inform the exhibitor that she would be asked to leave the event if she didn't comply. She immediately became confrontational and wasn't in any mood to listen to reason. When I stood my ground, she began to threaten me, and it became clear that I was going to need a little backup. Our team had created a code to use on our radio communication system that would immediately get the attention of a crisis response team that included the local authorities. Once I made a quick call ("I have a 'code red' at booth 140"), it was less than a minute before I had an entire squad of officials lined up behind me, including a couple of police officers. The exhibitor quickly backed off, left the event without further incident, and was not invited back.

The last thing you expect at an art show is to have someone in your face making a verbal or physical threat. This is a good reminder that event organizers have to be prepared for any eventuality and must have security measures in place to deal with any circumstance. Depending on the nature of your event and your crowd, you might want to consider working in teams of two so that no single person will be caught dealing with a dangerous situation on their own.

Have someone on your team monitor social media feeds, including those containing your event hashtag. If you pick up on a conversation thread that indicates that an organized protest or other controversy might be brewing at your event, alert your security team and local authorities so they can prepare. Remember that building security is primarily there to protect the building; it's your responsibility to protect your guests. If you don't feel comfortable with your existing security plan, hire an outside security firm to provide additional protection.

Part of hosting a public event, big or small, is making sure you have done everything necessary to keep those in attendance comfortable and safe. The times that we live in require us to be diligent. We must assess every possible scenario and risk and then come up with a plan to mitigate the risk to the best of our ability.

Marketing and Publicity

Many events don't have a built-in audience. You will have to promote your event in all of the right places in order to attract your attendees and convince them that this is an event they must attend.

REGISTRATION

The registration materials you produce for your event, whether printed, online, or both, are the best opportunity to provide all the information your guests need to know. One of the biggest mistakes an event planner can make is not providing the essential information people need as they decide whether to attend. Whether you send a formal invitation, an e-mail, or a flyer or you use a full-blown website or app where people can register, spend some time anticipating all of the questions your attendees may have and answering them before they are even asked.

I can't begin to tell you how many times I've received an invitation to register for an event where the actual date of the event was omitted! This happens when the person writing the invitation has become so close to the material that they actually stop seeing it. I recommend having someone unfamiliar with the event read the collateral you create and provide some unbiased feedback. They will often bring up questions

that you haven't thought of and help you assess whether your communications are thorough.

Dates and deadlines, event schedule, maps and directions, program
highlights, lodging options, and frequently asked questions should be
part of every communication you create.

A good place to start in developing your invitation and registration
form is to answer the big questions:

Who?

List all of the people who will benefit from attending your event.
Prepare a convincing argument for why your invitee is the one you had
in mind as you were planning the agenda and activities. This can be a
quite literal statement: "This conference is intended for those who . . ."

What?

Provide a full agenda that includes as much detail as possible without being too wordy or confusing. Your participants are making a significant investment of time and probably money to attend your event;
make it clear what they will receive in return. If your event includes
speakers or presenters, provide their bios and a thorough description
of what they will be speaking about. Also remember that many people
will have to gain the approval of others before attending; they may have
to prove the value of their attendance before their budget is approved,
so include information that will help them in their approval process.
Prepare a sample justification letter that they can copy and present to
their decision makers.

When?

There are lots of things you need to consider when setting start and
end times for your event. If most people will be driving into your event,
you will need to be familiar with area traffic patterns so you can alert
invitees to approximate drive times. If people are flying in to attend

your event, your start and end times will affect their travel and hotel reservations. Once you've landed on a date, send out save-the-date notices to generate some discussion and get people thinking about fitting your event into their schedule.

Where?

The location and venue you choose could weigh heavily in your attendee's decision to attend. How much time, money, and effort will they have to spend to get there? Is the venue in a city near a popular air hub? What will the average drive time be for your attendees? Is there a location that would be more central to your invite list? Are there plenty of restaurant, shopping, and entertainment options nearby? Remember that not everyone is comfortable navigating the one-way streets and parking garages of an urban downtown venue.

Why?

In order to convince your invitee to attend, you'll have to answer the WIIFM question—What's In It For Me? Why should your guest choose to attend your event over other options? Go back to your goals statement, and describe what your attendees will gain by attending your event.

How?

All important dates and deadlines should be front and center on your registration collateral. The event schedule, maps and directions, travel and lodging options, program highlights, and frequently asked questions should be part of every communication you create. FAQs could include:

- Dress code
- What to bring
- Cancellation policy
- How to access online information via websites, apps, etc.

- Availability of handouts and slide presentations before and during the event
- Availability of recordings, handouts, and slide presentations after the event

PUBLICIZING YOUR EVENT ONLINE

There are hundreds, perhaps thousands, of ways to promote your event online. First and foremost, you'll want to make sure your event is listed in every free site that publishes information on upcoming events. Here are a few to check out:

- Facebook Events and Facebook Groups
- Eventful.com
- Yelp.com
- AllConferences.com
- City, county, and state travel and tourism sites
- Community calendars on radio, television, and newspaper sites
- E-newsletters of corporations or industry organizations that share an audience with you

SOCIAL MEDIA

If you get a little overwhelmed when you hear the words *social media*, you're not alone. People who want to connect online have hundreds of options. If you are an event planner and want to promote your event, it's vital that you have a presence on social media. It can be a little tricky to navigate if you're not already familiar with the various platforms, and it does take an investment of time to do it right, but it is a fantastic promotional tool.

Some of the most popular social media sites are Facebook, Instagram, LinkedIn, and Twitter. I would recommend promoting your events on these platforms in addition to your own website or blog if you have the capacity on your team to do so. Once you've mastered these sites, and if you have the time and expertise to consistently post relevant content about your occasion, you can consider expanding to other sites such as Pinterest or YouTube.

GETTING DISCOVERED

If you've decided to promote your event on social media, create a unique hashtag that any interested party can follow to see updates on speakers or entertainers that have been confirmed and comments from people who have attended in the past and to communicate with others who have registered for the upcoming event.

Anyone who develops apps for Apple knows that #WWDC is *the* hashtag to follow if you want to keep in the loop on their annual Apple Worldwide Developers Conference. The same goes for the Las Vegas Market Show (#LVMKT) and the National Hardware Show (#NHS). These organizations know that creating a hashtag is the best way to increase their visibility on all social media platforms before, during, and after the event. Be sure to incorporate attention-grabbing images and video in your promotional campaigns, particularly of previous events. Post consistently, and encourage attendees to post as well.

It may not make sense to use every platform to advertise your event; which you use will depend on the type of event you are organizing and who your audience is. Here are a few tips to help you decide what might work best:

- *Facebook.* Posting information about your event on your personal Facebook timeline is a given, but creating a Facebook page specifically for your event can widen your reach far beyond your own list of friends. Invite all your Facebook friends to like the page. They in turn invite their friends, and so on. Make sure all your team members are clicking the "share" button every time there is a new post on your event page so all their friends are seeing it too.
- *Twitter.* This tool is used for microblogging messages that are very focused and concise. Share pictures, videos, and other content in short, quick posts.

- *Instagram.* One of the most popular social media platforms presently, Instagram promotes itself as a photo and video sharing app, so you must create a lot of image-based content in order to post consistently and get engagement on this site.
- *LinkedIn.* Think of this site as Facebook for business. Link to colleagues and business associates, and post content that will reach an entirely new audience.
- *Pinterest.* Use this fast-growing social media site to "pin" images and other content related to your event on a virtual bulletin board. Users pin these images to their interest boards, others follow those boards, and the sharing begins!
- *Blogging.* A blog is website that is written like a journal and usually focuses on a particular topic or theme. Those who follow your blog can receive a message in their e-mail inbox every time you post new content, whether it's a photo, a speaker interview, an agenda update, or updated registration information. A blog is only effective if you post consistently; I recommend creating an editorial calendar to plan a regular posting schedule.
- *Social media management platforms.* Use your website's blog as a launch pad to post content, and then use a tool like Hootsuite or Buffer to simultaneously send those posts to other platforms. This ensures that your event messaging is ongoing and consistent, since most platforms allow you to schedule and stagger posts for future publication. No new information equals no new or repeat visitors, so create the content once, post to your social media sites, and keep your message flowing.

With a simple online search, you can find all sorts of training resources, videos, and advice on using each of these platforms effectively. If you don't have a dedicated and experienced social media team, I would suggest that you learn enough to understand which platform is the best match for your audience demographic and start posting consistently on that single platform instead of diving into them all at once.

TRADITIONAL PUBLICITY

Contrary to popular belief, not everyone in the world has a Facebook or Instagram account . . . yet. While more people are looking to social media for their information, traditional advertising methods cannot be discounted.

- *E-mail.* This remains one of the most effective ways to reach your target audience. Use previous attendee lists and offer highly visible options on your website to join your e-mail newsletter.
- *Direct mail.* Create a mailing list for your potential audience. They should all get a direct invitation from you if possible.
- *Flyers.* Create a promotional flyer, and design it so it can be printed or mailed. It could be as simple as a piece of colored paper that is tri-folded and stapled, or it could be a more professional full-color brochure, postcard, or rack card. Have the flyer available in PDF format so it can be e-mailed as well. If your event is local or regional, ask to place stacks of flyers in doctor's offices, salons, libraries—anywhere with a waiting room or counter where people can see them and grab one. Many stores, especially independently owned stores, will place a flyer in each bag that goes out of the store if you ask.
- *Bulletin boards and marquees.* Location bulletin boards are still a great place to get your event notices. Think grocery stores, restaurants, beauty salons, churches, coffee shops, and libraries.
- *Yard signs.* This more recent trend is being used to publicize church festivals and other local events. The key is to keep the message concise so it can be digested as someone drives by—only what, when, where, and possibly a Web address where they can go for more information.
- *Newspapers, both print and online.* This doesn't necessarily have to be a paid ad, but make sure you're in all of the community calendars and "Things to Do" sections in your local papers. Is there a particular story or spin on your event that would make a great article?

Newspapers are always looking for interesting content; try pitching your idea to the reporters that cover the local news. If you've got a high-resolution picture to go along with your article, you'll have a better chance of getting published.

- *Industry magazines.* If you're organizing an antiques show, make sure it's listed in the *Antique Trader Magazine*. If you're planning an arts and crafts fair, be sure you've listed it in *Sunshine Artist Magazine*. These publications can only include events that are submitted many months before the actual publication date, so learn their dates and deadlines.
- *Newsletters.* Do you belong to any organizations that publish and distribute regular newsletters (churches, clubs)? Ask them to put a blurb in their newsletter about your event.
- *Radio and television.* Provide every news director at every station in your region with a fact sheet about your event, along with contact information for the persons that would be available for an in-studio or onsite interview. I once convinced a local weather personality to provide a "Festival Forecast" the day before my event and mention the website of the event in the process. This little on-air mention reached thousands of viewers and didn't take a penny from our very small advertising budget!
- *Press kits.* This is a perfect idea for a festival, especially food festivals. Deliver a goody bag filled with fact sheets, flyers, and other advertising collateral in person to the radio and television personalities in the area two to three days prior to the start of your event, along with some food samples that attendees could expect to enjoy at your event. Don't forget that you'll want a kit for the morning news crew, the noon crew, and the multiple evening crews. The goal is to get all of the on-air talent talking about the festival during their programming. Don't forget to include a treat for the gatekeepers, the front-desk folks at each location; they're the people who will be sure your press kits are delivered to the right people.

PHOTOS AND VIDEOS

Images are an important element in engaging an audience for your event. Think about all the places you can use photos and videos taken before, during, and after your occasion to encourage registration or attendance:

- Press releases
- Websites and blog posts
- Participant photos on Facebook
- Videos on YouTube
- Photos to add to Instagram or Twitter posts along with the hashtag devoted to your event
- Recognition of volunteers and sponsors
- Images for use in next year's registration forms and promotional materials

If you can't budget for a professional photographer to take shots of your activities, you should at least gain access to a quality, high-resolution digital camera and make a list of shots you want to make sure you get. But don't discount the spontaneous shots taken by your attendees on their smartphones or tablets: encourage them to click and share on their social media sites as well as your own.

Invest in a videographer to create sit-down interviews and on-the-ground footage in the hallways during your event. This raw footage can be edited into short videos and montages that can be extremely effective marketing pieces on your company's websites and social media pages and in future event promotions.

23

The Main Event

It's show time! This is the culmination of all of your hard work, when everything starts to fall into place and you begin to reap the benefits of all of your advanced planning. If you began your event planning process by creating a detailed action plan and following it to the letter, making sure that everyone on the team completed their tasks on schedule, the final days leading up to your event should be primarily a matter of confirming vendors, head counts, and arrival times; gathering supplies; completing a few last-minute tasks; and reviewing final details with your team.

The action items listed below are representative of the types of things that you will want to include on your plan if you're organizing a conference; your last-minute task list will vary depending on the type of event you're planning.

The timing of these tasks will have to be adjusted if you are planning a destination event; travel time and shipping schedules must be taken into account when determining when these items should be completed.

THE WEEK BEFORE

The sooner you begin finalizing your plans—dotting your i's and crossing your t's—the more smoothly things will run during the actual event. This is why I begin with specific instructions a full week out from your guests' arrival.

Confirm Everything

Contact everyone who has a role or responsibility in your event, and confirm the details. Reach out to speakers and presenters to confirm arrival times, transportation needs, and final payments. Talk to each and every vendor and service provider to confirm their load-in schedule and the names and day-of contact numbers for their onsite team. Check tracking numbers and delivery estimates for items that will be shipped directly to the event venue, and verify that the venue knows what to do with the items when they arrive.

Review traffic and parking logistics with the proper authorities, and confirm when barricades, cones, and directional signs will be put into place. Touch base with local authorities to ensure that their teams are ready and that all permits and permissions are approved.

Make Contact with Your Participants

Send a final e-mail to participants to provide additional information and work up some excitement about the event. Include any last-minute reminders and schedule changes, and reiterate check-in instructions, directions, hotel information, and a list of what they should bring (and what should stay home).

Include a link to the final agenda, as well as information on extras that are still available, such as tickets for an after-hours event or an open slot that is still available for a one-on-one training session or consultation.

Be sure to include the exact time that registration opens and the time and location for your opening sessions. Remember that attendees won't have an official program in their hands until they arrive, so help them out by providing details about how your event will begin.

Gather Supplies

Start collecting all of the items that you will either take with you or ship to the event site. Put everything in one place so it can be inventoried and checked off your list. The list could be long, including everything from signs to centerpieces and other decor, lanyards, extra badge supplies, and registration equipment. Prepare copies of handouts or survey forms, and label them so your team knows where they go when you arrive at the venue. Don't forget to label the box that contains the box cutter or scissors that will be used to open the other boxes!

Don't forget that emergency kit we talked about in chapter 17—a bin full of just-in-case supplies that will see you through most minor crises.

Make sure everyone on your team, including volunteers, has their parking pass, name badge, event clothing, meal vouchers, and anything else they will need prior to arriving at the event, or make sure that the items are labeled and ready to be transported to the venue and staged at a predetermined pickup spot.

Organize Paperwork

Bring all of the paperwork you may need to refer to throughout your event. Organize it in a ring binder or on a computer or smart device, but make sure you have easy access to copies of contracts and e-mails, countersigned banquet event orders, and emergency phone lists for participants, vendors, presenters, staff members, and volunteers. Keep this important information in a place at your command center where everyone on your team can access it.

Your paperwork will also include a final attendance list, exhibitor list, vendor list, and a list of anyone who owes you money or vice versa. Prepare copies of all speaker introductions to hand out to facilitators, and prepare thank-you notes or payments that will be distributed during the event. Prepare multiple copies of the event script and a debrief binder that people can use to enter comments, suggestions, complaints, or ideas for future events as they think of them or as things occur.

Finalize Participant Needs

At this point you should have your printed programs or agendas boxed up and ready to go, as well as any swag-bag items, giveaways, conference totes, and promotional items. This is the time to print registration badges (unless you're printing them onsite) and organize them so they can be easily retrieved on opening day.

Meet with Your Team

The final meeting you have with your team is your chance to prepare them not only practically but also emotionally. This is the moment when you must help them maintain their momentum by cheering them on, thanking them for all of the hard work they've done leading up to the event and for everything they will do in the coming days. Let them know how much you appreciate them, and encourage them to stay calm, keep focused, follow the plan, and ask for help when necessary.

In these meetings, you will confirm arrival times and initial tasks, distribute the completed event script, and answer any questions they may have about their responsibilities. Review all emergency procedures, and provide them with a written copy of the procedures that also includes emergency contact numbers.

THE DAY BEFORE

This is setup day, the day when your plan really starts to come together. As soon as you arrive at the venue, a preconference meeting with your event management team should be the first order of business. This is your chance to review the event orders and the agenda and to discuss any last-minute changes or issues.

When you gain access to your event spaces, start your load-in procedures. Start with the big items that will take the most time: the trade show floor team and the audiovisual team should be some of the first arrivals due to the potential complexities of their setups.

Place all directional signs, sponsor banners, and displays. Double-check meeting spaces to be sure they are being set up correctly, as well as any special event areas: the general session room, speaker lounge, meal spaces, and so on.

A lot of your time will be spent making sure that your registration area is completely installed and ready to go. All computers and badge-printing equipment must be installed and tested, and all participant materials must be assembled and ready for distribution.

As everything starts to fall into place, spend some time walking through the event area. Look at everything from the perspective of your participants: Is your event easy to navigate? Are your registration area, exhibit hall, and general session room easy to find? Are presentation screens easy to see? Are your sponsors appropriately recognized?

Are there any speakers or dignitaries that need attention during this time? Don't forget the airport pickups, welcome gifts at hotel rooms, and other hospitality items that need to be attended to.

Make sure that your team is being taken care of during this hectic time. Schedule food breaks and rest breaks throughout the day; no one is going to be any good to you if they're working without fuel and rest. This goes for you as well: Schedule time to get away from the madness for a while to take a few deep breaths and fuel up. It will do wonders for your frame of mind and your stamina.

OPENING DAY

Hopefully you got some sleep and are ready for action. Your go bag was packed the night before with your copy of the event script and all other paperwork, as well as the personal items you'll need throughout the day. If you want to keep your laptop with you as well as conference binders and supplies, use a wheeled briefcase or a rolling tote so you're not hauling around a heavy bag on your shoulder all day. Also take care to wear comfortable shoes; if there were ever a time to sacrifice fashion for comfort, today is the day!

Arrive early enough to do a final walk-through of the event spaces before your guests arrive. Make contact with your event manager at the venue, and confirm that everything is set up as agreed: storage rooms have been unlocked, meeting rooms are ready to go, the coffee is brewing, and the wait staff is preparing to serve the first meal of the day.

Confirm that your registration team members have manned their stations and are ready for early arrivals; you'll be surprised at how many people will show up thirty to sixty minutes earlier than the published registration window. Check in with the audiovisual team to confirm that the general session is powered up and ready to go.

Game On

The true test of a successful action plan is demonstrated by what you, the event organizer, are doing about one hour after the event begins. I recommend that you never assign yourself to any specific task during this part of the event. If you've done everything right, you will be standing off to the side, script in hand, smile on your face, observing your staff and volunteers taking care of business while the event is proceeding smoothly and efficiently. You will make yourself available to greet people as they arrive, answer questions, and provide guidance to your team, but the event is basically running itself because you've thought of everything and have put a plan in place for each component of the program.

A Well-Oiled Machine

As the event progresses, continue to refer to your event script and look ahead to see what is happening next. Confirm that your team is welcoming speakers as they arrive and taking care of their needs. Monitor activity at your registration center for any reports of problems. Check in on meal service and refreshment stations, and touch base with your A/V crew, trade show manager, and other service providers to be sure that things are running smoothly. Continue to work in this proactive state until every session and every activity have been successfully completed.

If everything is going smoothly, try to schedule an hour to two after lunch to step away from the event area and take a break. Set a timer, get off your feet, close your eyes, and try to relax. Taking this opportunity to catch your breath will help you generate the stamina you will need to power through the rest of the day and do it all over again tomorrow!

AFTER THE EVENT IS OVER

Congratulations! Your last session has concluded, and your last guest has left the building. Before you celebrate your success, there are a few items that must be taken care of.

Make sure your teardown team is taking care of business: dismantling signs and displays, boxing up and labeling supplies that will be sent to storage, and returning any equipment or supplies that were rented or borrowed. Review the policies established by your venue regarding such issues as trash removal, and make sure that you've returned the event space to its original condition.

If you decided to send out an electronic survey to your participants, send it out on the last day of the event so that it hits their inboxes while the event is fresh in their minds.

No event is complete until everyone responsible for its success has been thanked and acknowledged. This includes your presenters, vendors, sponsors, service providers, and participants. But most of all, take care to thank your volunteers and your core team. Do all of this as publicly as possible, using press releases, websites, and social media outlets. If you have the ability to offer a thank-you event for your team members, get it on the schedule as soon as possible.

Finally, complete your administrative tasks. Collect all revenue that hasn't already been received, and ensure that all service providers are paid in a timely manner. Review the final invoice from the venue, checking the details for additional charges that weren't included in your signed BEOs. Perform a complete bank reconciliation, and prepare financial and other reports required by your stakeholders.

There are some universal truths about event planning and many surprising twists and turns that you will encounter along the way. There will be many magical moments and a few downright dirty jobs. You may experience some frustration on your journey, but I've always found that these moments are far outweighed by the tremendous satisfaction realized from a job well done. There is nothing more gratifying than surveying your event in full swing, where everything is going according to plan, your guests are having a great time, and your goals have been fulfilled.

THE REAL SECRET TO EVENT PLANNING SUCCESS

Remember the times and the places when you have felt the most passionate, when that swell of joy and contentment bubbled up inside? At that moment, you were living in your sweet spot. The secret is making the decisions that will allow you to live in that sweet spot as much as possible: remove the obstacles, expect the unexpected, dive in, and live your life of passion! When you can put something of yourself into a project, it's no longer a job—it's a joy!

It seems as though every job, every organization, and every role I've ever had in my personal and professional life wound up having an event planning component to it, and that's okay by me. It's as though my soul draws energy from the process of creating an event and reveling in the results of its successful execution. I always receive more than I give when I'm planning a special occasion. I believe that will be true for you as well.

When the day comes that you find yourself in charge of organizing an event or project and become filled with anxiety and stress, when you feel unqualified or unprepared to successfully plan a special occasion, or when you would prefer to let someone else take charge while you just work behind the scenes, remember that the greatest failure is the failure to try. So give it a shot! As long as you are armed with an achievable goal and a solid plan of attack, you will be able to manage any obstacle that comes your way. You will have the ability to quickly adjust when the unexpected happens and to implement your alternate plan with confidence and a sense of humor, and your event will appear effortless.

Author Elizabeth Gilbert says, "Your life is short and rare and amazing and miraculous, and you want to do really interesting things and make really interesting things while you're still here."[1] She couldn't be more right; my life has been enriched and made more meaningful by the mountaintop moments that I've created and experienced. I propose that your life will be richer if you invest some of your precious time and energy into making some unforgettable events in your corner of the world.

24

Communicate Effectively

Every event organizer knows that their projects can only be successful if there is an effective communication strategy in place. The biggest problem in communication, it has been said, is the illusion that it has taken place.[1] I have found this to be true—so much so that I err on the side of overcommunicating, checking and double-checking to make sure that everyone I'm working with is on the same page.

While you may have your action plan finished and memorized, you must meet your team where they are in the learning process. Remember that your staff and your volunteers aren't going to know everything they need to know when they sign on. You must start at the beginning and introduce your plan to them in all your communications, both written and verbal. Assume that they don't know your schedule, your processes, your safety procedures, whom they report to, or what they will be required to do.

MEETINGS

Much of the communication with your team will occur in meetings. Meetings can be productive slots of time where decisions are made and measurable progress is attained; if poorly run, they can also be a colossal waste of time and energy!

For those times when a meeting is required, here are five ways to keep them meaningful and focused:

1. *Establish a set day and time for your meetings (for example, the first and third Thursdays of the month, at 10 a.m.).* This creates milestones for each team member; if they're expected to provide a progress report at each meeting, they'll work harder to complete their tasks rather than show up empty-handed.
2. *Always provide a written agenda.* It will help to keep the meeting on track. The sample Planning Meeting agenda included in the appendix contains a list of the components of a well-run meeting.
3. *Designate a facilitator and a notetaker for each meeting.* It's best if two different people fill these roles. The facilitator's job is to make sure the meeting isn't hijacked by sidebars and discussions that are off-topic. If this occurs, the facilitator must steer everyone back to the agenda. The notetaker records any votes or decisions, logs progress on existing action items, and documents any new action items and owners.
4. *Establish an end time for your meetings.* A well-run meeting should never go beyond ninety minutes in length. Attendees tend to lose focus and conversations to stray from the original topic if meetings go longer than an hour and a half. Let attendees know when the meeting will end, and then honor that commitment.
5. *Follow up each meeting by sending meeting minutes to each participant.* This is a written record created by your notetaker that reminds everyone of the decisions made, what action items are still pending, and who is the owner of each new action item identified.

Don't leave anything to chance; frequent communication through effective meetings will help minimize risk and maintain momentum on your essential projects.

For communication that must take place in between scheduled meetings, I suggest using an online collaboration tool to keep your teams informed and engaged. Many times a quick online conversation can help avoid additional in-person meetings and can instead push you ever closer to completion of your goals with less time and effort. Most of these tools have some file-sharing capabilities. They also allow you to create as many groups as you like so you can communicate specifically with the people who need to be included in the conversation. Create a different group for the logistics team, the publicity team, the sponsorship committee, the executive committee, and so on; the possibilities are endless. A few online collaboration tools to check out include Trello, Ryver, Slack, Asana, and Microsoft Teams, which is part of Microsoft Office 365.

E-MAILS

E-mail can be a very effective way to keep the momentum going in between your face-to-face meetings. If your team members all have an e-mail address that they check on a regular basis, this is probably your best tool for sending and receiving status reports, asking questions, and posting meetings notices or other announcements.

Here are my top ten rules for the effective use of e-mail:

1. *Keep your e-mails clear and concise.* Many people won't read an e-mail beyond the first or second line, so make sure you include vital information early in your correspondence, including what actions you require from the recipient.
2. *Always enter a meaningful subject in the subject line.* Effective use of the subject line will increase the chances that your e-mail will actually be read. The subject line "October 12 Meeting Reminder—RSVP Required" is more likely to be opened and a response received than an e-mail with the subject line "Meeting."
3. *Use good grammar and punctuation.* Follow the same sentence structure and grammar and punctuation rules you would use if you were writing an actual letter. E-mails are not texts, so keep them as brief as possible, but don't use too many shortcuts and abbreviations; it can

give your e-mails an unprofessional appearance, and recipients may not take them seriously.

4. *Avoid using all capital letters.* You will appear as if you are shouting your message.

5. *Sign your name to your e-mails!* If your e-mail address doesn't identify you, adding your signature line may be the only way that the receiver knows who is sending the message.

6. *Set up e-mail groups.* Create an e-mail group for each key committee, one for the core organizing team, and one for your entire planning committee. With one click, you can schedule a meeting, make an announcement, or gather input on a particular topic from the right people. You also don't have to worry about leaving someone out of the loop, which becomes more likely when you're selecting one person at a time from your contact list.

7. *Understand the differences between Reply, Reply All, and Reply All with History.* There are some very important differences between these options. *Reply* is a response that will be delivered only to the person who sent you the message. *Reply All* ensures that your response will go to everyone who received the original message; make sure that it's necessary that everyone receive your reply. *Reply All with History* means that all the text in the entire e-mail string will be attached to the bottom of your new e-mail. All of these reply types can have unintended consequences, so think about the messaging type you select, and be sure your new e-mail is going only to the people you want to receive it.

8. *Self-edit.* Before you hit *send*, read your e-mail again from start to finish, and utilize the built-in spell-check tool to make sure your message makes sense. My brain often gets ahead of my fingers, and I've sent more than a couple of nonsensical messages in my time. Misinformation is a huge time waster! Does your e-mail provide all the information you think the sender will need? Can you anticipate any questions the recipient might have after reading it? If so, will adding more information prevent multiple back-and-forth exchanges?

9. *Sleep on it.* If the subject of your e-mail addresses a sensitive or controversial topic, save it as a draft and sleep on it before you send it. Once you hit *send*, you can't get it back, so think it through before you do. You may want to consider picking up the phone instead. While you may think the tone of your e-mail is appropriate, someone else could interpret it differently. In those cases, a face-to-face or telephone conversation may be a better choice.

10. *Keep your in-box clean.* Wading through hundreds or thousands of e-mails in my in-box is not my idea of time well spent. Use the folders features of your e-mail account to categorize the e-mails you need to keep. I have folders set up for each project I'm working on; if I decide it's a message I need to save, once I've read it and taken any necessary actions on it, I immediately drag it into the project folder so I can quickly access it again. This ensures that the only items in my in-box are the things that still require action.

Again, you shouldn't assume that your e-mails are being read immediately or even at all. Your recipient may have dozens and dozens of e-mails going to each of their several e-mail accounts every day, and it can be difficult to respond right away (sound familiar?). There are others who have made it a rule to only check their in-box once or twice a day in an effort to not let e-mails become too distracting (admirable!). Then there are those who only open their e-mail occasionally but not as a regular practice (cringeworthy!).

Liz is a friend of mine who oversaw an overnight camping adventure for six hundred scouts. The leaders had to change the venue with little notice due to a strong storm that came through and damaged the original campsite beyond repair. Liz did everything in her power to communicate with the affected families, explaining the change in venue and providing detailed directions to the new facility. But because she understood that many people *just do not read e-mail,* to be on the safe side she had the presence of mind to post a volunteer at the original site of the event to redirect parents who hadn't caught on that there had been a change in venue. Sure enough, dozens of families showed up at the wrong location with bewildered looks on their faces; they had no idea that there was a problem.

Your stakeholders may have many different communication preferences. You will need to be quite persistent in finding the method that best suits your audience. This could include a combination of phone calls, e-mails, texts, snail mail, social media, and instant-messaging tools.

SO CLOSE AND YET . . .

Here's another example of a time when I had assumed that I'd been effectively communicating but in fact couldn't have been more wrong. I had asked an attorney to be a presenter at a conference I was organizing, and he graciously agreed. Through multiple e-mails and conversations, I provided him with all of the details, including the name of the venue (the beautiful Great Wolf Lodge), the date and time of his presentation, some information about his audience so he knew how to prepare, and so forth. I touched base with him one week out (as I do with all my speakers and presenters) to make sure that everything was good to go and checked him off my task list; we were all set.

On the day of the presentation, I started to get a little nervous when I realized I hadn't seen my speaker arrive with only an hour to go to his presentation. We had agreed that he would arrive early enough to get into the room to test his presentation equipment, so it seemed a little odd that he was still nowhere to be found. As I started to pick up the phone to call him (yes, I always have a day-of contact number for each of my presenters), my phone began ringing, and sure enough, it was him.

"Hi, John; is everything okay?" I asked. "Well," he said, "I'm at Great Wolf Lodge, but the parking lot is completely deserted, so I'm a little confused." After a little back-and-forth, we quickly understood what had gone wrong. You see, the Great Wolf Lodge family of resorts has a facility in Mason, Ohio, but also a sister location in Sandusky . . . about four hours north from where I was standing. John was sitting in the Sandusky parking lot, and I was in Mason.

Communication fail! I was mortified that I hadn't properly conveyed this ridiculously important detail. He was stunned and felt like he had let me down in some way (he hadn't; it was all me). Add to that the fact that in less than one hour we would have a large crowd assembled to hear his presentation. In the end, he was able to rush back to his office and conduct his session via conference call (thanks to the quick-thinking tech team members at Great Wolf who were able to set up a phone connection, including sound, in my meeting room), with a facilitator in the room to advance his slide presentation and assist during Q and A. This is a prime example of how not paying attention to a seemingly minor detail can create a lot of unnecessary stress and scrambling to solve a problem that with a little more care could have clearly been avoided.

25

Stay Organized

Becoming an effective event planner, or just becoming more effective period, starts with finding an efficient way to keep track of multiple dates, tasks, and deadlines. If you ever have trouble remembering things that need to be done or struggle to arrive on time to appointments or have difficulty maintaining focus on single task long enough to finish it, you may need to improve your time management skills.

Have you ever felt like a juggler, with so many balls in the air that you didn't know which to catch and which to let drop and roll away? If this sounds like the story of your life, it's important that you carve out a few minutes each day to create an organized plan that will help you accomplish your goals.

The action plan you've created for your event should already include a comprehensive list of prioritized tasks and deadlines in order to achieve success. Now it's just a matter of incorporating those tasks into your daily routine. Add each item to whatever calendar or to-do list works best for you. This sounds like a simple, perhaps obvious suggestion, but putting everything in writing in a prominent place, something you reference every day, can make a huge difference in keeping you on target, on time, and stress-free. Be sure to include enough information to jog your memory about what you specifically need to do for each task and to include a due date for each item.

For instance, if you're planning your executive team's strategic-planning retreat, you will start adding items to your calendar months in advance; you'll need to finalize the date, secure a venue and sleeping rooms, plan a menu, and send meeting invitations. As you get closer to the event, you'll need to pick a date to finalize the agenda and assemble all presentations. In the week prior to the event, you'll add reminders to contact the venue to verify final head counts, room configurations, and audiovisual equipment needs. You'll also want to send all of the attendees a communication with the final agenda, directions, dress code, hotel info, and other pertinent information. Two days before, you'll need to schedule some time to assemble everything you'll need to take with you to the site and connect with the venue manager to confirm that their part of the setup is under control. The day before will be spent setting up the room and taking care of any last-minute details.

I typically start from the date of the event and work my way backward, thinking through all of the elements of the event and what tasks are dependent on one another. This method helps me figure out what tasks I must focus on first and get them on my schedule in a logical order.

Write things down in a notebook that you carry with you, or use an app on your smartphone or tablet. Whatever you do, pick a method, stick to it, and update that list every day. Use your lists to record all of the smaller tasks and details for each event on your schedule.

As soon as you think of a task, write it down! Keep paper and pen by your bed, in your car, and in your purse or briefcase. If as soon as you lay your head on the pillow your brain starts spinning with the tasks facing you the next day, take a few minutes to "download" those items to a written list so your brain can rest.

When working on your schedule, think about the time of day when you are most productive, and use that time to tackle the most difficult or complex tasks. I know that I'm at my best in the morning; that's when my brain is firing on all cylinders. I use that productive time to review lengthy contracts or bite off big chunks of tasks that require a great deal of concentration, saving the more repetitive or mundane tasks for later in the day.

If your to-do list seems simply overwhelming, it may be time to delegate. The way to stay sane when managing multiple projects is to identify all of the tasks that can and should be delegated to others. It is imperative to the successful execution of your event that you assess all available resources and make sure that the work is divided appropriately. Micromanaging your team or becoming a martyr by doing everything yourself is self-sabotaging and will have devastating results on you and your project.

It's just as important that you keep anything off your schedule that is a drain on your time and has no measurable benefit to your goals. "Time is the coin of your life," said American poet Carl Sandburg. "It is the only coin you have, and only you can determine how it will be spent. Be careful lest you let other people spend it for you."[1] Think carefully about saying yes to extracurricular items, and avoid overbooking yourself to the point where you have no free time to think, breathe, and recharge. If you must, stand in front of the mirror and practice saying *"No!"*

Managing multiple tasks can be daunting. A comprehensive to-do list reinforced with a well-organized calendar is a killer combination and will help you to stay on track. The most important thing is to choose a system that you can maintain without spending a lot of time and effort. Whatever method you choose, it's important to select a one that is comprehensive enough for your needs but not so complicated that you can't keep it current.

CALENDARS AND PLANNERS

I love the time of year when calendars and planners hit the shelves. Each year the selection grows as manufacturers try to help us find a way to organize the chaos of our lives. Wall calendars with pictures of adorable puppies or breathtaking landscapes, niche planners for moms or students, and leatherbound executive planners with every imaginable customized insert—oh, how to choose? Big enough to record appointments, meetings, family stuff, and work deadlines but not so big that it's cumbersome to tote around.

Whatever you decide to use, you should plan to spend at least five to fifteen minutes each day maintaining a calendar and task list. Spend this time reviewing your calendar for the next week and adding any appointments, to-do items, or reminders. Reminders are simple notes that you should put in your calendar prior to an event (for example, entering a reminder on Tuesday to write thank-you cards for the speakers at your lunch and learn event on Friday). Just move backward from the date of the event, and put in that little memory-jogger to avoid scrambling at the last minute. Use the reminder tools on your online calendars to help you recall that your final head counts for the award ceremony are due next Monday or that your contribution to the company blog is due in ten days or that you need to make travel arrangements for the trade show in June.

There are dozens of ways to keep track of your schedule. If you're like me, you've tried various methods at one point or another. Some systems work better than others, depending on the stage of your life and how many different schedules you're trying to keep track of.

Review these common scheduling systems to find the one that suits you:

- *Wall or refrigerator calendar.* Typically with one month per page; available at office supply stores and bookstores
  - Pros—Highly visible to others
  - Cons—Lack of portability and limited writing space
- *Paper planners.* Typically offered with one month to a page and one week to a page; produced by Circa, Good Busy Planner, and Franklin Covey, among others
  - Pros—Extremely versatile; companies provide versions for different demographics (student, busy mom, professional, etc.)
  - Cons—Can be bulky and difficult to maintain; can also be a little pricey if you spring for all of the extras

- *Mobile apps.* Think Outlook Calendar, Google Calendar, or Informant
  - Pros—Sync across devices; can be updated no matter where you are, with automated reminders
  - Cons—Limited views and visibility
- *Project management databases.* This would include software like Microsoft Project or Basecamp
  - Pros—Perfect for keeping track of complicated, extended endeavors
  - Cons—Big learning curve; can be time-consuming to keep updated

If you find yourself copying appointments into multiple calendars, it's time to rethink your system. If you're not sure which is right for you, I would recommend starting with a midsize (eight and a half by five and a half inches) monthly/weekly calendar and a mechanical pencil with a good eraser. Out of all of the methods I have tried, these are some of the best tools I have found to manually keep track of a schedule and tasks. Unless you're a doctor scheduling appointments on the quarter hour, this size is probably big enough to keep track of work, home, and volunteer schedules while still small enough to easily transport wherever you go. Whatever system you decide on, never count on your memory if someone else is counting on you!

OTHER ORGANIZATIONAL TOOLS
Have you ever tried to slice a tomato with a dull knife or hang a picture without a hammer? Attempting to complete any task efficiently without the proper equipment is not only frustrating but a huge time waster as well. Equipping yourself with good-quality, basic organizational tools will ensure that you are making the most of your time and energy.

Ring Binders
The next time you head to a bookstore, take a look at the wedding-planning books. They usually take up an entire section that is chock-full of beautifully designed books in ring-binder format. Lots of checklists,

dividers, pockets to keep loose papers, and places to add fabric swatches, magazine clippings, and business cards.

This makes perfect sense to me; I'm a ring-binder girl. Ring binders are a great way to organize almost any project. You can get different sizes based on the complexity of your project and use different colors so you can easily identify the project you want to work on and grab it off the shelf. I use binders to store a master task list, time line, contacts, meeting agendas and minutes, ideas clipped from magazines for decor or other elements, and other important documents.

A variety of accessories make organizing with ring binders a breeze, including hole punches, sleeves for stashing business cards and pockets for loose items. Ring binders are inexpensive, versatile, and readily available and can be effective tools for keeping track of the majority of events discussed in this book.

Mechanical Pencils

You may think that a good pen is the way to go, but more often than not a mechanical pencil is a better choice—especially when it comes to maintaining a manual calendar, address book, or task list. Invariably meetings, appointments, contact information, and other details will have to be added, removed, or modified. Your planning documents will be much cleaner and less cluttered if you can erase an item instead of scratching out items written in ink and trying to force revisions into small margins.

Online and File-Sharing Tools

- *Google Drive and Google Docs.* These programs allow you to share large files with your team members via your Gmail account. Google Docs allows you and your team members to work on documents, spreadsheets, and presentations simultaneously with changes appearing in real time. It also saves previous versions in case you want to revert to a version prior to the latest changes.

- *Dropbox.* This tool allows you to access and share any file from your phone, tablet, or computer. Once you have an account established, just save your files in Dropbox folders. All of your devices will sync when new files are added or existing ones are modified. Create public folders, and then share them with your team so they can edit files or add new files. The motto of Dropbox is "Your life's work, wherever you are." I love it.

Stay Focused

A large service corporation planned a customer event at a grand hotel near their headquarters. Customers were flying in from all over the United States, and the event planning team had worked tirelessly on every detail. Then, two days before attendees were to arrive, the sprinkler system at the hotel malfunctioned, and all of the ballrooms were completely flooded, rendering them unusable.

Encountering a situation like this could make any event planner feel like curling up in a corner, but there was no time to panic. The planning team had to remain focused and determined to find a solution. Everyone got to work; the hotel team was able to find another local venue that had the space available to accommodate the conference. There wasn't a lot of sleep that weekend as event organizers moved their entire operation. They had to quickly familiarize themselves with the new facility, figure out how to utilize each new space, and notify the attendees about the location change, but by Monday morning it was as if the event had always been planned to be held at the new venue.

The reason this conference ended up being huge success despite this huge setback is because the planning team was able to regroup and improvise; they used the PARTY principles of successful planning:

- *Preparation.* Identify mission-critical activities, and create an action plan.
- *Agility.* Strive to think on your feet, and quickly adjust your plan when necessary.
- *Resolve.* Visualize your goals, and strive to delight your attendees.
- *Team.* Assemble a trusted team to implement your plan.
- *You.* Stay physically strong and mentally focused in order to maintain your momentum and persevere.

FIGHT PROCRASTINATION

A project with no target date is doomed to stretch on beyond any reasonable time frame for anyone prone to procrastination, and the event planner is no exception. Even if you've been given no official deadline to complete your planning work, set some milestones for yourself, and write them down. Use an accountability partner; let them know your plan, and ask them to help you to meet your goal by regularly meeting with you to assess your progress and provide support and encouragement.

BREAK TASKS INTO SMALLER PARTS

The secret to getting ahead is getting started, it is said. And the secret of getting started is breaking complex, overwhelming tasks into small, manageable tasks and then starting on the first one. This should be your mantra if you are a habitual procrastinator. The best way to solve a problem or complete a project is to unravel it, bit by bit. Some will save the most unpleasant tasks for last, but all that does is add to the level of pressure and stress as deadlines approach and the biggest "bite" is still staring them in the face.

You will increase your stress-free and anxiety-free time if you banish the elephant in the room altogether! Write down the list of tasks that will need to be completed before your project can be considered complete, and put a star next to the items that are causing you the most stress when you think about them. The quicker you can cross those starred items off your list, the better you're going to feel. The rest of the plan will be a breeze once you have the toughest jobs out of the way.

ELIMINATE DISTRACTIONS

Some believe that procrastination worsens when a person is unable to filter out distractions, which in turn decreases their ability to organize thoughts and keep their attention on the task. Assuming this is true, it becomes vital that you literally schedule time in your day to work exclusively on your project—and stick to it. If you have too many distractions where you are, grab your project binder or laptop, get away from the television and your other to-do lists, and get out. Go to the library, the bookstore, the coffee shop, a bench in the park—anywhere you can reduce the number of distractions and focus on the task at hand.

FIGHT THE URGE TO BE PERFECT

Many times, it's the fear of failure or of not measuring up to society's standards that can paralyze us into either delaying tackling a task or avoiding it altogether. Remember what I said earlier: the only true failure is the failure to try! Will some people be critical of your actions? Possibly, but the only way you will ever have a chance of succeeding is by continually moving forward on the road toward your end goal. I could write a marketing e-mail or thank-you note over and over and over again in an effort to find the perfect words and sentence structure to convey my message, but at some point I have to stop editing and move on. A completed task done well is far better than one that remains undone as you strive for perfection. Remember that each step you take will get you closer and closer to success, so do the best you can, and then let it go; it's a wonderful feeling!

LEARN YOUR LIMITS

Stress is probably one of the biggest factors in creating chronic procrastination. It can result from taking on too much or from miscalculating the time necessary to completing a task or project. So before you agree to take on any new project or task, look at your current schedule first, consider the time *realistically* necessary to do the task, and sleep on it before you decide to get involved. Don't get overwhelmed by pressure from outside sources; saying no is better than taking on more than you can reasonably handle.

As an event organizer, I've been in the position of having a key committee member drop out during the most critical time in the project because they put off their tasks to the last minute and then decided they had taken on too much. This kind of situation is devastating for the planning team and for the event. So before you say yes to a commitment, get a complete understanding of the job at hand, and then create a task list and time line, get help if you need it, and get cracking! There's no room for procrastination when you're an integral part of pulling off an extraordinary event.

REMEMBER THE BOTTOM LINE

Procrastination is something I fight regularly. I've had to deal with the consequences of watching too many *West Wing* reruns instead of meeting a deadline, but sometimes it just happens: I begin with the best of intentions, and three episodes later, I'm in panic mode because the afternoon is gone and my grand plans for a productive day have disappeared into thin air. My best advice is to continue to fight the good fight; try some of the tips listed above, remember the consequences of a job left to the last minute, and decide for yourself whether giving in to procrastination is really worth it.

27

Measure Your Success

As I settled in for a writing session at my local coffee shop a few months ago, a group of people began to gather at a large table nearby. As they passed around a tray of pastries and began their conversation, I realized that I was overhearing a debrief session of the organizing committee for a community event that had occurred the night before.

There are so many things to admire about this coffeehouse meeting. First, I was impressed that the organizers understood the importance of reviewing everything about their event—what went well and what could be improved. Second, although they were probably pretty tired from the night before, the team took the time to meet immediately after the event so that everything was still fresh in their minds.

Each member was given the opportunity to talk about their area of responsibility and what, if anything, they would change the next time around. Just as important was that members felt comfortable providing constructive analysis to each other, a healthy sign of an effective, high-performing team.

While all these things were impressive, the most notable aspect of the meeting was who was in attendance. Seated next to the person who was clearly the chair of the event was the person who would be replacing her next time around. This group understood the importance of identifying a replacement for each key role and ensuring that they shadowed the current officeholder to learn the intricacies of the job they would assume in the future.

If you are part of an event planning team, remember to take the time to review and assess after the event is over and to identify and train replacements for key personnel. It will help you create a stronger, more successful event in the future.

REVISIT YOUR GOALS

How will you evaluate the success of your event after it's over? How many attended? How much money was raised? What were the comments on the feedback forms? How many leads did you get? How happy did everyone seem as they left? How much product was sold? Get your team together one last time and revisit the goals you set at the very beginning. Did you achieve them? If not, what could you have done differently? If your event is recurring, addressing these issues should be the first thing on the action plan for your next occasion.

GATHER PARTICIPANT FEEDBACK

Data is important to any project, including event projects. Anyone who is planning a recurring event should find a method to collect constructive, meaningful information from previous attendees before starting to plan future events. You'll never have the opportunity to improve your next event if you don't ask your attendees what they liked and what they would change. Surveys are a great way to get the feedback you need to take your event to the next level. Use them to get to know your audience so you can create a program that creates value and encourages them to attend again and again.

Decide whether you will require a signature on the survey. Anonymous surveys might encourage more honest and open feedback. However, it will be difficult to address specific issues if you don't know who submitted the survey.

Paper Surveys

Smaller events often opt for paper surveys. I've attended conferences where there was a survey form to complete for each session I attended as well as a general survey for the entire event. They either provide the surveys in the conference bag provided at registration or have a survey waiting in each room as participants travel from session to session.

To ensure that a high percentage of your attendees participate in completing paper surveys before they leave an event, provide an incentive, such as entering them in a high-value prize drawing. Another idea is to offer a commemorative item to each person who turns in a completed survey—a premium promotional item, such as wireless earbuds or a power bank.

Polling

If you're interested in receiving instant feedback after every session, or even have the ability to poll attendees in real time during a session, look for a registration tool that also includes surveying capabilities, such as Whova or Cvent. Alternatively, you might consider investing in an engagement app such as CrowdCompass or Pathable, which offers not only instant polling and surveying from the attendee's smart device but also tons of other tools that can be used throughout your event.

Online Surveys

Another option is to have an online survey waiting for attendees in their in-boxes when they get home, using Web tools such as Survey-Monkey, Google Forms, or Crowdsignal. Here are a few things to keep in mind in order to create an effective online survey:

- *Timing.* Always send the survey out as soon as possible after your event has concluded. Waiting for even a couple of days could affect the percentage of returned surveys. Once your attendees are back in their regular lives and their regular routines, other tasks will take precedence, and your survey is more likely to end up unopened or in the trash. If your survey tools allow for it, create the survey prior to the event and schedule its delivery so that it's sitting in each attendee's e-mail in-box on the last day of your event so they can complete it right away.

- *Deadlines.* Include a deadline in the body of the e-mail or better yet in the subject line of your e-mail so it creates a sense of urgency to complete it if they want their input to be heard. Some survey tools will automatically send a reminder e-mail at a time of your choosing to people who haven't yet completed the survey, usually three to five days after the initial e-mail invitation.

MAKE YOUR SURVEY COUNT
Build a survey that will provide the insights you need to plan more effective events in the future.

Number of Questions
Be very deliberate about the number of questions you include on your survey. If you ask too many questions, or if your survey takes too long to complete, many potential respondents will give up before they hit the *submit* button, causing you to lose a lot of valuable input. Don't make it time-consuming or tedious. Each question must have a valid reason to be on the list. If the answers to the question won't impact future events, eliminate the question from the list.

Phrasing
The questions you ask will depend on the type of event held. If you've just held a customer conference, for example, you will want to ask questions about the value of the program content, about the effectiveness of your speakers, and about the venue (food, lodging, hospitality, etc.). You'll also want to provide space for suggestions for your next event (new topics, new speakers, and venue suggestions).

Keep your wording simple and direct. Don't ask leading questions that might color the answers one way or another. For instance, instead of "What did you like least about the conference?" ask "Would you recommend this conference to others?" and provide room for them to expand on their yes/no answer.

Ask a few team members to review the questions for content and clarity.

Evaluating the Results

Don't change your course because of one or two negative survey responses. Remember that if you get one negative response to each of your ten questions, all ten of those answers may have come from the same unhappy person. While it's sometimes difficult to accept criticism about an event that you put your heart into, don't fall into the trap of changing a venue, meeting format, session, or speaker simply because a small percentage of your audience didn't enjoy it. If 5 percent of your survey results are negative on a particular topic, that means that 95 percent of the feedback was good!

It's important to keep perspective when evaluating survey results. While you will definitely want to read and discuss those negative comments with your team, you mustn't give them more weight than they deserve when making plans for your next event. It's great to shoot for a 100 percent satisfaction rate, but the last thing you want to do is throw away a solid program to try to satisfy the vocal minority.

KEEP THE CONVERSATION GOING

All kinds of studies indicate that the percentage of information retained by people who hear a presentation once it's over is depressingly low. The more time passes, the less information is retained. If you want your attendees to retain certain key messages from your event, hammer them home by connecting with your guests after the event has concluded. Continue to leverage the online engagement apps you used during the event, or send out a series of follow-up e-mails. Make sure your attendees know where they can go to view any videos of your event or where they can download presentation slides.

THANK YOUR CREW

Anyone who has volunteered to help plan an event can attest to the fact that they usually receive far more than they give, but a little recognition for their efforts will always be appreciated.

While it's tempting to kick up your feet and relax after your event has concluded, you still have one more important task to check off your list: it's time to give thanks to those who helped make it possible. You will be glad you recognized the efforts of your team members the next time you need to ask them for help.

I once was part of an organization that planned a large local event. Each year, their core team is rewarded with a get-together a couple of weeks after the event has concluded. These are the folks who work tirelessly year-round to register vendors, negotiate contracts, organize trash crews, secure sponsorships, and on and on. They deserve a medal for volunteering to take on these tasks and make the event a success year after year. Instead, they are invited to a little shindig called the Never-Do-It-Again Party, and for a couple of hours they eat, drink, laugh, swap stories, and pretend that they will never, *ever* do it again! They are recognized for a job well done, and, without skipping a beat, they get to work the next day to start planning next year's event.

Make sure you take the time to thank everyone as personally and publicly as possible by mentioning them in the event's program, online forum, website, and newsletter. Consider placing a thank-you ad in the local newspaper, sending hand-written individual notes, or presenting them with a small token or gift during a wrap-up party or volunteer recognition luncheon. Placing these seemingly small "deposits" into your gratitude account will pay dividends later.

While you have your thank-you cards in hand, make sure to thank your speakers, sponsors, third-party vendors, friends, family, and anyone else who helped to make your event a success.

28

Learn from the Experts

Here it is—a compilation of some of the best advice from some of the best in the business! Soak up the wisdom and experience of these event industry professionals and use it to make your event a real triumph.

IT'S NOT AS HARD AS YOU THINK

Certified meeting professional Deborah Gardner is an author, speaker, and competitive-performance expert with three decades of hospitality experience working with thousands of meetings and events professionals. "Event planning doesn't have to be hard," says Deborah. "If things seem overwhelming, just remember that your stakeholders have all the answers you need. Questions are your friend; start strategically asking lots of questions so you know where to start, and before you know it, things will start flowing."

EVERYTHING IS NEGOTIABLE

Alexandria Tomayko, experience coordinator for Nomadic Planning, reminds us that "everything is open for discussion. Many event planners don't even think about asking for a discount. Remember that negotiation is a conversation; it has to be a win-win."

FIRST IMPRESSIONS COUNT

"You have two chances to make a first impression: on the registration website and at the registration kiosk. Wow the attendee, and the coffee will taste better the rest of the event," says Travis Tucker, president and CEO of GTR.

MAKE A DIFFERENCE

"How much would it change our work if we didn't consider a job complete until we saw evidence that a difference has been made?" asks David Sturt, author of *Great Work*. "If we kept on working tenaciously up to and beyond the moment of delivery to ensure that our recipients were truly delighted? It's taking the time to understand what worked, what didn't, and most of all *why*."[1]

LEVERAGE THE EXPERTISE IN THE ROOM

Certified speaking professional and author Andy Masters says that most professional speakers understand that meeting planners are sometimes stressed and overwhelmed, so he urges planners to take advantage of their experience. "Let us help," says Andy. "Trust us on how we can help you make the most successful agenda for your event and your attendees."

STAND OUT FROM THE COMPETITION

"Although it's a shame, often the simplest way to stand out from your competition is by keeping your word," says A/V ambassador Brian Monahan.

LEARN TO IMPROVISE

Shana Bryant is founder and CEO of Shana Bryant Consulting and regularly produces conferences for nonprofits primarily serving women and girls. She tells the story of an event she planned where building in some transition time between agenda items really paid off. "I had my decor specialist setting up an elaborate balloon garland and towers on stage the day before the event; she wasn't able to complete the work and had to come back the morning of the conference to finish, so we had to delay the start of the program," says Shana. "Fortunately, our registration and breakfast were being held in a different room. The other thing on our side was that we had an amazing emcee and deejay. With their help we were able to engage one hundred middle and high school students who just met each other for the first time by playing the Human Bingo game and then having a dance contest; they were both a hit! The program welcome and keynote started forty-five minutes late, but only the logistics team knew we were behind."

"It all worked out, and the remainder of the day stayed on schedule," Shana says. "I've learned to always incorporate more transition time, because you never know when you will need it. And ending an event a little early never hurt anyone."

TAKE A WALK IN YOUR PARTICIPANTS' SHOES

"Put yourself in the attendee's shoes as the user of the experience," says Alexandria Tomayko. "Walk through the event, and think about what they're looking for, what they want, what they see. If you're hosting a fundraiser, think about what's in it for your guest. Adding liquor, entertainment, a great experience, and value for them will help them loosen their purse strings and be generous in return."

EMBRACE THE TASK LIST

When it comes to getting the planning team organized, Deborah Gardner's best advice is to "Create a task list, and then assign and delegate each task. Make sure everyone stays in their lane—that they're focused solely on the tasks assigned to them. Clear communication of tasks and assignments will eliminate having too many hands in the pot and avoid having people working at cross-purposes."

FOCUS ON EDUCATION

"Be careful about the buzzword *engagement*," says Travis Tucker. "It's not necessarily always a good thing; it can take away from the most important factor, which is education. The conference that focuses on quality speakers and content is far more valuable and will get much higher survey results than those that focus on the 'it' things."

REIMAGINE YOUR MARKETING EFFORTS

Alexandria Tomayko recommends that you create content that can be used as advertising for your upcoming events. "Capture photos and video that can be used as free marketing for your event the following year," she suggests. "Host a 'Hackathon,' where each of your speakers or presenters shares their favorite hack, and share it on social media. Record some Ask-Me-Anything sessions, weekly one-hour interviews with featured speakers; then post them to your Facebook groups, VIP groups, and LinkedIn, or turn them into podcasts."

SEEK MEANINGFUL SPONSORSHIPS

Deborah Gardner says that the biggest mistake planners make when it comes to sponsors is not using them! "Some groups don't even think about sponsors," she says. "They can be a huge resource, helping you cover costs like speaker fees or after-hours activities. I recommend that you create a menu of various packages that give potential sponsors some options. Ask what you can do to showcase them and make their sponsorship more meaningful. They will have ideas too."

KNOW YOUR AUDIENCE

"Don't schedule a bunch of networking events if your audience is a bunch of introverts in the tech industry," advises Travis Tucker. "You'd be better off offering them a video-gaming room or some Pac-Man machines."

STAY ORGANIZED

"Always think ahead," advises event and meetings professional Erin Thomas. "I create a binder that contains everything about the event—emergency numbers, copies of contracts, all of it. I make sure that every team member and volunteer has access to it just in case something is needed."

DON'T PANIC
"Roll with it if unexpected things come up and take you by surprise," says meetings and events professional Tracy Zglinicki. "It doesn't help to panic. Always keep a level head."

MAKE YOUR SPEAKERS FEEL VALUED
Communication is the key to establishing a good relationship with the speakers and presenters who deliver your program. "As a speaker, I appreciate it when I receive a single document that includes everything I need to know—where I'm supposed to go when I arrive at the property, who I'm supposed to sit with at lunch," says Deborah Gardner. "Pick a liaison—someone whose sole responsibility it is to communicate with the speakers and take care of their needs. Speakers get stressed out too; do everything you can to minimize their anxiety and help them perform at their very best when they take the stage."

START EARLY, AND MANAGE YOUR TIME
Strategic event professional Karen Hartline recommends tracking the time it takes to plan your event so you can staff appropriately. "Most people have misconceptions about how much time it takes to manage the details of an event, as well as the length of time from inception to completion," says Karen. "Lead times are getting shorter and shorter. You might be able to find a venue in four months, but sponsor and speakers are tougher. You should plan at least nine months out; a year is even better."

Karen says she learned early on in her career to track time by each event component. "While it takes a lot of effort, I have a very clear picture of how long each part of the project will take to complete. It also helps when recruiting volunteers; you can give them a very clear picture about the time commitment they're signing up for."

MAKE IT A FAMILY AFFAIR

Meeting participants are seeking family-friendly events more than ever. "People struggle with having to leave family and friends behind to travel to events," Deborah Gardner says. "Add elements to your agenda that will encourage them to bring their family with them. Provide activities that family members can participate in during times when their loved ones are in meetings. Adding family-friendly components can often encourage participants to extend their stay, which could help you meet your room block guarantee."

STAY ON YOUR TOES

"I once organized the Draw Party for the World Figure Skating Championships, where each skater is introduced and brought on stage to draw for their spot in the upcoming competition," says meetings and events professional Margie Nolting. "Unfortunately, three of the most famous and anticipated skaters didn't show. Our entire program hinged on their appearance. Luckily I had booked a celebrity guest host and had provided them with copious notes on each of the skaters so they could improv when the absent skaters were called.

"While our guest host was improvising onstage, I noticed that none of the food was coming out of the kitchen. I went into the back and learned that there had been a small kitchen fire. The fire was out, and everything was returning to normal, but the fire department had already been called. We were able to cancel the fire run and avoid a complete evacuation of the facility, which would have ended the entire event."

MIX THINGS UP A BIT

Deborah Gardner recommends abandoning the typical meeting agenda and switching things up. "Surprise your attendees. Wow them. Spark things up! Try flipping the agenda, serving breakfast for dinner or scheduling the gala on the first night of the event instead of the last," she suggests. "Survey your attendees ahead of time, and let them drive the outcome by letting them choose from a menu of topics, interactive activities, and creative meal options. Keep things moving by incorporating games or other icebreakers into your networking events. Make it a memorable experience."

COMMUNICATE EARLY AND OFTEN

Karen Hartline urges event planners to use as many communication channels as necessary to stay in touch with sponsors, speakers, clients, and team members. "For speakers and sponsors, I create a hidden web page or portal on my event website where they can get all of the important details, including paperwork and due dates."

Karen always follows up via e-mail as well, but she creates an e-mail alias, such as speakerinfo@eventname.com, instead of having all e-mails coming into her personal e-mail in-box. That way, several people can monitor the e-mails and manage and respond to them instead of a single person. "I was once the organizer for a three thousand–person event, and my speaker manager had a sudden death in the family," recounts Karen. "E-mails were flying around like crazy, but I was able to tell her to go be with her family because I was able to access those e-mails and know exactly what the status was for each speaker and sponsor and what exactly needed to be done."

For her internal team, Karen uses an inexpensive collaboration tool called Slack. She creates a new "channel" for each event, sometimes multiple channels per event for different work groups or teams, where people can interact with the entire team, chat one-on-one, share files, and integrate other project management tools.

BE PREPARED TO PIVOT

A few years ago, Deborah Gardner was booked to be the keynote speaker for an event that boasted a *Wizard of Oz* theme. She was immediately inspired and decided to surprise the organizers by channeling her inner Dorothy with her clothing choice: a beautiful emerald green dress and red shoes. When she showed up early in the morning for the A/V test, she mounted the stage and began her walk-through. "The video crew was in the back of the room testing their equipment, and it wasn't long before they started to chuckle and point," says Deborah. "When I asked what was going on, they invited me back to see what they were seeing through their video camera lens. They played back the video, and I immediately saw the problem. The only thing that could be seen was my head, arms, and legs moving around; my dress was a perfect color match to the green backdrop, so my body had literally become invisible!"

Everyone started to freak out just a little; Deborah hadn't brought a change of clothes (the obvious plan B solution was out), so they had to go with plan C: take down the green backdrop and replace it with a black one so a quality video could be captured.

This was a huge learning lesson on everyone's part that day. Yet Deborah took that nerve-wracking experience and applied it to all subsequent speaking engagements. "First," she says she learned, "be transparent, and communicate with the organizers ahead of time about my wardrobe choice. Second, I always have a change of clothes. And finally, I ask the organizers for as many details as possible about the speaking environment and purpose and meaning behind their theme."

BLOW THEIR SOCKS OFF

Phil Mershon is events director for Social Media Examiner, as well as podcast host and experience designer. His advice? "Don't just plan for the things that could go wrong; plan for those things that go way beyond. What could go so well that would blow your socks off and your attendees' socks off and give them something that they're going to be talking about for days, weeks, months, years, decades to come?"

29

Rise to the Occasion

Any time someone asks me the secret to planning a great event, I tell them that it's all about building and strengthening relationships. I really don't think of it as creating an event as much as building a community, a shared experience built on a solid foundation of good communication, focus, and teamwork. But most of all, I believe that an event can't be truly successful without incorporating a generous dose of hospitality into everything you do.

IT'S ALL ABOUT HOSPITALITY

Today the word *hospitality* is associated with an industry more than a state of mind. A hospitality degree can prepare you for hotel management, food service, travel, tourism, and, yes, event planning professions. Those who excel in the hospitality industry do so because they have finely honed problem-solving skills. They know when to lead and when to delegate. They understand the importance of teamwork. They are outstanding communicators and are skilled in the art of negotiation. But most important, they understand what it really means to be hospitable.

A few years ago, when I was wandering through a little antique store and came across that well-worn copy of Betty Crocker's book on entertaining, I was immediately intrigued. As a self-proclaimed obsessive organizer of people, places, and events, I was curious to see what Betty had to say about hosting events back in the day.

Some of the advice that Betty provided in that book has certainly gone out of style. She provides tempting recipes for the buffet table like jellied chicken loaf and avocado mousse and delectable desserts such as broiled canned peaches with dollops of green jelly in the center. And let us not forget the exotic new recipe from Mexico she introduces called "gwah-ka-mole-ay" to be served as an appetizer with saltine crackers!

But much of Betty's advice still rings true today. She relied on the dictionary definition of the word *hospitality*—"being disposed to entertain with generous kindness"—and applied it to all of her events.[1] As a modern-day event planner, I believe that definition has withstood the test of time. When you break it all down, planning events in today's world is really not all that different from what it was in the 1950s. Planning a special occasion, whether for your family, your community, or your career, is as simple as rediscovering Betty's definition of hospitality and applying it to our twenty-first-century lives.

Being Disposed . . .

Being disposed is all about being ready in detail and in spirit. Behind every successful event is someone who has taken the time to establish goals, assemble a team, create an action plan, and execute with precision. This allows everyone to relax on the big day and enjoy it without stress or unpleasant surprises. Being disposed means you have taken the time to sweat the small stuff in order to make sure your guests have a great time.

. . . To Entertain . . .

The trick is figuring out how to entertain others while enjoying the event yourself. At every event I've ever organized, the majority of people in attendance have shown up wanting to have a good time and therefore have been pretty forgiving if everything wasn't 100 percent perfect. I'm sure that you've attended lots of events where everything wasn't necessarily going according to plan and you didn't even realize it. That's because the organizers were keeping their cool while implementing their plan B and everyone was having a good time in spite of the snags.

With a little advanced planning, you should be able to relax and have fun at your events. And if you're having fun, your guests will too. Planning ahead will lessen much of the stress that sometimes comes with hosting a special occasion. Notice that I said "lessen," not "eliminate." I'm not ashamed to admit that I have a little experience in this area; I've had my share of recipe failures and Pinterest failures and even a couple of minor personal injuries in my event planning adventures! So strive for excellence, but don't freak out if something goes wrong; just keep breathing, smile, and improvise!

. . . With Generous . . .

Planning an event with generosity means that you've provided event elements that exceed expectations. You revisit the reasons that you are having the event and then make sure that all of your time and resources are spent meeting that goal. Identifying and documenting your goals and objectives, and then making sure everyone involved understands those goals, is the best way to ensure that your time and resources are spent wisely and efficiently.

Betty says that hospitality isn't a contest; it is sharing the best you have, without apology. It's having a generous spirit and going into it knowing that your event is a gift that you are giving your guests without expecting anything in return. Planning an event with generosity doesn't mean you've spent a lot of money. It just means you've done everything you can to make your guests feel valued.

I lost my father a few years ago, and when I think of him, I think of the mountaintop moments that we shared. I remember the look on his face as he walked into his surprise seventieth birthday bash and the uncharacteristic speech he gave honoring my mother at their fiftieth wedding anniversary party. Those events involved a lot of planning and effort, but they were the best gift we could have ever given him. I wouldn't trade those moments of joy, love, and laughter for anything in the world. Those memories are worth everything to me.

... Kindness

Serve your participants with kindness so that they leave feeling treasured. When I plan an event, I always think about how I want my guests to feel when it's over. What do I want them to be thinking about on the way home? What will they tell their friends and colleagues? What memories do I want them to carry with them long after the event is over? Planning a special event can be a lot of work, but the rewards can be great. I'm always glad to see survey results from customers who say that our conference is the best one they attend all year.

Occasionally you will encounter someone who joins an event planning team and then decides to use their authority as an excuse to be overbearing or rude. These kinds of volunteers can do a lot of damage to your reputation and to the integrity of the event and should not be tolerated. Instead, fill your team with people who will look for every opportunity to treat your participants with kindness, and empower them to make decisions that will make your guests feel valued and respected.

WALT GOT IT RIGHT

If you've ever visited a Disney amusement park, then you have without a doubt seen true hospitality in action. All Disney "cast members" undergo extensive training for the express purpose of making sure that you and your family have a magical experience. Walt Disney once said that you can dream about creating the most wonderful place in the world, but it takes people to make it a reality.[2] He believed in instilling those dreams into all of his team members, and that philosophy is still working today. Every cast member learns to be emotionally invested in providing world-class service and has been empowered to go above and beyond to make their every guest's dreams come true.

Try adopting a Disney-esque attitude when planning your next event. Work with your team to make sure they're dedicated to creating an experience full of unforgettable experiences, heightened engagement, and pure delight.

HONORING A FRIEND

I knew Brenda first as a neighbor, then as a coworker and mentor. When you looked up the phrase *work ethic*, her picture should have been there; her customers loved her, and her coworkers respected and admired her.

When Brenda was diagnosed with cancer, it took our breath away. She was such an integral part of our team, and the thought of not having her by our side was chilling. In true Brenda fashion, she didn't let her diagnosis stop her from what she wanted to accomplish. When treatments compromised her immune system, she worked from home and continued to answer the phone with a smile in her voice. With her infinite patience, she helped her customers resolve their multitude of issues, never letting them know the intense personal battle she was fighting every day.

Eventually it became clear that Brenda was losing her valiant fight. Those who loved her began to prepare for the worst. As we tried to deal with our anger and bitterness at the thought of losing Brenda, it occurred to us that there was something we could do. We decided that we would do something to honor her while she was still with us instead of simply waiting for the inevitable.

That's when the Most Valuable Player celebration was born. We just knew in our guts that the very best way to honor Brenda was to celebrate her life and her contributions while she was still able to celebrate with us. She and her family were excited to hear about our plans, and she was determined to be there no matter what. We organized a fabulous luncheon for her and invited her family as well as all past and present coworkers. We worked with the venue to create a tasty menu and decorated the tables and the room with lots of color and sparkle. The way her eyes lit up when she came into the room is something I'll never forget.

We put together a slideshow chronicling Brenda throughout her career—at customer events, at employee picnics and other outings.

We showed the serious, the sweet, and the hilarious, including a montage of her outrageous Halloween costumes. People paid tribute to Brenda through numerous speeches and toasts. Thoughtful gifts were presented, and a few tears were shed, but smiles and laughter were the order of the day.

The entire event was emotional and beautiful, and Brenda was clearly touched by it all. She stayed with us longer than she probably should have that day, talking to everyone in attendance, sharing hugs and taking pictures. It was a special time and one that I know she treasured.

Brenda passed away less than a month after the MVP event. Our hearts were broken, but we were so glad that we'd had the opportunity to know her, work with her, and call her a friend. We were also so happy that we'd taken the time to honor Brenda while she was still here to share it with us.

IT'S TIME TO RISE

There are so many events worth having and so many events that need your unique skills and perspective. So what's holding you back? How many opportunities to create an extraordinary event have already been lost because you think you're too inexperienced or not organized enough? It's time to take a deep breath and rise to the occasion, my friends. Raise your hand and say yes to organizing the next association meeting, planning retreat, or client event. Shove the fear of failure behind a firmly closed door, and make it happen.

Seek out the first timer at a club meeting, take them under your wing, and ask them to join you on the committee for the next silent auction or fundraiser. If there is a corporate event or exhibition in your future, think all of the ways you can make guests feel informed, welcome, comfortable, and appreciated.

It's never been truer than it is today that our families, our communities, our workplaces, our *world* needs more "Betty-style" hospitality. So, no matter what, always, *always* be disposed to entertain with generous kindness.

Appendix

Worksheets and Checklists

The forms found in this section are representative of the kinds of documents you can use to stay organized and stay on track throughout the event planning process and the event itself. Having this information in one binder, computer file, or online system will save you from wasting your precious time wading through e-mails, trying to find that one phone number you need in a hurry.

You can find editable Microsoft Word and Excel versions of all of the documents in the appendix by going to www.LindaJoyceJones.com /worksheets. Use these editable versions over and over again to create and save custom forms for each of your unique events.

GOAL STATEMENT

Spend some time to get your goals down on paper. Create a goal statement—a short, easy-to-memorize "elevator pitch" that can be used in
press releases and advertising materials. Start by working together with
your core team to answer the following questions. Remember that there
may be multiple goals for your event, so don't limit yourself to a single
objective. Creating a unifying goal statement will make decision making
much easier for your entire team.

1. Who is this event intended for? Who are the stakeholders, the
   people who will benefit from the success of this event? (There may
   be many.)

2. What is the benefit that stakeholders will receive? What's in it for
   them?

3. What are your overall objectives? (What is the purpose of your
   event? What do you hope to achieve when all is said and done?)

4. What are your specific deliverables? (What specific things will you
   produce at your event in order to achieve your objectives?)

5. How will you measure success (e.g., tickets sold, dollars raised, number of closed sales, or survey results)?

6. What people and resources will be required to achieve success?

7. What obstacles exist to achieving these objectives? (Is there anything
   related to scope, time, or resources that will limit your ability to
   achieve your objectives?)

8. Once you've answered the questions above, create one or more goal
   statements below.

Goal #1 for this event:

Action steps required to achieve this goal:
     Action 1:
     Owner:
     Due date:

     Action 2:
     Owner:
     Due date:

Goal #2 for this event:

Action steps required to achieve this goal:
     Action 1:
     Owner:
     Due date:

     Action 2:
     Owner:
     Due date:

BUDGET

Creating a detailed budget is crucial to planning an event. Until you have a firm grasp of all sources of revenue available and all expenses you will incur, you are operating on nothing but guesswork, and that's a dangerous way to operate.

Use the worksheet below to list every possible revenue source and every expense you may incur. Some of your expenses will be required, and some will be discretionary; mark each item that can be eliminated if necessary. If exact prices or quantities are not yet known, do as much research as necessary to establish a reasonable estimate.

Revenue	Quantity	Price Each	Total
Ticket and registration fees			
Ticket level 1			
Ticket level 2			
Sponsorships			
Sponsor level 1			
Sponsor level 2			
Donations			
Fundraisers			
Corporate resources			

Expenses	Details	Required? (Y/N)	Estimate	Actual
Venue				
Room rentals				
Technology rentals				
Other equipment and supplies				
Permits/licenses				

Expenses	Details	Required? (Y/N)	Estimate	Actual
Decor				
Flowers				
Lighting				
Table decor				
Paper products				
Banners and signage				
Food and beverage				
Food				
Drinks				
Linens				
Staff				
Bartender				
Waitstaff				
Other				
Tax				
Gratuity				
Program				
Performers				
Speakers				
Hotel				
Transportation/parking				
Production				
Supplies for individual activities				
Prizes				
Auction items				
Goody bags				
Ribbons/trophies/certificates				

Expenses	Details	Required? (Y/N)	Estimate	Actual
Door prizes				
Thank-you gifts				
Publicity/promotion				
Advertising				
Publicity packets				
Graphic design				
Website/online registration				
Paper/stationery				
Photography				
Postage				
Printing				
Brochures				
Programs				
Staff and volunteers				
Shirts				
Badges				
Sleeping rooms				
Meals				
Miscellaneous				
Telephones/radios				
Fuel/mileage				
Insurance				
Safety equipment				
Security				
Contingencies				

Estimated total revenue $

Less estimated total expense $_____

= Estimated total profit $

TEAM AND VOLUNTEER DETAILS

Make a habit of keeping essential information in a spreadsheet for each of your team members, including volunteers. You will use it over and over again. It's best to store this information in a spreadsheet so you can sort it by committee to create e-mail groups or so you can sort it by last name for making name badges or for printing out phone lists and emergency contact lists to have on hand in your master binder at the event site.

First name:

Last name:

Title:

Primary phone:

Primary e-mail:

Day-of phone (cell):

Vehicle make:

Vehicle model:

Vehicle license plate#:

Emergency contact name:

Emergency contact phone:

Name badge done? Y/N

Clothing ordered? Y/N

Parking pass done? Y/N

Primary committee:

Assignment(s):

RFP TEMPLATE

Use this *request for proposal* template to communicate your event requirements to prospective partners. Provide this RFP to meeting planners so they can understand and provide a comprehensive response that will give you all of the information you need in order to make an informed decision and select the venue that is best for your event. You can use this format to create a custom RFP for other service providers, such as technology firms and trade show management firms.

Request for Proposal
2021 XYZ Fall Conference
September 15–17, 20XX

General information:
Company name:
Address:
Main phone number:
Fax number:
Primary contact name:
Title:
Direct phone number:
E-mail address:

Event summary:
Event name:
The XYZ Fall Conference is a three-day training and educational event for our clients, all of whom live and work in the tristate area. Our goals in hosting this event are to build and strengthen relationships with our clients, provide education on how to fully utilize our products to help them be successful, provide networking opportunities with their peers and other relevant service providers, and market new products and services that will help them work smarter while improving our profitability.

Attendee demographics:
Number of years the event has been held:
Date(s) of event:
Dates are flexible? Y/N
Start/end times each day:
Anticipated total number of participants:
Approximate # of sleeping rooms per night:
Number of sleeping rooms on the master bill (staff, VIP guests):
Individual sleeping room reservations tax-exempt? Y/N

Spaces needed:
- Registration area
- Storage/support room (need hardwire Internet capability)
- 7 meeting rooms for tracks as noted below
- General session room for Wednesday morning only
- Meal room that can accommodate minimum of 250 people
- All-day beverage station (coffee, tea, soft drinks, water dispensers)
- Exhibitor space in high-traffic area (no more than 25 spaces with a table, 2 chairs, and access to electricity for each)

Price quotes needed for the following:
- Full projection package for each meeting room, price per room
- Microphone on a stand or lectern, price each
- Lavalier microphones, price each
- Raised stage for general session meeting room
- Password-protected Wi-Fi for entire meeting area
- Hardwired Internet connection, price per room
- Copy of most current banquet menu

Does your facility provide the following amenities onsite? Please elaborate where needed, including hours of operation:
__ Complimentary parking
__ Complimentary transportation to local airports and local attractions

__ Restaurant
__ Bar
__ Pool
__ Spa
__ Exercise facility
__ Other

Draft Agenda
(All times are approximate.)

Tuesday, September 14   Arrive 3:00 p.m.
Requirements:
- Access to registration area
- Access to storage/support room
- Access to learning lab meeting rooms to set up computers (Tracks 2 and 3)
- Access to exhibitor tables for setup (no more than 25 exhibitors)

Wednesday, September 15
- 7:00 a.m.   Registration begins
- 7:30–8:30   Breakfast buffet
- 8:30–9:30   General session; needs to hold 275 people, theater-style
- 9:00–5:00   7 tracks running concurrently
  - Track 1   Training; minimum 100 people, either classroom or crescent rounds
  - Track 2   Training; minimum 60 people, classroom
  - Track 3   Training; minimum 60 people, classroom
  - Track 4   Lecture; minimum 80 people, classroom
  - Track 5   Roundtable sessions; at least 36, U-shape
  - Track 6   Training camps; 30 people, 6 crescent rounds
  - Track 7   Board room or small meeting room, U-shape for small-group software demonstrations
- 12:00 p.m.–1:00   Lunch buffet
- 6:00–7:00   Dinner buffet

Thursday, September 16
Identical to Wednesday, except:
- 6:00 p.m.–10:00   Dinner/gala, followed by after-hours event, in a space large enough to comfortably hold all participants; setup to be determined

Friday, September 17
- Registration and storage area, same as Wednesday and Thursday
- Breakfast buffet only
- Beverage service only until noon
- Tracks 1–4 only, running from 8:30 a.m.–12:30 p.m.
- Teardown and out no later than 2:30

Sleeping rooms:
We can guarantee a minimum of 100 rooms per night on Tuesday, September 14; Wednesday, September 15; and Thursday, September 16. The XYZ staff rooms (approximately 15–20 persons, each night) would go on the master bill; all other attendees will book and pay for their own reservations. We require a mix of room styles, including 2 queen and 1 king bed. Please provide information on other room styles you have available, as well as a price per room, including the current tax rate. Our participants will typically not be able to budget more than $175.00 per night for a sleeping room.

Food and beverage guarantee:
We can provide a food and beverage guarantee of at least $35,000.00. Please provide your most current banquet menu, including rates for taxes, gratuities, and service fees. Provide any information regarding off-menu food and beverage options that are available.

Date proposal due:
Decision date:

Industry references can be provided upon request.

VENUE EVALUATION

Complete one of these forms for each venue you are considering for your event. Customize the evaluation form to only include the items that are important to your particular occasion, and add other criteria as needed. If multiple people will be evaluating venues, devise a scoring system for each major component, and then tally scores to provide more structure to your decision-making process.

If the venue is a hotel or other facility that includes sleeping rooms, use the separate Sleeping Room Evaluation to assess that portion of the venue.

Name of venue:
Address:
Main phone number:
Website:
Primary contact name:
Direct number:
E-mail:

Facility Details

__ Parking:
Fee/free/valet
Paved and in good repair? Y/N

__ Transportation to airport and/or local attractions via taxi, limousine, or shuttle:

__ Loading dock? Y/N

__ Registration area:

__ Other event spaces:
    Space 1
        Max capacity:
        Setup style:
    Space 2
        Max capacity:
        Setup style:
    Space 3
        Max capacity:
        Setup style:
    Space 4
        Max capacity:
        Setup style
    Space 5
        Max capacity:
        Setup style

__ Meeting space equipment and amenities:
    Built-in audiovisual equipment
    Does venue provide pens, paper, mints, etc., as part of meeting room setup? Y/N

__ Exhibitor space? Y/N
    Number of spaces available:

__ VIP area:
    Security needs

__ Hospitality area:

__ Storage/prep area:

__ Quiet room:

__ Restroom facilities:

__ Business office:

__ ADA compliance:
    __ Parking and entrances
    __ Restrooms
    __ Meeting rooms
    __ Elevator required to access meeting rooms? Y/N

__ Outdoor spaces:
    __ Patio
    __ Food/drink permitted
    __ Seating
    __ Sound/lighting
    __ Temperature control (heaters, fans)
    __ Time-of-day restrictions?

__ Dining and entertainment:
    __ Restaurant
    __ Bar
    __ Pool
    __ Spa
    __ Exercise facility
    __ Other

Food and Beverage Worksheet
__ Banquet menu meets food and beverage needs? Y/N

Price range for the following:
    __ Appetizers
    __ Breakfast

   __ Buffet
   __ Plated
__ Lunch
   __ Buffet
   __ Plated
__ Dinner
   __ Buffet
   __ Plated
__ Desserts
__ Break food packages
__ Beverages (coffee, tea, water, soda)
   __ Pricing per person, per day
   __ Pricing by consumption

__ Alcohol permits and restrictions:
   __ Cash bar permitted?
   __ Liquors offered
   __ Minimum costs and hours for bartender

__ What additional charges are added to stated menu rates?
   __ Tax %
   __ Gratuity %
   __ Other

__ Restrictions on outside food and beverage?

__ Sustainable meetings compliance:
   __ Recycled paper products
   __ Bulk condiments
   __ Water pitchers and glasses instead of water bottles
   __ Recycle bins for paper/glass/aluminum
   __ Other

Equipment Worksheet

Check the items you will need, and determine whether the venue has access and what additional charges are applicable. Contract with a third-party rental company for the items that cannot be provided by your venue.

__ High-speed wireless Internet (in meeting rooms, sleeping rooms, and common areas)

    Password-protected option? Y/N

__ Access to copier, fax, printer

__ Audiovisual:

    __ Wired/wireless microphones with or without lecterns

    __ Wireless lavalier microphones

    __ Sound system

    __ Projectors (ceiling-mount or tabletop)

    __ Projection screens (wall, ceiling-mount, or floor stands)

    __ Projection packages

__ Stage/podium capabilities

__ Ballroom

    __ Dance floor

    __ Bar setup

    __ Seating

    __ Overflow seating

__ Technology

    __ Laptops

    __ Wayfinding monitors and other signage

    __ Other

__ Decor

    __ Linens

    __ Centerpieces

    __ Other

SLEEPING ROOM EVALUATION

When you are selecting the hotel, or hotels, that will house your guests, take the time to confirm the details below. Much of this information can usually be found on the hotel website. The last thing you want is to choose a facility and find that it doesn't offer basic amenities. During the RFP process, confirm the number of rooms available for your group during your event dates, including types of rooms available and price per night.

It's also useful to provide as many details as possible to your participants so they can prepare for their travels accordingly. If the facility has both smoking and nonsmoking rooms, for example, you'll want to be sure to let them know so they can specify their preference while making reservations.

Name of hotel:
Address:
Main phone number:
Reservations phone number:
Website:
Primary contact name:
    Direct number:
    E-mail:

Room Evaluation

Are all rooms nonsmoking? Y/N

Number of rooms by room style:
    __ 2 queens, standard
        Conference price:
    __ 2 queens, suite
        Conference price:
    __ King, standard
        Conference price:

__ King, suite
  Conference price:
__ ADA–compliant rooms
  Conference price:
__ Other room styles
  Conference price:

Deposit requirements at time of reservation:

Refund policy for cancellations:

Check-in/check-out times:

Credit cards accepted:

Checks accepted? Y/N

Tax-exempt requirements:

Transportation to airport and/or local attractions via taxi, limousine, or shuttle:

In-room amenities:
  __ Wireless Internet
  __ Coffeemaker
  __ Work desk
  __ Safe
  __ Refrigerator
  __ Microwave
  __ Hair dryer
  __ Alarm clock

Property amenities:
  __ Pool indoor
      Hours:
  __ Pool outdoor
      Hours:
  __ Exercise facility
      Hours:
  __ Breakfast available: Y/N
      Included in room rate? Y/N
  __ Full-service restaurant? Y/N
      Hours:
  __ Bar? Y/N
      Hours:

Area attractions:
  __ Dining
  __ Shopping
  __ Recreation

ACTION PLAN

The action steps listed on this worksheet will be used to make your vision a reality. Add as much detail as you need to paint a clear picture of what needs to be done, identify who is responsible for completing each task, set a target date, and record the actual completion date for each item. If you see that completion dates are starting to lag from the target dates that were originally set for the task, you are off schedule; you must evaluate whether you need to adjust the scope of the plan in order to avoid a critical misstep as you approach your event date.

Use a spreadsheet or other tool that you can sort by column to quickly organize the list by target date, completed date, or responsible party. Add other columns to help you see your plan in a way that makes sense to you. For instance, add a "Category" or "Team" column so you can easily see what needs to be discussed with each team at your next progress meeting. Add an "Urgency" column so you can indicate whether the task is a critical path item that requires completion before other tasks can begin.

The scenario below assumes that you have twelve months to plan your event. If your planning window is shorter, you will have to adjust your action plan accordingly. The example is a high-level list of action items; each item would most likely have many lines underneath it with each step necessary to complete that particular action and a person assigned to each step.

Action Plan
XYZ Fall Conference

Action item	Details	Who	Target date	Completed date
12 months prior				
Identify goals				
Prepare budget				
Secure venue				

Action item	Details	Who	Target date	Completed date
Send RFPs				
Site visits				
Evaluate all proposals				
Negotiate and sign a contract				
Pay deposit if necessary				
Form a core team				
Confirm event date				
Create a theme				
Create an invite list or target market				
Send out save-the-date announcements				
Create and launch marketing plan				
Select a registration method				
Launch event website				
Launch call for speakers				
Launch sponsorship campaign				
Collect sponsor logos and information and include in all collateral as early as possible				
Conduct initial planning meeting				
Create a schedule of planning meetings, and publish it to the entire team				
Conduct a risk assessment; add action items to your plan that are identified in the assessment				
6 months prior				
Secure keynotes, speakers				
Secure major vendors				

Action item	Details	Who	Target date	Completed date
Equipment rentals				
Technology and audiovisual				
Catering				
Security				
Inform venue of any third-party vendors that you have hired that will have onsite responsibilities at your event				
Secure entertainers and after-hours activities				
Finalize event agenda				
Create an hour-by-hour script for the entire event window				
Launch participant registration				
Set a deadline and pricing structure for early-bird price/ regular price/late price				
Launch exhibitor registration				
Secure additional staff and volunteers				
Secure all necessary transportation				
Create a sleeping room reservation list for staff and volunteers				
Monitor registration pace, and continue marketing campaign				
Continue to solicit sponsorships				
Continue to update event website with new sessions, speakers, activities, and sponsor details				

Action item	Details	Who	Target date	Completed date
3 months prior				
Secure additional supplies and minor services				
Badge-printing supplies				
Staff and volunteer clothing				
Continue marketing campaign				
Reminders published regarding early-bird deadline				
Collect speaker bios, headshots, presentations, handouts, etc.				
Continue to update event website with new sessions, speakers, activities, and sponsor details				
Order conference totes and other giveaway items				
Provide master schedule of events to venue				
2 months prior				
Reminders published regarding regular registration deadline				
Finalize menu, and provide to venue				
Begin to prepare printed conference program				
30 days prior				
Final marketing push for late registrations				
Confirm detailed banquet event orders (BEOs) with venue				

Action item	Details	Who	Target date	Completed date
Secure remaining speaker bios, headshots, presentations, handouts, etc.				
Deliver final conference program to printer				
Prepare copies of all handouts, signage, speaker lists, maps, other printed collateral				
Prepare speaker introductions, and identify facilitators who will introduce them				
2 weeks prior				
Send final details to participants				
Last-minute reminders				
Schedule changes				
Check-in instructions				
Directions and hotel information				
List of what they should bring (and what they shouldn't)				
Send final details to exhibitors, including arrival and setup times				
1 week prior				
Confirm everything				
Speakers and presenters				
Vendors and service providers				
Tracking and delivery estimates for shipped items				

Action item	Details	Who	Target date	Completed date
Review transportation, traffic, and parking arrangements				
Final meal counts to venue				
Gather supplies to be transported or shipped				
Signs				
Centerpieces, decor				
Handouts				
Emergency kit				
Team supplies (badges, parking passes, etc.)				
Organize paperwork				
Contracts				
Copies of banquet event orders				
Emergency contacts				
Attendance and exhibitor lists				
Speaker introductions				
Thank-you notes and payments				
Event script				
Finalize participant needs				
Programs				
Conference totes and contents				
Swag and promotional items				
Badges or badge-printing supplies				
Meet with your team				
Confirm arrival times and initial tasks				

Action item	Details	Who	Target date	Completed date
Distribute event script				
Review emergency procedures				
Answer questions				
Thank them for their efforts				
Day before				
These action items should also be included in more detail on the event script.				
Travel to event site				
Precon meeting with event staff				
Review BEOs				
Initiate setup activities				
Commence load-in procedures				
Exhibitor setup				
A/V and technology setup				
Sign placement				
Registration-station setup				
Complete walk-through of all spaces				
Welcome arriving guests, speakers, VIPs				
Arrange meals and breaks for team members				
Event launch				
These day-of activities will be detailed on the event script.				
After the event				
These action items should also be included in more detail on the event script.				

Action item	Details	Who	Target date	Completed date
Initiate teardown activities				
Dismantle signs and displays				
Box and label items for transport or shipping				
Return items that were rented or borrowed				
Initiate survey to participants				
Initiate survey to exhibitors				
Prepare thank-yous				
Presenters				
Vendors				
Sponsors				
Service providers				
Participants				
Administrative tasks				
Reconcile revenue				
Reconcile final venue invoice				
Reconcile other expenses				
Bank reconciliation				
Prepare financial and other reports				

SERVICE PROVIDER DETAILS

This information should be collected from every company and every person providing any service to your event. From audiovisual crews to catering, photography, florists, and entertainers, having this information will help you keep track of your pre-event activities with each provider as well as confirm day-of arrival times and contact numbers.

Company name:

Product or service:

Primary contact name:

Primary contact e-mail:

Primary contact phone number:

Day-of contact name:

Day-of contact e-mail:

Day-of phone number:

Contract signed? Y/N

Payment terms:

Arrival date/time:

Setup details:

Special needs:

EXHIBITOR DETAILS

There are several ways to organize your exhibitor details, depending on the size of your event. If you are more paper-centric, create a separate sheet for each vendor, and store it in a binder along with their signed contract and other documents, organized either alphabetically or by exhibit row. Another alternative is to create a spreadsheet and add a column for each of the pieces of information below, adding more as needed. Each row on your spreadsheet will represent one exhibitor.

A spreadsheet is easy to sort by any column; sort it by the "Contract Received" or "Deposit Received" column to see which vendors have action items that haven't been completed. If you consistently host much larger events (one hundred or more exhibitors), you may choose to track your year-over-year exhibitor information in a software product specifically designed for managing exhibitor and trade shows.

Company name:
Primary product or service:
Category:
Primary contact name:
    Primary phone:
    Primary e-mail:
Day-of contact name:
    Day-of phone (cell):
    Day-of e-mail:
Contract received? Y/N
Deposit amount:
Deposit received? Y/N
Logo received? Y/N
Company profile received? Y/N
Sponsorship?
Details:

Arrival date/time:
Setup details:

    ___ Single booth
    ___ Double booth
    ___ Corner booth
    ___ Electricity required

Other setup details:

Special requirements:

Booth assignment:

SPEAKER DETAILS

There are dozens of details that must be maintained for each speaker or presenter you invite to your event. This is an example of the specifics you or an assigned team member must manage for each person on your agenda.

Speaker name:
Primary phone number:
Day-of phone number:
E-mail:
Mailing address:

Presentation name:
Date/time/location of presentation:
Contract received? Y/N
Payment terms:

Presentation received? Y/N
Handouts made? Y/N
    Quantity needed:
Special audiovisual needs or room setup? Y/N
    Details:

Bio/photo received? Y/N
Meals? Y/N
Lodging required? Y/N
    Number of nights:
    Hotel:
    Room requirements (i.e., lower floor, bed preference, accessible, etc.):
    Confirmation number:
Transportation required? Y/N
    Air travel:
    Date(s) of travel:

Airline:

Arrive/depart:

Flight number/confirmation number:

Car rental or pickup:

Date and time of travel:

Car company:

    Phone number:

Confirmed:

Other transportation required:

Details confirmed one week prior:

With speaker? Y/N

With hotel? Y/N

With transportation provider(s)? Y/N

With staff re: handouts, audiovisual needs? Y/N

Day-of tasks:

Welcome gifts/thank-yous ready and in place

Payment is prepared

Speaker badge is prepared

Team member is assigned to welcome speaker and direct them to speaker lounge, meal rooms, and restrooms

Team member is assigned to introduce the speaker and facilitate their presentation

Speaker has seen the room and has tested the audiovisual equipment, including volume, clicker, etc.

Handouts are printed and in the room; someone is assigned to pass them out

Evaluations forms are ready

Books or other items for sale are in place

Book signing details (if any) are in place, including rope line, signage, etc.

Transportation for speaker has been arranged, if needed

PLANNING MEETING PREPARATION

Prior to Meeting

__ Establish goal/purpose

__ Establish attendee list

__ Secure meeting location

__ Send invite—date, time, location, anticipated length

__ Prepare agenda (see Planning Meeting worksheet)

__ Prepare any supporting documents—presentations, handouts

__ Secure technology, audiovisual, teleconferencing needs

__ Assign a notetaker, or secure a recorder or videographer

__ Purchase/rent necessary office supplies and equipment

__ Arrange for food and beverages, if necessary, and all required serving/eating equipment and utensils

Day of Meeting

__ Prepare each room

    __ chairs

    __ tables

    __ note taking materials

    __ podium, microphone if needed

    __ lighting

    __ temperature control

    __ power up and test computer

    __ power up and test audiovisual, conferencing equipment

__ Confirm food and beverage delivery (or prepare in advance if being taken care of in-house)

__ Begin on time!

__ Stick to agenda and timetable

__ Establish action plan/next steps

__ Assign an owner and deadline for each step

__ Establish date/time for next meeting, if necessary

After the Meeting

__ Transcribe meeting notes

__ Distribute notes and action plan (including owners and deadlines)

__ Send invitations for next meeting

PLANNING MEETING

Meeting Title
Date
Time
Location

Organizer:
Attendees:
Purpose:

1. Introductions (if necessary)
2. Explain purpose of meeting, and review agenda (organizer)
3. Review and adoption of minutes from previous meeting (if applicable)
   a. Changes/corrections of previous minutes
4. Reports (from teams that have progress reports due)
   a. Report 1
   b. Report 2
5. Other old business (updates from owners of actions identified in previous meeting)
   a. Old business 1
   b. Old business 2
6. New discussion items and/or presentations (in order of priority and relevance)
   a. New business 1
   b. New business 2
7. Action items
   a. New action item 1
      i. Owner
      ii. Deadline
   b. New action item 2
      i. Owner
      ii. Deadline

    c. New action item 3
      i. Owner
      ii. Deadline
  8. Other business
  9. Set date and time for follow-up meeting (if necessary)
10. Adjourn

(If the meeting will last longer than 1–1.5 hours, insert time for restroom and refreshment breaks.)

EVENT SCRIPT

Creating a day-by-day, hour-by-hour, minute-by-minute script not only helps draw out forgotten details during the planning process but also is an essential tool during the actual event. The ability to prepare a comprehensive script is evidence that you have fully developed your action plan and left absolutely nothing to chance. It is a separate, more detailed document that will help you and your team execute your vision with accuracy and precision.

Create your script in a project management or spreadsheet tool such as Microsoft Excel. This is a living document that will be continually updated throughout the planning process; using a spreadsheet makes it easy to insert rows in the middle of the schedule as additional tasks are identified during the planning process. The rows represent dates and times, and the columns contain at the very least the following: time, activity name, location, who is responsible, and additional details.

I make sure that the spreadsheet is configured so that it can be easily reproduced and handed out to the entire team prior to the event so they can review it, ask questions, and mark all of the details they need to pay particular attention to.

I carry my script with me everywhere I go, usually on a clipboard, so I can cross things off as they are completed, and pencil in my own notes and additions as needed. Inevitably, a participant or a sponsor will want to schedule an impromptu meeting; a quick glance at the script tells me that I have a free hour from 2:00 to 3:00 on Day 2. The script gives me the confidence to schedule a meeting during this time, knowing that I am not dropping the ball on something else.

Event Script
XYZ Fall Conference

Time	*Activity Location*	*Who*	*Additional Details*

The Week Before:
Tuesday, September 7
Final team meeting
    Distribute script
    Confirm arrival times and initial tasks
    (name) to review emergency procedures

Wednesday, September 8
Gather, box, and label items to be shipped to venue:
    Signs
    Centerpieces and decor
    Handouts
    Team clothing and name badges
    Programs
    Conference totes and contents
    Swag and promotional items
    Badges or badge-printing supplies

Thursday, September 9
Speaker committee confirms details with each speaker
    Speaker #1 contacted by (name)
    Speaker #2 contacted by (name)
    Speaker #3 contacted by (name)
Logistics committee confirms details with each vendor and service provider
    Vendor #1 contacted by (name)
    Vendor #2 contacted by (name)
    Vendor #3 contacted by (name)

Logistics committee ships items to venue today
  Box #1 containing:
  Box #2 containing:
  Box #3 containing:

Friday, September 10
Gather supplies to be transported:
  Contracts
  BEOs
  Emergency contacts
  Attendance and exhibitor lists
  Thank-you notes
  Payments for speaker or services
Final head counts to venue for each event:
  9/14 Early-arrival networking event:
  9/15 Day 1 breakfast:
  9/15 Day 1 lunch:
  9/15 Day 1 afternoon break:
  9/15 Day 1 dinner:
  9/16 Day 2 breakfast:
  9/16 Day 2 lunch:
  9/16 Day 2 afternoon break:
  9/16 Day 2 dinner/gala:
  9/16 Day 2 after-hours event:
  9/17 Day 3 breakfast:

Monday, September 13
Pack up supplies for transport
Travel day

The Day Before:

Tuesday, September 14, Setup day

12:00 p.m.	Arrive at event site
	Precon meeting with (name) and (name) from venue
	Review BEOs
	Complete walk-through of all spaces to confirm initial configurations
	Confirm arrival of all shipped items
	Set up activities
2:00	A/V load-in begins
2:00–8:00	Exhibitor load-in
	Place directional signs
	Place sponsor signs
	Set up registration station
	Stuff conference totes
	Badges
	Programs
	Debrief binder
	Emergency kit
	Set up quiet room
	Set up speaker lounge
	Set up staff/volunteer hospitality room
	Welcome speakers arriving today
4:45	Speaker #1 pickup at airport
5:30	Speaker #2 approximate arrival
(time)	(name) to join Speaker #1 and #2 for dinner at (place)
(time)	Dinner break for team at (place)

Day 1

Wednesday, September 15, Day 1

6:30 a.m.	Confirm final presentation room setups
	Room 301 Details confirmed by (name)
	A/V is on and working

Presentations for each session is installed
on laptop and working

Room is configured correctly

Daily agenda sign posted by door

Introductions for each session are on lectern

Handouts for each presenter are labeled
and on front table

Room 308 Details confirmed by (name)

A/V is on and working

Presentations for each session is installed
on laptop and working

Room is configured correctly

Daily agenda sign is posted by door

Introductions for each session are on lectern

Handouts for each presenter are labeled
and on front table

7:00   Registration table opens

Staff assignments:

    #1 (name)

    #2 (name)

    #3 (name)

7:00–8:00 Breakfast

Welcome given by (name)

Hospitality announcements by (name)

8:00   Speaker #1 greeted by (name)

Speaker #2 greeted by (name)

8:15   Conduct sound check in presentation room 301

Conduct sound check in presentation room 308

8:30–9:30 Session 1

Track 1   Room 301, "Tips and Tricks for the Advanced User," Speaker #1

Introduced by (name)

Facilitator/notetaker (name)

Handouts? Y/N

Special needs: Will use his own laptop; have IT staff on standby for testing

Track 2   Room 308, "Essentials for Beginners," Speaker #2

Introduced by (name)

Facilitator/notetaker (name)

Handouts? Y/N

Special needs: Needs a lavalier microphone and a flipchart with markers

9:30–10:00   Break

10:00–11:00   Session 2

Continue creating this kind of detail for each activity throughout the day. Indicate miscellaneous entries—for instance, when a room needs to be reconfigured for a different activity or when and where sponsors need to gather in order to be introduced at lunch.

Final Day/Teardown:

Friday, September 17

Teardown

11:00 a.m.–2:00 p.m.	Exhibitor teardown
11:00 a.m.	Box up directional signs
	Box up sponsor signs
	Tear down staff/volunteer hospitality room
1:00	A/V teardown begins
	Tear down registration station
	Tear down quiet room
	Tear down speaker lounge

Remove all trash to appropriate location

Ship boxes back to headquarters

Final walk-through of all event spaces

Touch base with venue representatives before departing

Relax, and celebrate a job well done!

EVENT DEBRIEF MEETING
Date:
Time:
Location:
Attendees:

Agenda

1. Review goals
   a. Read goals set at beginning of event
   b. Overall, did we meet our established goals? Why or why not?
2. Budget
   a. Did we achieve our revenue goals? Why or why not?
   b. Did we stay within our budget? Why or Why not?
3. Evaluate team performance
   a. Staff
   b. Volunteers
   c. Third-party vendors
   d. Other
4. Evaluate logistics management
   a. Setup
   b. Teardown
   c. Parking
   d. Signage
   e. Other
5. Evaluate communications
   a. Promotion
   b. Registration
   c. Team communication
6. Evaluate program
   a. Sessions
   b. Keynotes
   c. Entertainment

7. Evaluate survey results (if available)
8. Evaluate team feedback
9. Identify any action items/follow-up that needs to be done

EVENT PARTICIPANT SURVEY

E-mail subject line: 5-Minute Survey for the XYZ Conference—We Need Your Feedback!

E-mail body:

We hope you enjoyed this year's XYZ Conference and hope to see you again next year! In order to continually improve, we need your feedback. Please take a few minutes to answer the questions in the short survey attached. Your input will be considered when planning future events. Thank you in advance.

Sincerely,

The Conference Planning Team

Sample General Survey Questions:

Are you a first-time attendee? Y/N

Please rate the ease of the registration process on a scale of 1 to 5, with 5 being the highest. 1 2 3 4 5

Please rate your overall satisfaction with the venue. 1 2 3 4 5

Please rate your overall satisfaction with the food. 1 2 3 4 5

Please rate your overall satisfaction with the program. 1 2 3 4 5

Please rate your overall satisfaction with after-hours events. 1 2 3 4 5

What aspect of the event did you like best?

What aspect of the event would you change?

What is the likelihood that you will attend this event again? 1 2 3 4 5

Would you recommend this event to others? Y/N

    Why or why not?

What suggestions for improvement do you have?

Are you interested in being on the planning team for next year's event? Y/N

    If yes, please provide your contact information, and we will be in touch.

Sample Survey Questions for Individual Sessions

Please rate the following from 1 to 5, with 5 being the highest. Use the space provided for additional comments.

The speaker was knowledgeable. 1 2 3 4 5
The speaker was professional. 1 2 3 4 5
The speaker delivered content effectively. 1 2 3 4 5
The distributed materials were useful. 1 2 3 4 5
The content met my expectations. 1 2 3 4 5
There was adequate time for questions. 1 2 3 4 5
Overall I was satisfied with this presentation. 1 2 3 4 5
I would recommend this speaker to others. 1 2 3 4 5
I would recommend this session to others. 1 2 3 4 5
Comments to improve this session:
Other sessions you would like to see:

Acknowledgments

To Suzanne Staszak-Silva and the entire Rowman & Littlefield team for believing in me and this project. Your support and guidance is what made this book reach its full potential, and I thank you for it.

To my event planning posse, the people I've had the pleasure of working with over the years to create events of all shapes and sizes. I'm looking at you, Dawn, Barb, Gus, Kim, Chad, Tom, Pam, Mark, Bob, Beth, Karen, and so many others too numerous to mention here. We've shared laughter, hard work, blood, sweat, and tears, but most of all we've celebrated the successes and experienced the joy that comes from a job well done. You inspire me.

To the teachers, guides, and mentors who have touched my life and encouraged me in so many ways, including Marisa, Carol, Kevin, Kelley, Kim, Shaun, Cheryl, Quiana, Terry, Al, Rick, and the entire SSI team. I appreciate you more than you will ever know!

To those who agreed to share their wisdom in this book. Thank you from the bottom of my heart. I already know that that those who spend their lives planning extraordinary meetings and events are generous, smart, kind, and passionate about what they do, but you just proved it to the world. I am forever grateful.

To my mother, my sisters, my mother-in-law, my extended family, and my dear friends. Thank you for your love and encouragement. It means the world to me. I love you all!

To my daughter Kelly, who is well on her way to creating a life full of mountaintop moments for her sweet family. You are a truly amazing woman, wife, and mother!

To my daughter Amy, my champion, my sounding board, and my secret weapon. Thank you for your patience and insight. I am so proud of everything you've become and can't wait to see what the future holds. "What's next?"

Finally, to my husband, Matt, who provided his love and support not only through the creation of this book but also through a lifetime of wonderful adventures. Here's to many, many more!

Notes

INTRODUCTION

1. Alice Waters, *40 Years of Chez Panisse: The Power of Gathering*, fore. Calvin Trillin, aft. Michael Pollan (New York: Clarkson Potter, 2011), 9.

2. Ann Lamott, *Bird by Bird: Some Instructions on Writing and Life* (New York: Pantheon Books, 1994), 204.

CHAPTER 1

1. Betty Crocker, *Betty Crocker's Guide to Easy Entertaining: How to Have Guests and Enjoy Them*, illus. Peter Spiel (New York: Golden Press, 1959), 8.

CHAPTER 4

1. Cy Wakeman, *No Ego: How Leaders Can Cut the Cost of Workplace Drama, End Entitlement, and Drive Big Results* (New York: St. Martin's Press, 2017), 39.

CHAPTER 8

1. First attributed to Margaret Mead by Donald Keys in *Earth at Omega: Passage to Planetization*, intro. Norman Cousins (Boston: Branden Press, 1982), 79.

CHAPTER 9

1. David Allen, *Getting Things Done: The Art of Stress-Free Productivity* (New York: Penguin Books, 2001), 38 (emphasis original).

CHAPTER 20

1. Jon Petz, *Boring Meetings Suck: Get More Out of Your Meetings, or Get Out of More Meetings* (Hoboken, NJ: John Wiley & Sons, 2011), 14.

SECTION V

1. Elizabeth Gilbert, *Big Magic: Creative Living Beyond Fear* (New York: Riverhead Books, 2015), 27.

CHAPTER 24

1. Attributed to George Bernard Shaw by William Hollingsworth Whyte in "Is Anybody Listening?" *Fortune* (September 1950): 174.

CHAPTER 25

1. Sandburg apparently offered this gem to the guests assembled at his eighty-fifth birthday party, on January 6, 1963, as reported by syndicated columnist Ralph McGill, later collected in *The Best of Ralph McGill: Selected Columns*, ed. Michael Strickland, Harry Davis, and Jeff Strickland (Atlanta: Cherokee Pub. Co., 1980), 82.

CHAPTER 28

1. David Sturt, *Great Work: How Make a Difference People Love* (New York: McGraw-Hill Education, 2013), 138.

CHAPTER 29

1. *Betty Crocker's Guide to Easy Entertaining*, 7.

2. The Walt Disney Company is fond of repeating one of its founder's most beloved pieces of wisdom, which reads in full, "You can design and create and build the most wonderful place in the world. But it takes people to make the dream a reality." See, for example, https://www.disneyinstitute.com/blog/leadership-lessons-from-walt-disney—how-to/.

Index

accessibility, 62. *See also* Americans with Disabilities Act

action plan: assembling team, 71–79; designing, 81–94; finding right venue, 57–70; identifying goals, 37–42; understanding budget, 43–55; worksheet, 282–89

acts of God, 198

administrative tasks, 219

agendas, 86–87, 215; draft, 272–73; flipping, 254; in registration material, 204

airports. *See* transportation

Allen, David, 83

amenities, 62, 67–68

Americans with Disabilities Act, 62, 184

appetizers/finger food, 104

art shows, 50

association (club, organization) events, 4–5

athletic connections. *See* sports-themed events

attendance boosting, 84–85

attendee tracking, 192–93. *See also* participants

auctions, 48–49, 89

awards: for attendees, 84–85; for companies, 84; for contest winners, 53; for exhibitors, 146; for past participants, 84–85; presentation of, 32, 114; for teams, 115

bake sales, 50

banquet event orders (BEOs), 95–97, 219

banquet facilities, 57–58

banquet tables (themed decor), 115–16

bar foods, 107

basket raffles, 47–48

BEOs. *See* banquet event orders

beverages. *See* food and beverage

Bill Emerson Good Samaritan Act (1996), 100

bingo card, 144

blogging, 208
boxed meals, 105, 109
breakfast, 109, 123, 254
Bryant, Shana, 250–51
budget, 33–34, 35; expenses, 51–54; for
    food and beverage, 108; managing
    scope creep, 24; money saving
    tips, 54–55; and revenue, 43–51;
    stretching resources, 33; worksheet,
    266–68. *See also* fundraising
bulletin boards, 209
business meetings. *See* meetings
buttonhole sessions, 141

cake walks, 51
camps, 59
cancellation policies, 64, 91, 180, 205;
    due to weather (acts of God), 60,
    198; force majeure, 181
carnivals, 50
car washes, 51
Catchafire, 75
caterers, 170
club events, 4–5
coffeehouse atmosphere, 135
communication, 223–29; with clients,
    255; emergency plan for, 197; with
    event manager, 99; in meetings,
    223–25; with participants, 214; with
    service providers, 173–75; skills,
    18–19; with speakers, 151, 152–53,
    228–29, 255; with sponsors, 255;
    with team members, 255. *See also*
    e-mail
company events, 4
concealed carry permits, 97

concerts, 50
conference centers, 58–59
conference rooms, 116
conferences, 112; livestreaming, 189;
    planning, 29; script for, 88–89; for
    writers, 39
confirmations: for attendees, 207; early,
    26; with event managers, 217; with
    hotels, 279; with service providers,
    173–75, 214, 290; with speakers, 82,
    88, 154, 214; with team, 216, 218;
    transportation, 160; with vendors,
    213, 214; with venue managers, 232
conflict management, 17–18
contingency plans: for emergencies,
    167; emergency kit, 166–67, 215; for
    equipment failures, 163; for extra
    expenses, 54; for inclement weather,
    60, 161–62, 172–73
contractors, 171
contracts: Americans with Disabilities
    Act, 184; attrition, 182; clauses
    prohibiting changes, 183;
    common terms, 178–84; food and
    beverage/liquor license policies,
    182–83; force majeure, 181;
    indemnification, 181; minimums
    and commitments, 181–82;
    modifications to contract, 184;
    organizing and filing, 86; other
    considerations, 184–85; for services,
    178; severability, 183
convention centers, 58–59
conventions, 29–30, 103. *See also* trade
    shows
corporate events, 38

corporate sponsors. *See* sponsors, corporate
Create the Good, 75
Crocker, Betty, 15–16, 257–58, 259
CrowdCompass, 245
Cvent, 245

damages, 180
date selection. *See* time component
deadlines: communicating to attendees, 204–5; contest, 140; for critical path items, 83–84; early bird, 84; for exhibitors, 147; missing, 16; planning process, 14, 17, 26, 231, 234, 240; for publications, 210; for speakers, 88; for survey return, 246; for venues, 64
debate formats, 128
debrief binder, 87
decor: allowable methods, 102; in BEO, 96; bringing in to restaurants, 59; expenses, 52; ideas, 236; purchasing, 32, 89, 215; rented, 169, 170, 171, 173; repurposing, 33, 101; selection of, 26, 89; supplied by venue, 58; for tables, 96, 261; tied to theme, 8, 67, 119, 121, 122
delegation, 19
deliverables, 38–39
deposits, 179
dine-arounds, 55
directions, 160
direct mail marketing, 209
Disney, Walt, 260
documentation, 85–87; agendas and meeting minutes, 86–87; contracts, 86; debrief binder, 87; planning documents, 86. *See also* contracts
donations, 46
door prizes, 53
downtime (activities), 137–38; quiet zone, 130
dress code, 145, 205
Dropbox, 237

education, focus on, 251–52
education pavilion, 144
electricity, 164–65
e-mail, 214, 225–28, 255; for event participant survey, 307–8; follow-up, 247; marketing, 209. *See also* communication
emergency exits, 197
emergency kit, 166–67, 215
engagement, 251–52
entertainment and entertainers, 8, 50, 52, 137; for coffeehouse setting, 135; for registration area, 132
epidemics, 181
equipment, 163; audiovisual, 96; extra fees for, 65; failure, 180; needs, 32–33; rental, 52, 60, 82, 147, 169, 171; worksheet, 278
ethical code, 19–20
evacuation, 195
event cancellation. *See* cancellation policies
event coordinators. *See* event professionals
event managers. *See* event professionals
event planning: after event is over, 219–20; annual events, 30–31;

assessing available resources,
15–16, 29–34; by association
members, 4–5; breaking tasks into
smaller parts, 240–41; by business
management, administration, and
staff, 4; by community organizers,
4–5; day before, 216–17; eliminating
distractions, 241; by family and
friends, 5; fighting procrastination,
240, 242; fighting urge to be
perfect, 241; focus on details,
13–14, 140–41; gathering supplies,
214–15; including significant others,
254; learning from failure, 90–92;
leveraging connections, 31–32;
limits in, 241–42; meeting with
team, 216; opening day, 217–19;
PARTY principle, 240; scope of
event, 21–24; targeting audience,
252; time component, 25–28; week
before, 213–16; where to begin,
11–12
event professionals, 5–6, 10–11;
event coordinators, 95, 101; event
managers, 66, 98–99, 217; meeting
managers, 95. See also project
managers
event script, 299–304
exhibition management companies,
147–48
exhibitions. See trade shows
exhibitor appointments, 144–45
exhibitors: awards for, 146; connecting
with participants, 146–47; contests
for, 146; details about (worksheet),
291–92; feedback from, 145;

invitations to, 145; needs of, 145–
46; thanking, 146; at virtual events,
147. See also vendors
expenses: contingencies, 54; for decor,
52; food and beverages, 52; freight
and storage, 54; gratuities, 54;
hidden, 53–54; labor and overtime,
54, 179; logistics, 53; merchant
fees, 54; prizes and giveaways, 53;
program costs, 52; publicity and
promotion, 53; service fees, 53–54,
97; taxes, 53–54, 97; venue, 52
expert advice, 249–56
expos, 143–48. See also trade shows

Facebook, 206, 207, 211. See also social
media
family and friends: activities for, 5,
131–32; as event organizers, 5; as
resources, 31
FAQ page, 27
fashion shows, 50–51
feedback, 244–47. See also surveys
festivals, 50
file-sharing tools, 236–37
firearm policies, 97, 197
fire extinguishers, 197
Firsdon, Lori, 153
first impressions, 250
flyers, 209, 210
food allergies, 107–8
food and beverage: alcoholic, 22, 52,
58, 104, 107, 108, 164, 182–83, 251,
277; appetizers and finger food,
104; bar foods, 107; BEOs, 95–97,
219; boxed meals, 105, 109; breaks,

105–6, 107, 217; bringing your own, 103–4; buffets, 52, 100, 104–5, 209; build-your-own food bars, 106–7; clauses, 64; contract issues, 182–83; cost of, 52, 103, 108; special dietary considerations, 107–8; dine-arounds, 55; drinking water, 52, 88; finger food, 104; innovations in service, 107; hosting, 50; open bar, 52; options for, 36; plated, 22, 100, 104, 104; reducing time needed for serving, 108–9; safety regulations, 199; for speakers, 154; ticketing, 100; trucks, 30; worksheet, 276–77. *See also* special diets

formal events, 115

freight charges, 54

fundraising, 23–24, 47–51; auctions, 48–49, 89; donations, 46; donor solicitations, 23; government grants, 24; raffles, 41, 47–48, 49; registration fees, 43–44; sponsorships, 23, 35, 44–46; ticket sales, 43–44. *See also* revenue

games of chance, 51

Gardner, Deborah, 249, 251, 252, 255–56

gathering, reasons for, 2–3

generators, 164–65

Gilbert, Elizabeth, 222

giveaways, 53

goals, 7, 35, 37–42, 125; clarifying, 42; creating change, 42; deliverables, 38–39; objectives of event, 37–38; obstacles, 39; revisiting, 244; and

room configuration, 117; success criteria, 39; unexpected results, 41–42

goal sponsorships, 49

goal statements, 39, 264–65; sample, 39–40

Google Drive/Google Docs, 236

gratuities, 52, 54, 97

Great Wolf Lodge, 228–29

GTR (event technology firm), 192

handouts, 89, 100, 117, 154, 166, 206, 215

Hartline, Karen, 253

Hawks, Greg, 153

head count, 83–84, 170

health emergencies, 199–200

HelmsBriscoe, 69

hospitality, 257–60, 262

hotels: available, 30; confirming with, 279; information about, 145; as venues, 58

improvisation, 250–51

indemnification, 181

industry magazines, 210

injuries, 200

Instagram, 31, 206, 208, 211. *See also* social media

insurance, 198, 200

Internet availability, 59, 63, 69–70, 99, 271, 278, 280; Wi-Fi, 68, 188–89

introductions for speakers, 88, 151

invitations, 145; what to include, 203–6

jigsaw puzzle, 138

Kalahari Resorts and Conventions, 67–68
keynotes, 149–50
kindness, 20, 260, 262
Kosins, Lysa, 172, 173
Kosins Tents and Events, 171–73

labor fees/rates, 54, 179
Lamott, Anne, 10
lectures, 126–29
lighting, 30, 188
lining out, 183
LinkedIn, 31, 206, 208. *See also* social media
liquor licenses, 58, 104, 182
live auctions, 48
load-in procedures, 216
locations. *See* venue selection
lodges, 59
logistics, 8, 53, 157–58; electricity, 164–65; preparing for unexpected, 166–67; restroom facilities, 30, 53, 59, 62, 163–64; for trade shows, 147; trash removal, 53, 165–66. *See also* equipment; transportation

Manning, Peyton, 150
maps, 160
marketing, 252. *See also* promotion/publicity
marquees, 209
Masters, Andy, 155–56, 250
McKnight, Allison, 45, 72, 73

Mead, Margaret, 71
meals. *See* food and beverage
mechanical pencils, 236
media kits, 85
medical emergencies, 199–200
meeting managers, 95
meetings: business, 116; event debrief, 305–6; event planning (worksheet), 297–98; event planning preparation (worksheet), 295–96; minutes from, 86–87; online, 48; reminders, 27; with team, 216, 223–25
merchant fees, 54
Mershon, Phil, 42,151, 256
Meyer, Leslie, 67, 68
Midwest Writers Workshop, 140
Monahan, Brian, 46, 190, 250
mountaintop moments, 1, 3, 222
music: copyrighted, 188. *See also* entertainment and entertainers
music festivals, 30
mystery auctions, 48

name badges, 133, 154
negotiation, 185, 249
networking opportunities/events, 31–32, 133–36; coffeehouse atmosphere, 135; roundtable experience, 135; table topics activities, 136; team building events, 135–36
newsletters, 140, 210
newspapers, 209–10
noise restrictions, 184
Nolting, Margie, 33, 69, 254
nonsmoking facilities, 184

offsite events, 129

Ohio Sauerkraut Festival, 78

Ohio State University, 139, 157–58

one-on-one sessions, 140–41

online collaboration tools, 225, 255

online engagement apps, 247

online registration, 52, 53, 191–93. *See also* registration

open flames, 184

opening day, 217–19

organization, 231–37; using calendars and planners, 83, 233–35; using Dropbox, 237; using mechanical pencils, 236; using notebooks, 83, 232; using online and file-sharing tools, 236–37; using project management tools, 83, 235; using ring binders, 235–36, 252–53; using smartphone/tablet, 232, 235; using spreadsheets, 83

orientations, 130

outdoor venues, 60, 115, 129; music festivals, 30; and severe weather, 172–73, 197–98

pandemics, 181

panel discussions, 128

paperwork, 215. *See also* contracts

parking, 30, 62, 160–62, 214; fees for, 58

participants: awards for, 84–85; communicating with, 214; connecting exhibitors with, 146–47; engagement of, 251–52; feedback from, 244–47; needs of, 215–16;

survey for, 307–8; thanking, 219; tracking, 192–93

party favors, 53. *See also* swag bags

Pathable, 245

payments, 179

Petz, Jon, 136, 187

photo release, 184

photos, 211

Pinterest, 31, 208. *See also* social media

planning professionals. *See* event professionals

plated meals, 22, 100, 104, 104

portable restrooms. *See* restroom facilities

presentation format, 128–29

presenters. *See* speakers and presenters

press kits, 210

press releases, 211

Prestige AV and Creative Services, 46, 190

prizes. *See* awards

procrastination, 240, 242

procurement specialists, 69–70

programming decisions: athletic connections, 139; considerate events, 130–33; ideas, 125–26; learning from success, 140–42; meaningful experiences, 129; networking opportunities, 133–36; schedule of events, 126; time for fun, 137–39; value with a twist, 136–37; workshops vs. lectures, 126–29. *See also* scheduling

programs (printed), 52, 215

project management: concepts, 7, 15; tools, 83

project managers: ability to delegate, 19; business acumen of, 18; communication skills of, 18–19; conflict resolution skills of, 17–18; essential traits of, 16–20; ethical code of conduct of, 19–20; kindness of, 20; as leaders, 16–17; organizational skills of, 17; positive attitude of, 18; as problem-solvers, 17. *See also* event professionals

promotion/publicity, 53; using social media, 206–8; traditional, 209–10. *See also* marketing

protestors, 201–2

public transportation, 132, 160

quarantine, 195

quarter auctions, 49

quiet zones, 130

race sponsorships, 49

radio marketing, 210

raffles, 41, 47–48, 49

receptions, 5, 22, 45, 52, 57, 58, 98, 103, 108, 115, 134

recycling, 99, 277

referrals for speakers, 151

registration, 203–6; area for, 132–33; badges, 216; early registration discount, 84; essential information, 203–4; fees, 143–44; online, 52, 53, 191–93

rental companies, 101, 115, 116, 164, 169–72, 278

request for proposal (RFP), 51, 61, 62–63; template, 270–73

resources: connections, 31–32; equipment, 32–33; money, 33–34; people, 30–31; space, 29–30

restaurants, 59–60

rest breaks, 217, 218–19

restroom facilities, 30, 62, 163–64; outdoor, 164; portable, 53; primitive, 59

retreat centers, 59

retreats, 38, 77, 90–92, 101; management, 4; for planning, 10, 39, 232, 262

revenue: from donations, 46; from fundraisers, 47–51; from sponsorships, 44–45; from ticket sales/registration fees, 43–44. *See also* fundraising

RFP. *See* request for proposal

risk assessment, 196–97, 200

road closures, 199

room configurations, 111–17; 360-degree stage, 114; banquet seating, 113; business meetings, 116; classroom, 114; conference rooms, 116; crescent rounds, 113–14; hollow square, circle, or rectangle, 114; room temperature, 117; theater or auditorium, 113; unconventional seating, 115; U shape, 114

room temperature, 117

roundtable experience, 135

safety services, 30

Samit, Jay, 76

Sandburg, Carl, 233

save-the-date announcements, 85, 205

scheduling: after-hours activities, 138–39; attention to detail, 140–41; downtime, 137–38; including significant others, 131–32; memorable, 141–42; offsite events, 129; orientation, 130; outdoor spaces, 129; quiet zones, 130; registration area, 132–33; shopping time, 131; social media moments, 131; tactile experiences, 129; thoughtful, 126, 130; time for fun, 137–39; time to move, 131. *See also* programming decisions

scope creep, 24

script creation, 87–90

security issues, 97, 195–202; attendee tracking, 192–93; in contracts, 180; insurance, 200; and local authorities, 198–99; medical emergencies, 199–200; protestors and other threats, 201–2; risk assessment, 196–97

service fees, 53–54, 97

service providers, 169–75; communicating and confirming, 173–75; confirming with, 173–75, 214, 290; contractors vs. vendor-partners, 171–73; details about (worksheet), 290; selection process, 170; thanking, 219. *See also* vendors

setting up, 216–17

shopping, 131

signage, 162, 216

silent auctions, 48; script for, 89

Simon, Jerry, 67–68

Six Degrees of Kevin Bacon, 77

Slack, 255

sleeping rooms, 178, 182; evaluating, 279–81

snacks, 105–6, 107

social distancing, 65

social media: monitoring for threats, 201; publicizing through, 206–8; moments, 131, 140; social media management platforms, 208; use to solicit volunteers, 75. *See also specific sites*

Software Solutions, Inc., 120

sound systems, 30, 187–88

speakers and presenters, 217; communication with, 151, 152–53, 228–29, 255; confirming with, 82, 88, 154, 214; details about (worksheet), 293–94; expertise of, 250; fees for, 52; introductions for, 88, 151; and keynotes, 149–50; local, 22; locating, 154–55; needs of, 150–51, 153–54, 189–90; no-shows, 155–56; as potential assets, 250; referrals for, 151; in registration material, 204; respecting and valuing, 153, 253; sharing with other events, 54–55; thanking, 53, 219, 248; transportation for, 154, 214, 217; use of technology by, 190

special diets, 107–8

splitting the pot, 48

sponsors, 7; communicating with, 255; corporate, 44–45; thanking, 219, 248 sponsorships, 23, 35, 44–46, 92, 142; goal, 49; meaningful, 252; promotional, 45; tournament or race, 49; by vendors, 32–33

sports-themed events: at Ohio State University, 139; team banquets, 5, 21–22, 115

spreadsheets, 83

staff, 35, 71–73

storage fees, 54

stress, 14, 240, 241–42

Sturt, David, 250

success criteria, 243–48

Super Bowl XLVII, 90

supplies, 214–15

surveys: designing, 246–47; before event, 254–55; evaluating results, 247; number of questions, 246; online, 245–46; paper, 245; for participants, 307–8; phrasing, 246–47; polling, 245

sustainability, 99–101, 277

swag bags, 53, 100, 142, 215

table design, 115–16. *See also* decor

table topics activities, 136

tactile experiences, 129

task list, 251

taxes, 53–54, 97

team: committee members, 31; communicating with, 225–28, 255; details, 269; expanding, 28; meetings with, 216, 223–25; teardown, 219; thanking, 248;

troubleshooting issues, 27. *See also* volunteers

team assembly: networking events, 77–78; staff, 71–73; volunteers, 73–79

team-building events, 135–36

teardown team, 219

technology, 187–93; event management, 191–93; Internet, 59, 63, 69–70, 99, 271, 278, 280; lighting, 188; online registration, 191–93; partners, 190; presentation needs, 189–90; sound systems, 30, 187–88; Wi-Fi, 68, 188–89

television marketing, 210

temperature control, 141

thank-you gifts, 53. *See also* swag bags

themes, 8; corporate, 120–22; decade party, 122; foodies, 123; inspiration for, 119–20; matching to audience, 123; representing brand, 122; sports, 132–33; viewing party, 122

Thomas, Erin, 64, 98, 252–53

ticket sales, 43–44

time component: communicating date to attendees, 203–4; determining date, 25–26, 82–83; for feeding guests, 108–9; restrictions in contracts, 184; understanding dependencies, 28

timelines: after event, 219–20; in BEO, 96; creating, 83; day before, 216–17; opening day, 217–19; proactive, 26–27; week before, 213–16

time management, 253

time/quality/cost triangle, 21–23, 26, 28

Tomayko, Alexandria, 125, 189, 249, 251, 252

tournaments, 49

trade shows, 143–48; bingo card, 144; driving booth traffic, 144–45; equipment for, 32; prioritizing event organization, 145–47; soliciting help, 147–48; surveying exhibitors, 145

training events, 81, 103

transition time, 131, 162, 250–51

transportation: airports, 159; confirming, 160; directions, 160; golf carts, 32; to and from hotels, 58; information about, 145; maps, 160; navigating venue, 162–63; parking, 160–62; public transportation, 132, 160; shuttle buses, 160; signage, 162; for speakers, 154, 214, 217; utility vehicles, 32; for volunteers, 75

trash removal, 53, 165–66

Tucker, Travis, 192, 250, 251–52

Twitter, 31, 206, 207, 211. *See also* social media

unexpected issues, 253

universities, 74; Ohio State, 139, 157–58

unusual venues, 60–61

utility vehicles. *See* transportation

vendors: confirming with, 213, 214; as partners, 171–73; offering reduced rates or sponsorships, 32–33; thanking, 219, 248. *See also* exhibitors; service providers

venue details, 274–76; BEOs, 95–97; evaluation of, 274–78; expenses, 52; listening to experts, 98; security issues, 97; sustainability, 99–101

venue managers, 232

venue selection, 205; additional fees, 65; amenities, 62, 67–68; assistance with, 68–70; attention to detail, 63–64; banquet facilities, 57–58; cancellation policies, 64; cleanliness and safety, 65; conference and convention centers, 58–59; creating RFP, 62–63; hotels, 58; in-person visits, 59, 61–62; local locations, 101; lodges, camps, and retreat centers, 59; restaurants, 59–60; unusual venues, 60–61; virtual locations, 101. *See also* outdoor venues; venue details

videos, 211

VIP lounge, 145

virtual events, 30, 48, 101, 147

virtual meeting platforms, 52

Volunteer-Match, 74–75

volunteer opportunities, 139

volunteers: community, 74; details about (worksheet), 269; among event participants, 75; expenses for, 53; internal, 73–74; meetings with, 223–25; motivations of, 76–77; online, 74–75; overbearing or rude, 260; recognizing, 211, 261–62; recruiting, 73–75, 262; from schools and universities, 74; taking care of, 75–76; thanking, 219, 248. *See also* team

Wakeman, Cy, 29
Warrick, Scott, 151–52
Wartan, Patrick, 177–78, 180, 184–85
water bottles, 100
Waters, Alice, 3
weather contingencies: severe
    weather, 60, 161, 173, 197–98; and
    transportation, 161–62
website, 140; FAQ page, 27; media kit
    or newsroom page, 85
The Wedding Planner (film), 166
welcome gifts, 217
Whova, 245
Wi-Fi networks, 68, 188–89
worksheets: action plan, 282–89;
    budget, 266–68; equipment, 278;
    event debrief meeting, 305–6; event
    participant survey, 307–8; event
    script, 299–304; exhibitor details,

291–92; facility details, 274–76;
food and beverages, 276–77; goal
statement, 264–65; planning
meeting, 297–98; planning meeting
preparation, 295–96; RFP template,
270–73; service provider details,
290; sleeping room evaluation, 279–
81; speaker details, 293–94; team
and volunteer details, 269; venue
evaluation, 274–78
workshops, 126–29
Writer's Digest Annual Conference, 133

yard signs, 209
yoga sessions, 131
YouTube, 207, 211. *See also* social
media

Zglinicki, Tracy, 62, 97, 98, 253

About the Author

Linda Joyce Jones is a self-proclaimed obsessive organizer of people, places, and events. Her passion for planning events has been used in orchestrating special occasions in her personal and professional life for over twenty-five years. Her pragmatic approach and knack for sweating the small stuff has helped her organize successful corporate conferences, community events, retreats, fundraisers, and more. This includes serving multiple years as chairperson for the Ohio Sauerkraut Festival, a nationally recognized food and crafts festival that attracts 450 artisans and 250,000 visitors annually. Linda resides in Waynesville, Ohio, with her husband, Matt.